MW01037233

ABOUT ISLAND PRESS

Island Press is the only nonprofit organization in the United States whose principal purpose is the publication of books on environmental issues and natural resource management. We provide solutions-oriented information to professionals, public officials, business and community leaders, and concerned citizens who are shaping responses to environmental problems.

In 2002, Island Press celebrates its eighteenth anniversary as the leading provider of timely and practical books that take a multidisciplinary approach to critical environmental concerns. Our growing list of titles reflects our commitment to bringing the best of an expanding body of literature to the environmental community throughout North America and the world.

Support for Island Press is provided by The Bullitt Foundation, The Mary Flagler Cary Charitable Trust, The Nathan Cummings Foundation, Geraldine R. Dodge Foundation, Doris Duke Charitable Foundation, The Charles Engelhard Foundation, The Ford Foundation, The George Gund Foundation, The Vira I. Heinz Endowment, The William and Flora Hewlett Foundation, W. Alton Jones Foundation, The John D. and Catherine T. MacArthur Foundation, The Andrew W. Mellon Foundation, The Charles Stewart Mott Foundation, The Curtis and Edith Munson Foundation, National Fish and Wildlife Foundation, The New-Land Foundation, Oak Foundation, The Overbrook Foundation, The David and Lucile Packard Foundation, The Pew Charitable Trusts, Rockefeller Brothers Fund, The Winslow Foundation, and other generous donors.

RANCHING
WEST OF
THE 100TH
MERIDIAN

RANCHING WEST OF THE 100TH MERIDIAN

Culture, Ecology, and Economics

Edited by
Richard L. Knight
Wendell C. Gilgert
Ed Marston

ISLAND PRESS
Washington • Covelo • London

Library of Congress Cataloging-in-Publication Data
Ranching west of the 100th meridian : culture, ecology, and economics /
edited by Richard L. Knight, Wendell C. Gilgert, Ed Marston.
    p. cm.
Includes bibliographical references (p.   ).
    ISBN 1-55963-826-5 (cloth : alk. paper) — ISBN 1-55963-827-3 (paper :
alk. paper)
1. Ranching—West (U.S.) I. Knight, Richard L. II. Gilgert, Wendell C.
III. Marston, Ed.
    SF196.U5 R36   2002
    636.08'45'0978—dc21   2001006931

British Cataloguing-in-Publication data available.

Printed on recycled, acid-free paper ✹

Manufactured in the United States of America
09 08 07 06 05 04 03 02   8 7 6 5 4 3 2 1

The editor and authors gratefully acknowledge permission to reproduce
poems, a drawing, and photographs. Five poems by Drummond Hadley are
used by permission of the poet; the drawing by Andrew Rush is used by permission of the artist; and the photographs by Charles J. Belden are courtesy
of Charles J. Belden collection, American Heritage Center, University of
Wyoming.

To Maria Sandoz and J. Frank Dobie,
who knew well the West's natural and human histories

| Contents

ix

| Preface

Our book has three parents. It has an academic parent who cares about the West's principal plant communities—grasses and shrubs—and the fact that their main use is livestock grazing. It has a land-use parent who cares about the increasing economic value of the grasslands and associated water and the fact that ranches are being converted to subdivisions and commercial use at an alarming rate—in Colorado alone we see the equivalent acreage of Rocky Mountain National Park go out of farm and ranching each year and reappear as prairie castles, seasonally occupied condos, and a vast array of commercial developments. And it has a moral parent who values ranching as one of the few western economies that approaches sustainability and has multigenerational ties to the land. Ranching has persevered for the last four hundred years, going back to Juan de Oñate and his *entrada* of *pobladores* who settled at the confluence of the Rio Chama and the Rio Grande in 1598. Beaver trappers, buffalo hunters, loggers, miners, water developers, and recreationists cannot make that claim. Indeed, the length of time that husbanding livestock has been practiced in the West makes it one of our most intact cultures and allows it to stake out the terrain covered under the rubric of sustainable land use. Ranching—except for the halcyon days of the late 1800s—has always existed on the economic margins. Sustainability acknowledges both intergenerational use of land and modest economic returns. Therefore, ranchers may have something to teach us regarding how the West can be used in a sustainable fashion.

This book is also intended to repay part of the debt we owe the many ranch families who have enriched and educated our lives. Whether trailing cows in summer to distant mountain ranges, sitting in their kitchens and hearing the retelling of stories that stitch together lives that span up to nine generations, or simply being impressed with their understanding of animals, grass, water, terrain, and tools, we have seldom encountered Americans who have such a strong sense of family and of belonging to a place. We wonder what our region would be like if other westerners accepted ranchers into their lives as readily as ranch families welcomed us into theirs . . .

On another level, this book joins the ever-widening effort to promote conversations over the role of ranching in the West. Because our contributors believe that ranching can be more ecologically sustainable, more economically viable, and more culturally robust, we share a hope that they the essayists and you the reader may help speed the transition to a ranching tradition that is better than before. We did not invite writers who have no room for livestock in their New West. Nor did we invite those who have no room for public lands because of their private-property rights hysteria. Our contributors are from the radical center—they prize a mix of people with long-term tenure on the land, healthy grasslands and streams, and a public/private blend of lands. The goal of this book is to examine family operations whose thinking and working are linked to the land through husbandry and stewardship. We hope that these poems and essays help to revive a conservation attitude that has been withering for fifty years or more. Environmentalists have been attacking ranching from a perspective detached from the land; conservatives have been striking out in anger at anything that hints of cooperation and collectivism. In response, ranchers have been wondering why no one seems to see that they not only produce food that we need but also guard open space that we covet.

If the conversations offered here are reasonable and address our ecological commitment to the land, our cultural commitment to American society, and the economic role ranching plays in sustainable food production and land conservation, then perhaps this book will contribute usefully to the ongoing debate on the future of the New West. These essayists explore how the ranching culture can do these things better. We should not shrink from the fact that ranching, done wrong, has the capacity to hurt the land. But if done right, it has the power to restore ecological integrity to western lands that have been neglected too long.

| Acknowledgments

This book was possible due to the support of many individuals and organizations. We most heartily thank Dave Armstrong, John Baden, Tom Bartlett, Ben Brown, James Brown, Fred Bryant, Indy Burke, Stephanie Gripne, Rod Heitschmidt, Glenda Humiston, William Lauenroth, Jeremy Maestas, Bill McDonald, Curt Meine, John Mitchell, Eric Odell, Pat and Sharon O'Toole, Bernard Rollin, Bruce Runnels, Andrew Rush, Lynne Sherrod, Larry Van Tassell, Jack Ward Thomas, and Allen Torell. Through their actions and intellectual energy they are ensuring that the theory and practice of ranching will be more culturally robust, ecologically sustainable, and economically viable in the New West.

Many organizations and agencies have supported our work: the Wildlife Habitat Management Institute of the Natural Resources Conservation Service; the Grazing Lands Technology Institute of the Natural Resources Conservation Service; the Gallatin Writers of Bozeman, Montana; the American Farmland Trust; the National Fish and Wildlife Foundation; the Agricultural Research Service; the Animas Foundation; the Colorado State University Agricultural Experiment Station; the Caesar Kleberg Wildlife Research Institute; the Western Center for Integrated Resource Management at Colorado State University; *High Country News*; the Central Colorado Educational Endowment; and the Department of Fishery and Wildlife Biology at Colorado State University. The American Heritage Center at the University of Wyoming in Laramie and Jack and Lili Turnell graciously made available the remarkable photographs of the late Charles Belden of the Pitchfork Ranch, Wyoming.

It is a privilege to acknowledge our long-term relationship with Barbara Dean and Barbara Youngblood of the Covelo, California, office of Island Press. By their loyalty, good cheer, and distinguished scholarship they deserve more than our friendship. If ever two angels touched the ground, Barbara and Barbara are they! Don Yoder as copyeditor and Jennifer Alt and J. Randall Baldini as production editors are sincerely thanked for their attention to detail and loving diligence.

RLK owes a debt to Stan and Junior (Ernest) Berg, ranchers from the Okanogan Highlands of Washington who befriended him when he first came West. They shared with him their lives of living simply, with love enough for the land and for their neighbors. It was then that he began to see how ranching blended human and natural communities, a working recipe for long-term sustainability. Catherine and Evan Roberts, neighbors in Livermore, Colorado, are also remembered as confidants and heroes. They believe people fit into one of two categories: "takers" or "caretakers." Through their commitment to land health, they clearly belong to the latter. Special thanks also to George and Nancy Wallace, Ted and Cheryl Swanson, and Al and Virginia Johnson, neighbors in the Livermore Valley and Buckeye country north of Fort Collins, for days "ahorseback" moving cows and evenings around campfires talking about land and community health. WG thanks ranchers in the Upper Stony Creek watershed in northern California for teaching him that long-term and reasoned change is incremental. A debt of gratitude also to Wayne Elmore, John Buckhouse, Doc and Connie Hatfield, and the rest of the Oregon Traveling Riparian Show, for bringing a message of hope to those same ranchers, and to Jack and Jeff Somerville of the 4-J Ranch for hearing the message and applying it on the ground. EM thanks Doc and Connie Hatfield, for showing him that the West is composed of people and families who care for its human and natural communities, and Sid Goodloe for spending many hours explaining how he brought his New Mexico ranch back to life. And, finally, EM thanks the readers of *High Country News* for supporting his work for going on twenty years.

Part One

INTRODUCTION

Cuando el buho canta el Indio muere.
No es cierto, pero sucede.
When the owl calls the Indian dies.
It is not certain, but it happens.

Rafael Quijada Sierra Madre Sonora Mexico

DRUMMOND HADLEY

I go now to see my cuñada la que me repechó
She who gave me her breast when my father was killed
When my mother went to live with another man
Now my cuñada is dying she is not sick but only old
When she goes we will place her body in a sack
To bury her in the ground
A sack or the mountain wind waits for me as well
Even as I climb the steep cedar breaks
I feel calambres in my legs
Calambres are the pains when one walks
When the nerves in the legs tighten
I grow down and old like the tail of the cow
Someday I will not be able to go to find work
From the borderline as far as Pueblo Colorado
When that time comes I will need a patron
A boss who will not try only to ganar
To win all he is able from my back and my hands

I do not like the towns in the mountains the head is clear
If I could stay in a jacal a hut of bear grass near the canyon spring
I would wake in the mornings and walk to the ridgeline
To look toward those blue valleys and cradles of the Sierra Madre
There I would remember those touches of my women
The long circles the roundups the rock footed horses I'd ridden
There I would wait to drift again
With the spring wind through these mountain passes
There I would wait until the owl calls

Chapter 1

Ranching: An Old Way of Life in the New West

PAUL F. STARRS

For decades proposals have been floated to arrest grazing on federal lands. And today, in our interesting times, arguments are actively being made—consider one published quotation—to "remove livestock from public lands to conserve native biodiversity."[1] Although this statement invokes an epic ecological simple-mindedness that only a law professor could muster, the spirit is as undeniably and quixotically valiant as the conservation biology is primitive. In fact there is a distinguished tradition of ganging up on the livestock industry (as a structural entity), on cattle and sheep (as agents of change), on grazing (as a practice), and on livestock ranchers (as convenient and visible foils). All bear examining.

The theme isn't close to new. The bumper sticker campaigns of the 1990s exhorted "Cattle Free by '93," "Out the Door by '94," "Boycott Public Lands Beef." An entire catalog would take up column-feet of text. Still easily available are volumes with titles as carefully charged with inflammatory power as habanero chile bins at a Tucson farmer's market: *Sacred Cows at the Public Trough, Waste of the West, Beyond Beef.* None of them (surprise!) is by an ecologist. In Elko, Nevada, a couple of years ago—a stronghold of ranching and wildlife and diverse federal lands if ever there was one—a billboard was installed at the southern end of town where it loomed, unsubtly, over every citizen's entry and exit. "Our public lands, ground into hamburger," it read. Studiously (and uncharacteristically), the Shovel Brigade and the Wise Users ignored it. There is nonetheless a great deal of heat generated on the theme of public lands grazing—an anger and skepticism that extends to ranching generally in the American West, whether it involves public lands or not. Vast eddies of hot rhetoric swirl about this topic, which insists on the removal of livestock, and so, tacitly, livestock ranchers, from the use of western public lands. Opening up on the subject can get you into at least a shouting match in any bar in the New West. Certainly it merits discussion.

Even more insidious today is the percolation of that benevolent pro-wilderness, antihuman sensibility steeped into those of us who grew up in the 1970s, started college in the 1980s, and graduated to become observers and students of the public domain in the 1990s. We watched, agape and eventually aghast, as the sides spread wide apart, ever intransigent, often absurd in their militancy (or militant in their absurdity?). To use or not to use: This was the polarization betwixt proponents and opponents of grazing. There are voices in between, but few. The debate, Manichean in philosophical terms, is polarized black versus white and lodged against the detents of reason. The splits are extreme: full use or none, wild or domestic, city slickers or rural rubes, federal or private, small or big, endangered species or livestock. In these terms, the hand dealt is typically all-cows or no-cows. But this doesn't need to be so—as a number of entirely reasonable conservation and biodiversity groups have made clear by meeting ranchers and other western interest groups more than halfway. Innovations are happening in support of not just biodiversity but also working landscapes and a central terrain of shared use and purpose. The question is: How are these innovations being recorded, acknowledged, tested for results, and, if good, passed forward?

There are intriguing programs designed to use the stewardship practices of ranchers—and the actions of grazing animals, and the habitat they use, for part or all of the year—for larger aims. These aims may be personal goals, open-space goals, ecological goals, watershed goals, fuel-hazard-reduction goals, economic goals, community goals, government goals. But they flow in an atmosphere that still includes a proportion of cow haters. And change is occurring with sufficient speed on the ground—let a thousand ranchettes blossom from one historic ranch property—that this is no time to dither.

Ranching's very practice, formation, and history make for an extraordinarily multicultural and diverse way of life that is rife with harsh compromises and yields sometimes opulent, sometimes disappointing, results. In moving away, we break clear to a suitable viewpoint; fog lifts. Gaining a sight line is, in no small degree, what this essay is about.

RANCH FITS AND STARTS

Ranching in the United States is a singular mix of the resolutely practical and time-honored as well as features that are dreamlike and elusive, feats of imagery and the fantastic and the romantic. The product is a distinctive landscape, extensive in its territory, yet often subtle, or at least remote, in its humanized features. The ranching landscape is a subject of almost infinite complexity about which much has already been written.[2] But the essence of twenty-first-century ranching—and the cowboy, and the ranch economy, and the landscape of the ranch—is complicated adaptation. And that is nothing new. It's been so for a century and a half, maybe even five hundred years, since cattle and the elements of ranching practice were brought to the New World in Columbus' second expedition in 1493. That's a long tradition, in which change is about the only expected and standard rule, with challenge a close second to change as agent and force. It's odd that a lifeway whose supporters are so given to espousing tradition is, in fact, completely dependent on tacking before countervailing political, ecological, and economic winds. Ranchers tend, pretty much of necessity, to be ultimate pragmatists. It is their supporters who wear the big hats, never having choused a cow, and it is often rancher-wannabes who prove notoriously inflexible, hidebound, and doctrinaire. Because ranching requires access to so much land and because its incomes are at best small, ranching has rarely had a strong built-in economic constituency in places of power. Instead ranchers have through the years had to make cultural converts. And they continue having to do so, with surprising and ongoing success.

The roots of ranching in the American West are stunningly ancient, extending back to practice in the Iberian Peninsula, North Africa, and the Mediterranean realm. But ranching is also the most swiftly adapting and changing land use in the West—largely because it has to be (Figure 1.1). There is little alternative. Ranch land and public lands are under unceasing pressure—in the past from farmers and homesteaders and dis-

FIGURE 1.1. The ranch in the American West routinely embodies complex foreground/background relationships, evident in this 1950s view of the Bar 99 Ranch in Fish Lake Valley, Nevada. The ranch fields are in the foreground: the irrigated pastures surrounding the ranch buildings. In the middle distance are dry fields and a considerable reach of BLM land grazed as a lease. And in the distance are the White Mountains (including White Mountain Peak, 14,242 feet), where ranch cattle would graze in the early summer and nearly into the fall on Forest Service (USDA) land. The ranch is dependent on many parts, therefore, none easily controlled—"a piece of the continent, a part of the whole," as John Donne put it. (Photograph from Bar 99 Ranch, Nevada, by Paul F. Starrs)

tant elected representatives, today from environmentalists, real estate developers, politicians and planners, and sundry others. And ranchers respond to these challenges, continuing a practice of improvisation and circumstantial change that keeps ranching, in all its variations, very much among the contending forces of the New West.[3]

It does not hurt that almost everyone is in some way enchanted by the lifestyle (though there are violent contrarians). Ranching has forever involved people of varied ethnicity, race, income, and gender. To each one's own: The newly rich flock to trophy ranches in Montana, Wyoming, Colorado, New Mexico, Nevada, and slap down conservation easements and land trusts and buffalo herds that are profoundly of the present, much akin to what the nineteenth-century "remittance men" did when they carved out their part of the frontier and put it to use. And for the middle class there remains the image of the ranch house, the ranchette, and all the colorful histories and nostalgias that time and place can build. The ranch, then, is intrinsic to the western past but intimately part of the New West's future. Ranching embodies, still, American ambitions: dreams of community, dreams of avarice, dreams of control or compromise, dreams of family, dreams of authority, dreams of dominance, dreams of paternalistic arrogance. Not all are pleased—but that too is part of the story.

The ranch, in its varied parts and people, remains interesting to many Americans because the cowhand, the ranch, the federal grazing permit, are telling features of our time. This notion is echoed in Kinky Friedman's timeless line—a bit of prose graven not in *High Country News*, not in some local penny-saver magazine, but in the op-ed pages of the venerable *New York Times*—which holds that "cowboys are America's gift to the children of the world."[4] The ranch gets written off episodically, of course, just like the cowhand. The ranch merits attention precisely because it is controversial and aggressively lacking in diffidence. The ranch grows more interesting because it impinges on aspirations and clashes with visions of what we might want the world to become. Because the ranch and ranch land (and the land that ranchers borrow from the American people) are under pressure, they have always a currency and vigor that less brazen places and landscapes lack.

Ranching is our figurative scarlet "A," a badge variously of courage and shame and fortitude. If we cannot make the ranch work in the twenty-first century, then I would say we will have proved we cannot have a rural future in the urban West. Across this western terrain, Gertrude Stein's words resound: "In the United States there is more space where nobody is than where anybody is, that is what makes America what it is."[5] Through the classic images that reveal the American West as a place of lights, ranch country dwells in the bower of darkness (Figure 1.2). The large metropolises in this image are strikingly evident: here Denver, there Phoenix, Vegas, Albuquerque, Salt Lake. But they are fireflies, clots of photoluminescence, compared to the great darkness that is ranch land and wild land, which share one fundamental attribute: a paucity of people.

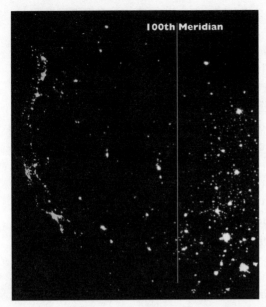

FIGURE 1.2. Western United States at night with the 100th meridian added for orientation. This classic image captures the split between city and rural places. It takes a conurbation of roughly 20,000 people—hardly a large city—to show up from space, but there are surprisingly few of even these small dots in this image. (AVHRR Image, NASA, 1987)

Is the West "an immense landscape . . . going from one set of uses to another set of uses, from one way of life to another, in an astoundingly short time?"[6] This is the way Ed Marston, publisher of *High Country News*, put the matter in a recent essay. Or, restating the case, is the ranch about to disappear? Or is the ranch, instead, an essential landscape feature, the physical expression of long-standing human values, and an ever-developing fact? Ranching will not disappear. But it risks retreat from the city edge into distant redoubts where it might grow all but forgotten. Obviously the ranch has survived so far by redefining itself, and to some degree this is happening now. A ranch is more than a couple of cows; it is more than a ranch house; it is other than a 15-acre ranchette. And though there certainly can be llama farms or bison outfits or subdivisions or bordellos that dub themselves "ranches," it should probably be agreed that the ranch is more than something owned by a gal or a guy sporting a big hat and a belt buckle nearly as large. A ranch is in its essentials extensive—a use of sizable acreage to produce something from forage grown on the ranch itself. That something can include wildlife, of course, or beef or *cabrito* or wool, or watershed protection or biodiversity banking. The essence of the ranch is absolute acreage, never easily obtained. And this acreage requirement is precisely what separates the western ranch from its eastern private-pasture-based forebears. It is also what connects the ranch to its traditional Hispanic roots: Hispanic ranchers had to have acreage too, although the Hispanic (or Canadian) world has fewer overt concerns about the private use of large acreages than the founding fathers of the United States.

The subdivision of sizable properties into small parcels is happening everywhere across the West, a doleful expression of our millennial pathology. Many a recently platted subdivision adopts the moniker "ranch"—a slew of them, for instance, exist in a dozen-mile radius of downtown Reno, Nevada, mostly named for this or that historic family ranch recently sliced and diced at high per-unit profit into coveted ranchettes. Once a subdivision arrives the size, the forage, the vistas, and the abstract quality of open range are gone: Lights loom. Yet ranching in its diverse nomenclatural modes is the litmus of the New West, a most interesting realm. For some of its fans, the ranch is a state of mind. They love the chance to own a piece of the old, the wild, West. It would be foolhardy to grow grim-countenanced about this. Let's instead rejoice in the evolving possibilities.

ALTERNATIVES

What would happen if those who object to western ranchers making use of public lands for grazing domesticated animals were actually to get their way? Remove western ranchers as land stewards, and what have you got? Although there's no immediate risk that the use of 330 million acres of western lands will be withdrawn from ranchers, horns are being raised by latter-day Gabriels to trumpet just that possibility.[7]

Of course, there are those who say the cat's been watching the canary for too long already, since the late nineteenth century, with ranchers granted a large role in public land management by the U.S. Forest Service and the Bureau of Land Management. A hundred years ago there were massive abuses of unclaimed public lands by grazing animals— enough to cause real ecological damage from which recovery is slow, but ongoing. With the days of catastrophic abuse past, who is the appropriate steward of public lands? And if public lands ranching were actually to stop, who would gain dominion over these lands? In the last couple of decades, things have been getting better. And new dialogues have begun that make the early twenty-first century especially exciting for land managers.

Consider the alternatives. The military is the solution that the early preservationist John Muir offered. In a wonderfully overt letter contributed to *The Century Magazine*, he explained that "one soldier in the woods, armed with authority and a gun, would be more effective in forest preservation than millions of forbidding notices. I believe that the good time of the suffering forests can be hastened through the War Department." And: "Let the forests on all the head waters of all the rivers in the country be reserved and put under the charge of the War Department, the most reliable, permanent, unpolitical, and effective department in our Government,—and then forest affairs will definitely be settled, and all our living trees will clap their hands and wave in joy."[8] But in Nevada, where branches of the armed services in the year 2000 directly control almost 30 percent of the public land (and overfly far more acreage), there is sparse—and waning—confidence in military management. Nevadans live year-to-year with the likelihood, a specter, of a military/civilian entente that will load fifty years of nuclear waste into the fractured tunnels underlying Yucca Mountain—already home to a couple of generations of atomic and nuclear testing. Yet it should be noted that often the best-preserved and best-managed wildlands near many an American city are on military reserves. But the military's mandate is specific. And the techniques of military usurpation have, in general, been applied through the years to other kinds of projects as well: building dams, policing parks, sanctifying wildlife reserves, suppressing fires.[9]

Wildlife biologists have been especially vocal in slamming ranching. But verifiable management successes, in restoring habitat and in dramatically boosting the quantity and quality and variety of wildlife living in reserves, are few indeed despite the respectable acreage in the West devoted to refuges. Although the federal government became the official steward of unclaimed public domain lands only in 1976, it is still duty-bound to admit that its longtime management served at best as a holding action. Yet a broad administration of public lands was instigated by the U.S. Congress from the 1890s to the 1930s because ranch, timber, mining, and farming interests were deep in the pocket of development interests; vesting administrative control in federal agencies was part of the Progressive movement. Washington, D.C., remains far from the

West in thought and fact. Too few are the wildlife biologists whose conception of "community" and "economy" actually extends to the human side. And there are prominent failures of wildlife management to go with some few successes.[10]

Who should mind the henhouse of public lands? Foxes abound. And there are plenty of Sir Galahads who insist that their strength is off the charts because theirs is the virtue. There are cow-haters and midge-lovers, tree-huggers and native plant puritans, human opponents and pro-nature jihadists of every stripe. We all have our druthers. But the fact is, no one deserves to have it all. The only virtue is in the community of shared effort. And the first effort involves coming to the same table to attain some common results—not an easy trick.

AMERICAN LESSONS

Good students recognize good teachers. In the United States there have been public figures who tendered deep lessons that might have been absorbed and heeded. But Americans have not always listened well, a pattern dating well back into the nineteenth century. The paragon of western sense and sensibility was, of course, none other than John Wesley Powell (Figure 1.3).[11] His views were in spirit Jeffersonian—Powell believed in communities connected to the land—yet at a firm remove from Thomas Jefferson's eastern agrarian physiocracy of autonomous virtuous farmers. Powell recognized that what had worked in the West required more than individual action; it had to gestate into a concerted group effort. The West, Powell believed, needed to be a place of community.

The essence of a seasoned public servant, Powell contended that the federal government should oversee the distribution of land into a complex mix of private and communal landholdings with forests held in reserve. But he believed that it was distribution—the rules—that had to be changed. And with those changes, the West could then control its own domain and destiny. Though elegant and reasoned, Powell's arguments would prove too high-octane, and certainly too heretical, for his time.[12] Still, the lesson that Powell offers is important. It is a reminder that while some of the plights of ranching are of its own difficult and speculative making, other problems are the product of American circumstance.

FIGURE 1.3. John Wesley Powell, seen here in his later years, was a powerful influence in debates over how the American West should be occupied by the spreading forces of European-American ambition. He held out for a more reasoned, and appropriate, form of settlement with a far more complex land tenure system than would prove the case. His arguments fell upon deaf ears. But the fundamental soundness of his argument is today largely beyond dispute. (Photograph from National Archives)

Powell objected to speculation. He despised land developed for buying and selling—land that could only be privately held, in the West, in inadequate amounts. All was to be diced into quarter-sections. He warned that the West risked being dissected into small speculative packages by the township and range land division system. He feared that vast industrial interests would gather and harvest resources subject to minimal control and accountability. Instead he suggested emplacing a land system that was deliberate, different, and durable. Powell spoke for a more permanent, an enduring, community. It was not to be. But he pursued this goal for two decades, through founding of the Bureau of American Ethnography, into directorship of the U.S. Geological Survey, and beyond.[13]

Powell brought the voice of community defense and what might now be called a bioregional ethic to the U.S. Congress, where it was shouted down, flamed out, and came to nought. His *Report on the Lands of the Arid Region* was, in fact, almost buried in the archives until found and republished in the 1960s. But Powell's admonitions keep coming back, and ranchers could do worse than read him and his modern-day biographers and supporters—and pay heed. There is a burgeoning watershed consciousness and bioregional movement in the American West. And it is inclusive—at least for those who recognize its larger message.

The dominant western economic force today is the so-called New West, overtly a series of urban, high-density oases of city people, many aspiring to suburban or rural gentry. The denizens of this suburban Shangri-la have little knowledge about how to manage public lands; the cities are doughnut holes of urban civilization set in vast surrounds of sparsely used land. Even fervent friends of the New West are becoming alarmed at the proliferation of real estate ranchette developments—once curious impositions on the landscape but ever increasingly, in area and economic dominance, the most potent force for landscape change in the West. Paving is permanent. Although the formal studies are just begun, there can be little argument that ecologically the effects of ranchettes spell trouble indeed for the future of western diversity.[14]

RANCHING AND SPAIN

Long before I was recognizably a westerner, I was an adoptive Spaniard. For seven years I lived on the high meseta, the central tableland of the Iberian Peninsula, and resided there long before setting foot in Nevada or Utah or California or Colorado. And I go back every couple of years; the cross-cultural images rattling about my head are often Spanish. When I look to lessons learned, I think about words from the distinguished expatriate English writer Gerald Brenan, who lived and traveled throughout southern Spain in the 1920s and 1930s. His words lead to some surprising, but no less significant, conclusions about cultural contrasts:

> The United States is a country where the compressed gases of Europe have been released and have then expanded suddenly to fill a vast, half-empty region. This has created a climate of euphoria and optimism as well as much goodwill and friendliness, but operating in a vacuum with no historical background to channel it. Except in some corners of the [American] South there is little feeling for place, home, or material possessions in spite of many attempts in the past to create them. The landscape is too continental to encourage the putting down of roots and the pressures that make for a continual change of habitat are too many.[15]

Americans are rootless, in Brenan's reckoning, and singularly pressured. Yet in a kind of market-driven slash-and-burn mentality, unforgiving of inefficiency, what is at risk are resources and attributes that people elsewhere treat very differently. Placing greater value on cultural resources—and permitting a good landscape to have people who stimulate its variation and health—might merit more American attention. Sustaining biodiversity, then, is anything but one and the same as "wilderness preservation."[16] Boosting biological diversity by using land, not quarantining it as wilderness, is an idea that has not really arrived in the United States. But ranching's partisans favor preserving diversity with a tempered way of life grounded in the capacity of the land itself. Or so the hope goes.

From the 1970s on, the European Union has attempted to inoculate its member countries with a supercharged impulse toward homogenization. But, strikingly, city people and country people in southern and western Europe do resist. The knowledge economy is almost as vigorous in the Iberian Peninsula, France, or Italy as in the United States. But there is also a contrasting Mediterranean world that accedes to older impulses and breaks out the leather traces, hames, and a collar, harnessing the old cart of what might be called the "landscape economy," based on the fruits of the earth and a continuing interest in local products and the lay of the land. The goal is the large-scale preservation of a distinctive and favored landscape. There are lessons here that can be transferred from Old World to New. Everything, for a start, is "natural." European lay folk and scientists engage in no discussion of pristine nature: Both sides recognize the absurdity of claiming to know of a place where man has not set foot. Every landscape is presumed to have been civilized by the presence and timeless activity of humans. For European scientists and policymakers, the question is not the recuperation of a perfect environment, human bereft, but instead what each person might wish to see on the landscape (Figure 1.4). These are consensual decisions, with science and politics added. Thus everything from a cork oak to a field cleared of brush is considered a valued element of the natural world. Human activity is part of that world, and considered a good part, and the end product is not single but many: fine habitats and a world that did give rise, after all, to much of the culture of the United States.

There are primitivists who would rather acclaim a world of the perfectly pristine. Ecological historians in the United States are beginning to side with their European colleagues, however, and admit that wild

FIGURE 1.4. The concept of the "natural" is, for Europeans in general and certainly for Spaniards, a kind of irrelevance. Humans are part of nature, and what is seen is the world we have created. This is self-evident. Scientists now recognize that the effects of human activity are everywhere visible in the world—no place is "pristine." Here some cork oaks have had their bark recently removed; other oaks are preserved for their heavy fall of acorns; the understory is cleared of woody shrubs. The landscape is engineered, therefore, but also prime habitat for wildlife and domesticated animals. So it has long been.
(Photograph by the author, Extremadura, Spain, 1999)

land and habitat are everywhere, even in a backyard. Some of the places thought to be least touched by human activity turn out to be carefully maintained and humanized landscapes developed and sustained by aboriginal fire, by hunting, by self-transporting weeds, by settlement. No realistic scientist can even begin to say what a "pristine" world—or even a place—might look like. And not very many of the world's 6 billion people will volunteer for eradication in order to make more room for the remnant preindustrial 1 percent that occupied the globe fifty centuries ago.

A compelling and scientific argument can be made that in Europe, even today, there are still prolific endemic species, valued flora and fauna, and a biodiversity that is, in fact, quite a bit richer than anything in the United States. Why? Precisely because Europe has seen the effects of human activity for hundreds of generations—activity that has produced a variety of disturbances that increase biodiversity, part of the "intermediate disturbance hypothesis," which holds that in disturbance is created diversity.[17] Some species go; others come in. And by maintaining a middling level of pressure on an environment, a higher degree of diversity is produced, though at some cost to precarious disturbance-hating endemic plants, which must be otherwise preserved. In fact, the greatest danger is a monospecific obsession that excludes diversity from the landscape. Landscape is a mix, with a vehement and active human presence at some locales and far less in others. In the meld lies magic.

Let me note, finally, that the mix of urban and rural landscapes characteristic of a place like Spain, which includes by some estimates 70 percent of the "wild" land in western Europe, is not unlike that of the United States today. European scientists—and environmentalists—are loud in their praise of "low-intensity farming," which includes ranching and other extensive but not especially efficient uses of land. This enthusiasm represents a dramatic departure from American attitudes: Human activity is not regarded as something vile, dangerous, or forlorn in the Mediterranean realm. Not for Spaniards, or for other Europeans, is the notion of humanity as corrupt and something to be extirpated from the earth, a bedrock belief of modern ecoradicals. Think about what Albert Camus said: "If there is a sin against life, it consists perhaps not so much in despairing of life as in hoping for another life and in eluding the implacable grandeur of this life."

There have been ecological mistakes, environmental plights, and everyone remembers them. But human activity on the land across most of the world is not regarded as something bad. The human presence adds an element of interest to the natural world. There are people who have rooted—especially in that most elongated and sparsely populated of American regions, the West. And the people who have done this most effectively are of two sorts. First there are city people building metropolises that are monuments (especially of late) to an aggressive reshaping of the natural world into arcane models of occupancy. How else do we explain the proliferation of golf courses in Palm Springs, lakes in Las Vegas, allergen-laden mulberries in Phoenix? Second there are ranchers who have chosen as their way of life a practice of formidable historical depth, ecological ingenuity, and roots that date back to the earliest movements of pastoral people along North Africa, to Iberia, and thence, of course, to the Americas. But ranch land is also the setting for urban sprawl, where cities and especially suburbs bite off chunks of the modified world and turn them into smaller, more intensively used properties subject more to destructive exploitation.

GEOGRAPHIC IMPERATIVES

Why is ranching so oddly displaced an activity? Well, the economics of ranching is pretty wretched—unless you take into account a variety of positive externalities that make the phrase "voodoo economics" seem the stuff of Nobel Prize science. The community of ranching is an isolated, intense, dispersed few rather than a concerted and unified whole. Ranching is adaptive, poorly subject to standard rules. This makes it an unreliable marriage partner to hegemonic government edict and regulation. Often on the outs with government, ranchers have made up rules as they go along, sometimes to good effect, at other times bad.

Among the most effective philosophers of postmillennial life, it seems to me, are the experts who recognize what Bill deBuys has called the "radical center," a great ebbing body of practitioners committed to results. At both ends of the spectrum, far left and far right, we find a degree of intransigence that is paralyzed by orthodoxy. There is no ideological purity in the center—its compromises preclude that—but flexibility and realism make it possible to attain real accomplishments. Alas, at the two extremes we find a share of ranchers and certainly wildlife partisans. But I like the advocacy of Gary Nabhan—a MacArthur Fellowship recipient—and his coauthor Stephen Trimble, who in a fine book titled *The Geography of Childhood: Why Children Need Wild Places* assert:

> If we value what can come from living a rural childhood—
> from riding through cow pastures and playing in sagebrush
> rather than on lawns, from tending horses rather than hamsters—we must act to preserve the possibility of such a life.
> It is disappearing fast, and those who are aware of its endangerment are fighting over the scraps and remnants.[18]

An argument for ranching, in short, can be cultural. Some will not like it; Debra Donahue devotes much of a chapter in her recent book to rebuking those who speak of livestock ranching as something with an innate worth. But there are many arguments that can be made against an impulse toward cultural extermination, an acquiescence toward geno-cide, and these arguments are best mounted well before the disappear-ance is entire. What livestock ranching faces right now, in the vast upswing of land and water prices, a booming demand for exurban ranchettes, and a relentless pressure to sell, is but the latest in a 150-year history of selective pressure. Ranching's essence is change and adapta-tion. It is what ranchers do, what livestock do, and what makes ranch-ing more vocation than job. Its economics are poor, and the alternatives are not generous. If ranchers are to continue to serve as the first-line conservators of the working landscapes that we call rangeland, they will need ingenuity and help. In striking ways, everyone can benefit.

The public benefits from fewer subdivisions—and from better eco-logical management of subdivisions that are in place (the ecology of the subdivision is a nightmare) (Figure 1.5). There will be retained open space, better air, better water. The opportunity for recreational hiking will exist. But even more important, other uses are preserved: bird-watching and spotting game, increased access to scenery, protection of native plants and rare and endangered species. The flow of products is varied: perhaps hosting guests, producing sought after crops and prod-ucts. (Look at the sixty different cheeses produced in Marin County, California, by members and supporters of the Marin Agricultural Land Trust alone.)[19] More and more of the scholarly biodiversity literature, in the United States and abroad, holds that livestock is better a part of a biodiversity solution than a barrier to it. There's also an argument, not to be ignored, that the existence of human cultural and economic diver-sity amounts to something significant.

But there will also have to be a growing degree of public support for ranchers and their stewardship role. Among the blessed oddities of ranching is its informal structure for dealing with problems and com-munity issues. Resolution of most problems is sought in the networks of connections and personal relationships that the ranching community values so highly. Ranchers are accustomed to working things out; this, too, can be good news for the diverse constituents of public lands. Ranchers have adopted cooperative management agreements, collabora-

FIGURE 1.5. A classic yet omnipresent scene in the American West is the subdivision going in with great sight lines. It is difficult to argue against the desirability of owning a house in such a setting. But plunking a house into the middle of rangeland is also an act of stern finality: It can safely and surely be said that this place will never be the same. (Photograph by the author, near Lamoille, Nevada, 1998)

tive fencing and riding, 501(3)c's, as in the Malpai Borderlands, or inter-agency work. Ranchers are, further, there already. The good ones will learn. The bad, or improvident, or mulish will fail and disappear. They deserve to have the public and the government land agencies fire shots across their bow—and then act. There will be others more capable. Landscape use—working landscapes—is necessarily a compromise, never absolute. For every rare species affected by grazing there are also the grazing obligates—species that appear only in landscapes where grazing takes place. But this is simply the latest selective pressure on the ranching community, and who would have it otherwise?

RANCH EXIT

Western public lands and private ranching are not, in short, likely to disappear. Ranching exists in a complex tenure relationship: public and private, farm and forest, remote and suburban. Ranches are open lands, biodiversity niches, watersheds, archaeological reserves, archives of settlement history, endangered species habitat, diverse ecosystem pools, biodiversity banks—and, just incidentally, vessels for livestock feed. Ranchers live close to the land, choosing to do so and making many sacrifices to stay there. They have been there in some cases for generations; in other spots, only for a few years. This guarantees them nothing.

Livestock ranching in the twenty-first century exists in many meaningful modes. None is an unvarnished good or entirely bad. In fact ranching in its ambiguity mirrors the sheer difficulty of sorting out the human relationship with the physical world. It is our best parable of postmodernity. Ranching is analogous to an intricate astrophysical mirror: It exists to reflect light back; but to construct a perfect mirror, getting that flatness, polish, and shine to conform, requires huge labor. Perhaps as a millennial resolve we should quit wishing for simplicity when the complex is at once more challenging and more realistic. For better than a dozen reasons, the fact of ranching is a conundrum in a new century: We carry it around with us, mull over its possibilities and difficulties, deliberate over what it means. Ranching is a suitable koan—a problem from which we can learn. In coming to understand it, we grasp something else, better, and broader. There is nothing wrong with that.

Stewardship is, fundamentally, a tectonic process: slow and, if pursued, virtually unstoppable. But the results are clear: cessation of hostilities, cooperation (a Sesame Street value if ever there was one), and, ultimately, peaceful cohabitation. In concluding, then, let's rely on something old. For ranching to continue, and succeed, as a force for enhanced stewardship in the American West, cooperation and compromise are needed. We may have hopes, but perhaps also one small prayer. After all, the Book of Isaiah 11:5–7 does read: "And the leopard shall lay down with the young goat, and the lion with the lamb, and a little child shall lead them."

NOTES

1. The quotation, a casual example of cow loathing, is actually the subtitle of D. L. Donahue's *The Western Range: Removing Livestock from Public Lands*

to Conserve Native Biodiversity (Norman: University of Oklahoma Press, 1999); Donahue is a law professor in Wyoming.

2. Three works date from the 1990s alone, which is notable because there has been something of an analytical sea change in the study of ranching. These three works are: R. Slatta, *Cowboys of the Americas* (New Haven: Yale University Press, 1990); T. G. Jordan, *North American Cattle-Ranching Frontiers: Origins, Diffusions, and Differentiation* (Albuquerque: University of New Mexico Press, 1993); and perhaps my own *Let the Cowboy Ride: Cattle Ranching in the American West* (Baltimore: Johns Hopkins University Press, 1998).

3. *The Atlas of the New West* is a complicated product; supervisory editing by W. Riebsame and J. Robb with essays by P. Goin (photography), P. N. Limerick, and C. Wilkinson (New York: Norton, 1997).

4. K. Friedman, "God's Own Cowboys," *New York Times*, 18 March 1991, p. A-11 (national ed.).

5. G. Stein, *The Geographical History of America* (Baltimore: Johns Hopkins University Press, 1995), pp. 45–46; originally published in 1936.

6. The quotation is from Ed Marston's lead editorial in a New West edition of *High Country News*, the authoritative newspaper of the Mountain West: "Beyond the Revolution," 10 April 2000, quoting p. 1.

7. The list is long and odd, but some of the most anti-cattle-obsessed would have to include the following: D. Ferguson and N. Ferguson, *Sacred Cows at the Public Trough* (Bend: Ore.: Maverick Publications, 1983); R. Symanski, *Wild Horses and Sacred Cows*, foreword by E. Abbey (Flagstaff, Ariz.: Northland Press, 1985); L. Jacobs, *Waste of the West: Public Lands Ranching* (Tucson: self-published, 1991); J. Rifkin, *Beyond Beef: The Rise and Fall of the Cattle Culture* (New York: Dutton, 1992); and surely, most recently, D. L. Donahue, *The Western Range*. The list could be longer, but this is a good cross section of the belligerents.

8. The comment by J. Muir is in a letter to *The Century Magazine* on the theme "A Plan to Save the Forests: Forest Preservation by Military Control," February 1895, pp. 626–634; Muir's comments are on pp. 630–631. The other contributors are not without distinction: G. Pinchot, T. Roosevelt, F. L. Olmsted, B. Frenow, and N. S. Shaler. Yet the spirit of Muir's contribution is as militant as the writing of the others—perhaps more so.

9. The move toward military use goes back to the late 1800s; this need underlay the topographic surveys of G. M. Wheeler, of the U.S. Army, in his "Great Surveys" of the 1870s. Yet more recent authors have scored the dif-

ficulties of government management, including the following: P. Goin, *Nuclear Landscapes*; D. Loomis, *Combat Zoning: Military Land Use in Nevada*; S. Pyne, *Fire in America: A Cultural History of Wildland and Rural Fire*; and the sometimes difficult to credit A. Chase, in his highly original *Playing God in Yellowstone*. All remain easily found.

10. There is much discussion in the scholarly literature of problems and failures associated with different kinds of single-purpose wildlife reserves— not just in the United States but even more generally abroad. The recent doctoral dissertation by N. Sayre would certainly count as one distinguished example; his study of a wildlife preserve south of Tucson is appropriately cautionary and reveals the fallacies of monospecific wildlife management as readily and broadly as it slams certain kinds of community effort. See "Species of Capital: An Anthropological Investigation of the Buenos Aires Ranch (Pima County, Arizona) and Its Transformation into a National Wildlife Refuge" (Ph.D. disssertation, University of Chicago, 1999).

11. See J. Powell et al., *Report on the Lands of the Arid Region of the United States, with a More Detailed Account of the Lands of Utah* (Washington, D.C.: Government Printing Office, 1879). For Powell's own words, a convenient summary is *Seeing Things Whole: The Essential John Wesley Powell*, edited by W. deBuys (Washington, D.C.: Island Press, 2001).

12. According to D. Worster, *A River Running West: The Life of John Wesley Powell* (New York: Oxford University Press, 2000).

13. For a most intriguing treatment of Powell's nineteenth-century ideas, updated to our twenty-first-century context, see A. Phillip, "John Wesley Powell's Watershed Commonwealths: Mapping a West That Might Have Been," *Cascadia Planet* (Portland, Ore.), 1998 [http://www.tnews.com/text/powell_story.html].

14. The research by D. Theobald and R. Knight at Colorado State University, Fort Collins, on the geographic mapping and ecological effects of the widespread ranchette phenomenon in the American West may finally add full numbers to this debate. See E. Odell and R. Knight, "Songbird and Medium-Sized Mammal Communities Associated with Exurban Development," *Conservation Biology* 15 (2001): 1143–1150; and D. Theobald et al., "Estimating the Cumulative Effects of Development on Wildlife Habitat," *Landscape and Urban Planning* 39 (1997): 25–36.

15. G. Brenan, *Thoughts in a Dry Season: A Miscellany* (Cambridge: Cambridge University Press, 1978), p. 159.

16. For an intelligent essay see S. Sarkar, "Wilderness Preservation and Biodiversity Conservation—Keeping Divergent Goals Distinct," *BioScience* 49 (1999): 405–412.

17. On the significance of the intermediate disturbance hypothesis and its influence in the Mediterranean realm see A. Perevelotsky and No'am Seligman, "Role of Grazing in Mediterranean Rangeland Ecosystems," *BioScience* 48 (1998): 1007–1017. Additional treatments and discussions suggest just how much we have yet to establish. See, for example, A. Hector et al., "Diversity and Productivity Experiments in European Grasslands," *Science* 286 (1999): 1123–1127, and O. Sala et al., "Global Biodiversity Scenarios for 2100," *Science* 287 (2000): 1770–1774.

18. G. P. Nabhan and S. Trimble, *The Geography of Childhood: Why Children Need Wild Places* (Boston: Beacon Press, 1994), p. 124.

19. The comment on the vast array of cheeses is thanks to the assurances of S. Fairfax, professor in environmental sciences, policy, and management at the University of California at Berkeley (June 2000).

Chapter 2

Lay of the Land: Ranch Land and Ranching

Martha J. Sullins, David T. Theobald,
Jeff R. Jones, and Leah M. Burgess

Through boom and bust periods, the western ranching business has faced many challenges. Although ranching is a resilient business, today it confronts a fundamental change that is eroding the very foundation of the ranching enterprise—a rapidly shrinking land base. This essay explores the continuing transformation of cattle ranching in the Rocky Mountain states of Arizona, Colorado, Idaho, Montana, Nevada, New Mexico, Utah, and Wyoming and looks at strategies for shaping its future.

THREATS AND OPPORTUNITIES

Ranchers have always faced a wide range of challenges to their land and livestock: recurring drought, blizzards, pests and predators, poisonous and invasive plants, diseases, and more. Perhaps the greatest threat facing the future viability of ranching in the West is the declining availability of land. Because of the West's aridity, ranching traditionally requires large amounts of land so that cattle have sufficient forage for most of the year.[1] This acreage includes a home ranch of privately owned land and, most often, access to public grazing lands through permits to ensure adequate seasonal forage. Thus western ranchers have become stewards of large tracts of both private and public lands.

Rangeland covers almost 336 million acres or 61 percent of the total land base in the eight western states, and half of that is privately owned.[2] In fact, agricultural lands comprise the majority of all lands under private ownership—from 63 percent in Idaho to 90 percent in New Mexico. Federal agencies, primarily the U.S. Forest Service and the Bureau of Land Management, manage most of the West's public rangelands.

Grazing on public land is essential to the viability of western ranching. In 1994, USDA researchers reported that ranchers with federal grazing permits received higher net returns above cash costs per cow and per hundredweight than those without permits.[3] Roughly 97.7 million acres of agricultural land were tied to grazing permits in 1997, compared to 103.4 million acres in 1992, representing an average of 43 percent of all acres in production.[4] In recent years, however, a growing number of people with different land-use values have tried to limit ranchers' access to public lands or exclude them entirely.[5] Private grazing lands are also shrinking in availability as they are removed from production and put to other uses.

Not only is the land base for ranching decreasing but so too is water. Without water, much of the West's rangeland can no longer support cattle. Although it is difficult to determine precisely what is happening to water used for ranching, there is keen competition for it from municipal users. Estimates reveal that 80 percent of the water in Colorado's South Park, for example, has been purchased for the Denver metropolitan area.[6] Over the last several decades, 40,000 acres of irrigated hay meadows supporting South Park ranches have been taken out of production as the cities of Aurora, Denver, and Thornton purchased surface and groundwater rights. The prices are lucrative too. Water in Otero County, Colorado, now goes for about $56,000 per share. Drying up the water dries up the land, causing agricultural land values to plummet. In Otero County, land served by irrigation water is now worth from $1,750 to $2,000 per acre, whereas an acre without water brings about $300. Thus acre by acre and drop by drop, ranchers are inexorably losing their most valuable input to production—land.

CONVERSION OF RANCH LANDS

The U.S. Census of Agriculture lends historical perspective to changes in the agricultural land base.[7] Total acreage of farm and ranch land in the eight western states peaked in 1964 at 268 million acres.[8] Since then, agricultural acreage has consistently declined by an average of about 1 million acres per year. By 1997, there were approximately 228 million acres under production—a reduction of 15 percent from 1964. Arizona, for example, loses over 300,000 agricultural acres annually, Montana has lost almost 200,000, and Colorado has lost 154,000 acres each year since 1964. Although there is some variability in the data between census years, the long-term trends are fairly stable and consistent.

County-level statistics reveal additional information about agricultural land loss. Overall Colorado has lost 15 percent of its agricultural land base since 1964. But thirteen of its counties have lost more than 50 percent of their agricultural land, and just over half of the counties in the state have seen reductions of 25 percent since 1964.[9] The Colorado counties experiencing the greatest decline in agricultural acres are those found along the Front Range or those containing a high percentage of public land (for example, the mountain communities).

According to the census data, over the last ten years land used for grazing in the Rocky Mountain West has been declining at a rate of 1.6 million acres per year. USDA National Resources Inventory data reveal that while cultivated pastureland has been increasing gradually, rangeland (primarily native grasses, forbs, or shrubs or introduced forage similar to range species) has declined by almost 292,000 acres per year since 1982. From 1982 to 1997, about 45 percent of the pasture and rangeland taken out of grazing was converted to urban development; the rest remained in rural uses, including crop production.[10]

As rapid population growth is projected to continue, the landscape of the Rocky Mountain West is poised to undergo further transformation. This region grew three times faster from 1990 to 1999 than the rest of the United States.[11] In fact, fourteen of the fastest-growing counties in the United States are in the Rocky Mountain West.[12] Ten western counties are growing so fast that their populations will double by 2010, while the populations of an additional thirty-two counties will double by 2020. Although most of the current population still lives in urban areas, rural population growth exceeds urban growth in over half the counties (1990–1997). This phenomenon of strong rural growth patterns is unique to the Rocky Mountain region.

An unfortunate parallel trend is increased land consumption per

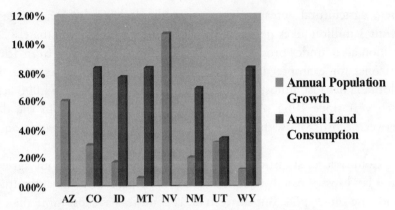

FIGURE 2.1. Population growth and land consumption in the Rocky Mountain West: 1960–1990. Land consumption data for Arizona and Nevada were unavailable.

capita. Throughout the Rocky Mountain West, land is being consumed for residential development much faster than the population growth rate (Figure 2.1). From 1960 to 1990, for example, annual rates of land consumption reached 7.2 percent—far surpassing the 2.8 percent annual population growth rate. Much of the new growth across the West is in second homes. In fact, up to 70 percent of the housing in and around towns like Vail, Park City, Tahoe, Sedona, and Steamboat Springs is owned by nonresidents who vacation periodically in these communities.[13]

HOW WILL RANCHING SURVIVE?

In areas with higher land values, many ranchers have stayed in business because rising land prices have increased their equity and net worth and allowed them to borrow more.[14] In 1997, per acre values for agricultural land and buildings averaged from $121 in New Mexico to $633 in Idaho.[15] State-level averages, however, mask the true range of land values that ranchers face (FIgure 2.2). Although 14 percent of the western counties had land values over $1,500 per acre, higher land values are a mixed blessing for the ranching industry because they also increase the pressure for land conversion to "higher and better uses."

To stay solvent, ranchers across the region are finding they need to diversify and develop other operations based on marketing their land

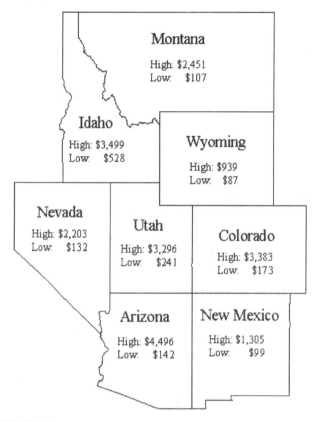

FIGURE 2.2. Average county-level per acre values of land buildings
in the Rocky Mountain West: 1997.

and livestock resources, including plants, animals, or scenery.[16] A rancher
in Arizona is opening a bed and breakfast, for example, in addition to a
new pasture poultry operation.[17] Other ranchers are trying niche marketing of natural, kosher, or conservation beef. Still other income-gen-
erating strategies include selling hunting leases, running a dude ranch,
offering trail rides, or allowing some public access for hiking, wildlife
watching, camping, cross-country skiing, and other recreational pur-
suits.[18] In today's economy, a rancher's management of land, water, and
livestock varies considerably from how business was conducted at the
end of the nineteenth century. Ranchers frequently find themselves marketing their stewardship practices to their nonranching neighbors in

terms of the soil conservation, water supply improvement, or wildlife habitat protection they can provide.[19]

Although land conversion is not a new threat, it is a growing one with permanent repercussions for ranching. Today many people value ranch lands as sites for second homes more than for their traditional commodities. What, then, will ensure a future for ranching in the West?

STRATEGIES FOR TOMORROW

The outlook for ranching in the West depends on the strategies we develop today. These strategies must be applied where ranching faces the greatest challenges: protecting the land base, offering economic development programs for ranch businesses, and promoting public education about ranching.

To focus strategies and programs, we need a clear picture of the forces driving ranchland conversion, including the causes, location, and intensity of conversion pressure. This process involves improving techniques for estimating ranchland loss and developing new data sources on land transfers (for example, using county-level real estate transaction data to identify ownership patterns and trends). Further research on these issues is particularly critical in light of an American Farmland Trust report titled *The Last Roundup*, which highlights the federal, state, and local policies, in addition to pervasive economic pressures, that lead to the subdivision of large ranches.

Developing appropriate land protection programs is a logical outgrowth of understanding the nature of land conversion. These programs must address the long-term viability of ranching by employing techniques that value nontraditional commodities—such as scenic vistas, wildlife habitat, and watershed protection—and promote sustainable ranching practices. Such techniques include the purchase of agricultural conservation easements, transfer of development rights, donation of conservation easements, and other tools to compensate ranchers for benefits they provide that are not always capitalized in land values.

Ranching is first and foremost a business that sustains families and communities. In addition to ranching's traditional commodities, there are newer and perhaps more valuable ones today. Ranchers should be encouraged to explore these new commodities. Agricultural economic development programs can help ranchers develop and market new products and services in response to changing economic conditions. This process involves combining the traditional service providers (Cooperative Extension Service, community colleges, agricultural organizations) with business consultants who can offer on-ranch expertise in economic development strategies.

Finally, we need to engage state and local governments, ranchers themselves, and the nonranching public in our efforts to protect ranch lands and the many commodities they produce. There must be education on the short- and long-term effects of converting ranch land to other uses, including the ecological and economic impacts, as well as the options that exist for protecting the land base. Education should highlight the many valuable products and services that well-managed ranch lands produce that yield community, and sometimes regional, benefits. Other education services should target new purchasers of ranches (for example, conservation buyers) who are unfamiliar with the management skills needed to preserve the ecological and open space values of their properties.

Ranching, especially as a family enterprise, is buffeted by powerful and often conflicting forces that threaten its very existence. Only a strategic, balanced approach to protecting the land base and the business will ensure that ranching is indeed in our future.

NOTES

1. Forage production varies according to the ecosystem and land management. Pinyon-juniper, desert shrub, and grasslands, for example, typically produce less than 1,000 pounds of forage per acre, while prairie, annual grasslands, and wet grasslands may produce more than four times that amount per acre. See L. A. Joyce, *An Analysis of the Range Forage Situation in the United States: 1989–2000*, draft (Washington, D.C.: USDA Forest Service, 1989), pp. 1-7c and 1-7d.

2. USDA Forest Service, *An Analysis of the Land Base Situation in the United States: 1989–2040* (Fort Collins: Rocky Mountain Forest and Range Experiment Station, 1989), pp. 36–37.

3. K. H. Mathews Jr., W. F. Hahn, K. E. Nelson, and T. L. Crawford, *Cow/Calf Ranching in Ten Western States* (Herndon, Va.: USDA/ERS, 1994).

4. U.S. Census of Agriculture, 1997 [http://www.nass.usda.gov/census].

5. E. Riebsame, "Ending the Range Wars?" *Environment* (May 1996):4–29.

6. S. Lipsher, "Showdown in South Park: Angry Residents Agree to Pay to Draw Firm Line in the Dust," *Denver Post*, 4 October 1998, p. H-7.

7. There are advantages and limitations to using U.S. Census of Agriculture data. Census data only capture *net* changes in "land in farms" and do not explain what happened to land taken out of production or where additional acres came from. The National Resources Inventory (NRI) is the best source for agricultural land conversion data because it reports on all land-use changes over a given period. NRI data have been collected only since 1982, however, and therefore cannot provide a historical perspective as can the census data. Finally, because the two data sets are collected using different sampling methods, it is difficult to compare them, although they do approximate each other.

8. U.S. Census of Agriculture, 1964 to 1997 [http://www.nass.usda.gov/census]. These data are from "land in farms," which consists primarily of agricultural land used for crops, pasture, or grazing and includes acres in the conservation reserve and wetlands reserve programs.

9. Ibid.

10. USDA Natural Resources Conservation Service, National Resources Inventory, 1982 to 1997 [http://www.nhq.nrcs.usda.gov/NRI/1997/summary_report/original/contents.html].

11. J. S. Baron, D. M. Theobald, and D. B. Fagre, "Management of Land Use Conflicts in the United States Rocky Mountains," *Mountain Research and Development* 20 (2000):24–27.

12. U.S. Census Bureau county-level population estimates, 1990 to 1999.

13. W. E. Riebsame, H. Gosnell, and D. M. Theobald, *Atlas of the New West: Portrait of a Changing Region* (New York: Norton, 1997), pp. 104–106.

14. J. M. Fowler and L. A. Torell, "Economic Conditions Influencing Ranch Profitability," *Rangelands* 9 (1987):55–58.

15. U.S. Census of Agriculture, 1997 [http://www.nass.usda.gov/census].

16. W. Scaling, "Developing Opportunities for Marketing Rangeland," *Rangelands* 10 (1988):159–160.

17. B. Graham, "Blood, Sweat and Steers," *Phoenix New Times*, 19 March 1998 [http://www.phoenixnewtimes.com/issues/1998-03-19/feature.html].

18. Scaling, "Developing Opportunities," p. 159.

19. Ibid., p. 160.

Part Two

THE CULTURE
OF RANCHING

Alma de mi Alma
A Song of the Vaqueros of Mexico

DRUMMOND HADLEY

El sauce y la palma se mesclan con calma
Alma de mi alma que Linda eres tu
The willow and the palm
They gently touch each other
Alma of my soul soul of my soul
How beautiful you were

Alma born about 1953 to Don Cruzita Alonzo
Vaquero in the Cañon de Dimas
Where the swallows come nesting
By the red cliffs in the springtime Sonora Mexico

Where do the swallows go passing with the west wind
By the red cliffs they stay for a while and then go
When she was a young girl her mother didn't want her
So took her to town to Doña Petra

Where do the swallows go passing with these west winds
Where do they nest for a while and then go
When she was sweet sixteen Doña Petra didn't want her
So she went to live with her Uncle Peru

She was shot through the heart by Peru's jealous wife
She's buried in the cañon at El Ranchito
Where do your hates and your jealous loves go
Who are we here . . . wanting to know

Who are we here . . . wanting to know

Shy whirling Alma dancing your young old eyes
The carousing vaqueros chased all night
Till the sunlight lit their camp on the town street
Between the roundup jefe's house and hers

Como un águila bajando a un lepe
Roberto bailó con las señoritas in Agua Prieta

Like an eagle dropping down on a doggie calf
Roberto danced with the senoritas in Agua Prieta

Where will the old Earth take you dancing through the starlight
Whirling you on and on while she goes
Where will the old Earth carry us dancing through the starlight
Whirling us all on and on while she goes

Danced her through that old white house where she lived one room
Adobe mud the other of cardboard and rusting pieces of rattling tin
Where Petra served us frijoles and carne
As though we'd come driving steers along the dusty trails as kings

Whirling you on and on while she goes
Whirling us all on and on while she goes
West from the San Bernardino River through Gallardo Pass we rode
In the dusk light lost two steers in the night time

Rode on again another day into Agua Prieta
Through dirt streets and Mexico kids
Running by the sides of the road throwing rocks at stray steers
Until we came to the border corrals

Then with tequila and corridas floating through the cantinas
And the women and the songs we forgot the dust the wild cattle
The cold of the mornings the winding trails and changed the town
To some whirling place we didn't remember or know

Where do those nights and the singing in your memories
And the crossing of these valleys and the sandy rivers go
Where do those nights and the singing in our memories
And the crossings of these lands and the sandy rivers go

And the vaqueros who rode whistling
In those soft dark eyes
While the swallows circled and drifted in the winds
Calling by the red cliffs in the Cañon de Dimas in springtime

Where will those loves and your laughing black eyes
And the winding river go
Who are we here wanting to know
Who are we here wanting to know

Chapter 3
Colors and Words

BOB BUDD

Ranchers talk in questions—arm out pickup window, elbow on saddle horn, head scratching, cap moving, hat adjusting, dirt digging with toe of old boot questions. It's just easier to start a conversation with a question than an answer. Questions can be simple, innocuous, as bland as observations on weather, but they are often deeper, harder, and impossible to answer directly. When you talk in questions, sanity can remain intact. Answers are sometimes certain death—of mind, heart, and bottom line.

"Suppose a guy was really worried about losing his place? He had a note at the bank, say, and he was in pretty good shape on the land, and he could cover the operating note with fifty more mama cows, but he hasn't got enough summer country. He can winter more cows, but he can't do that if the cows are coming off his summer country in August. Now, suppose a place that makes his ranch *really* work good comes up for sale, but the price is for houses? I hear some of that stuff is going for three thousand an acre. Maybe it's only two thousand, but cows make it a hundred at best, don't you think? So what do you tell that feller to do? Sell out? Or buy land high and lose it later?"

Sometimes the questions can get sort of long and complicated. This may be the curse of an open mind, or the agony of too much tradition. Simple statements end with a rising pitch, as if to place a question mark where none would normally be found. This is a relic of reality, of swings in weather that drive the thermometer one hundred degrees in hours. Speaking in questions is a simple reflection of people who live on the land. We don't know as much about this landscape as we wish, and we learn through questions. We can say with certainty and honor that we don't know all the answers, and we can say with equal certainty that simple solutions in a complex landscape are prone to failure.

Dave Gardner, a rancher friend, was aggravated by a particularly long dry spell when he was a younger man. In frustration he asked his father-in-law, a Shoshone elder, if he thought it would ever rain.

"It always has," was the answer.

Reality can be hard to live with. Some pray for rain while others relish reports that the weekend will be "great—dry and warm." In ranching, reality has a way of burning itself into a man's hide, creating a paradox of pessimism on the outside and blatant optimism on the inside that it will, indeed, rain. Management of natural lands requires the patience of glaciers and the ability to rebuild a framework from pieces scattered on the ground. Ranching is built as much on appreciation of decay as on lush grass in springtime. In our human obsession to control everything, we err by hoping for stability where chaos rules. Successful ranchers manage for a range of options, from drought to perfect moisture regimes, and then adapt, and adapt, and adapt.

The culture of ranching is a dichotomy of certain knowledge and total acceptance of random chance. In a "normal year" cows do certain things. Grass grows a certain way. Hay produces. Deer behave the normal way. But a normal year is a moving average, built on how many years the rancher has lived on a piece of land. In business circles and culture, the term "adaptive management" has become the buzz. In a century and a half of ranching, no one ever thought to coin the phrase because they were too damn busy adapting.

Of late it seems ranching is counterculture at its apex, out of step with the mindset of the time. When the national passion was farming and settlement, ranching was some sort of fanciful retrogression to nomadic days of following grass and water. John Iliff herded cattle from the safety of the Colorado plains into the heartland of Wyoming. Charlie Goodnight followed grass to Montana. Pan Phillips and Rich Hobson chased grass beyond the mountains to British Columbia. Like a colt in halter, there was a great deal of pulling back and lurching forward.

Society said settle down, make a go on a single piece of ground, build a town. Stay put. Hunker down. But instinct said follow grass. Maybe early ranchers had more in common with the Crow and Shoshone than they did with plow and post.

Suddenly ranching epitomizes sense of place: units of land that hold vast landscapes of the West together. But one ranch alone can't support the frame, any more than a single nail can anchor four boards around a photo of the past. Ranching has been depicted as a world of lonely independence, cocksure and superior wisdom, lined up in the face of battle, whether against interlopers, thieves, or weather. Always there was a tremendous payoff at the end of the road, whether that road was the Goodnight-Loving Trail or a simple path from sod hut to gate built from mesquite. At times, ranching is like that.

At times, there *is* loneliness—a sense that you are alone against the world. With this comes very real knowledge of vulnerability, usually hidden behind a veneer of machismo, marketable image of the silver screen. Ranching is called a battle sometimes. It feels that way when the end of the day brings yet another political attack, when the day was spent working on the land, doing everything in your power to make it better, failing as often as succeeding. Conservationists feel the same way when their muscles and hearts ache, so why is it that instead of sharing a common aim we rise to battle? In battle we fight with words our "opponents" don't understand, concepts they fear, hard lines in erosive soil. We hurt, and we give hurt back, despite the fact that we want the same thing in the end.

Ranching is an understanding—an acceptance that clouds bring many things: rain and snow, essential moisture to plants, fire and wind, and false hope. But clouds carry shade from the hot sun. And children on horses watch clouds, describe them, see wind miles over their heads, and grow from tiny horsemen to fighter pilots in an instant. In these clouds are tiny signals that tells bugs to hatch on water so that fish rise and let parents and children share pure joy. Clouds can carry frustration, and they can carry hope. Sometimes both come out of the same clouds.

The reality of ranching is manifest in the uncertainty of a new day, rain or dry wind, cattle happy or not, water plentiful or gone altogether. As much as the joys which come with a day that goes well, the hell of ranching is why people stay. It is a masochistic, manic-depressive career choice perhaps, but these good days are so good that they fade realities to gray and illuminate the mind. Ranching is no place for pessimists; they will be rewarded daily until they have no greater horror to foretell. Stewardship is for optimists, those who see flames as dancers, new growth in the ashes of fire.

Therein lies a great oddity, paradox for a sphinx. In the public eye, ranchers are often portrayed as greedy, pessimistic, ready-for-battle warriors hell bent on controlling their part of the planet. In their element—cracked hands immersed in snow melt, patient hands massaging the uterine wall of a nervous first mother, soft hands on the head of a tired border collie, worn hands holding tiny hands—the same people don't quite measure up to that image. As we continually gain speed in society and communication, we seem to lose our ability to see into hearts and listen to minds. It takes patience and time to know people, and few seem to have either the time or inclination.

It doesn't help that ranchers are lousy communicators. They've been trained that way. For all of eternity, economics, politics, and sameness have defined their existence. They may have cussed the neighbors, but they were there in times of need. The average age of ranchers in the West is something like sixty-three years old; more have ridden in horse-drawn wagons than in airplanes. Today flocks of people fly to ranches to ride in wagons. A good percentage of ranchers lived through the Great Depression, fought in World War II or Korea, then stood in awe when their house had a telephone, even a party line. They came home from a war that made ranching profitable, then found themselves mired in an economy where nothing seemed to work. Inflation and intolerance rode the same horse, and the whole world went through an upheaval never before seen by modern man and woman.

The single most important meeting of the year was with the banker. Everyone who could borrowed money, just as ranchers borrow money now. We're talking *lots* of money, more money than most dotcoms need to start up and operate for a couple of years. There were no investors, no markets for sharing risk. There were kids who worked for nothing; there were hands who wanted to be paid weekly even though calves were sold only once a year; and there were calves that weighed something and buyers who wanted them to weigh something else.

Merchants were gracious, but they kept their pencils sharp and looked at the bottom line. In a community, you paid your bills. You met your obligation to your neighbor, though you might speak quietly to the merchant at the high school football game, and ask for time—just a little more time—to pay for bolts and nuts and nails and wire. Nothing else carried the stress or importance of making ends meet. Kids learn from parents. They see stress, and the stress they see in ranching has a lot to do with money. The joy comes from the land.

"I miss the ranch," an elderly woman told me, and her eyes looked through me to snowy peaks and memories—frogs caught in bogs, fossils found on hillsides, boys kissed under trees while the river roared. Her voice trailed off, and I saw her mind wander briefly, until she turned and addressed me again, this time eyes clear and strong. "I *don't* miss the pressure," she said.

When a group of people talk, they speak of what is most important to them at the time, the thing that is on their mind. When you are losing money and losing the place you know as well as the birthmark on your daughter's leg, you tend to focus on money. The fact that society has seen this side of ranching foremost is sad, but it is the last piece of reality ranchers would wish to share. But they've been trained to talk about money, business, and success. Survival is continued existence, and this means an extended line of credit, nothing more or less. It is a shame that most people, even in the West, don't interact with ranchers often. The greatest contact is usually hunting season, the same time ranchers are shipping cattle and dealing with bankers. Tensions are high, and time is ebbing for both hunter and rancher. Neither gets a clear picture of the other.

There is a hidden culture in ranching. Sadly it is the intimacy people feel with land on which they live. Sadly because this is truly the way most would choose to be seen and remembered, the gift they offer their children and grandchildren. Saddest of all because the greatest gift to society, perhaps, is a subject not spoken of, and in the void a cultural chasm is allowed to widen. Instead of showing pride in the habitat they provide, ranchers run silent and deep. There is true fear in knowing where certain mice live, where grizzly bears den, where black-footed ferrets roam, for soon an agent of government may come prowling.

Only when trust is absolute will most landowners share these pieces of their heart, then only in confidence, and more often than not with a certain sense of embarrassment. I've had plants brought to me in styrofoam cups, cared and tended horseback for a full day, to see if they are rare. The phone rings at daylight with a description of a new bird at the feeder. We speak of deer, and grass, and water. For most, the health and vigor of their calves is an indicator of the health of the land, wild things, plants and water. Many monitor other things as well. Fish as big as footballs are important, as are hatches of grouse. Big deer indicate an adequate number of small deer. Ducks on ponds and elk in meadows mean something. When my neighbors and I smile and kick dirt, these are the things of which we speak. Sometimes for hours. Sometimes for days.

When we talk of calf weights, percentage of cows bred, prices, and how much feed we have left, it is almost a competition to see who is worst off. Business news, really. How cattle do in our own backyard is a barometer—sometimes an indication of problems, sometimes confirmation that the year was really pretty good. The general public hears the discussion of calves, calculates the value, assumes wealth, and walks away.

In the advance of darkness, where ranchers let their breath out slowly, hang arms over pickup beds, and speak of deer and ducks, there are few witnesses. These are discussions rooted in uncertainty, fear, and vast knowledge. The talk bounces erratically, irrationally, emotionally. It is both friendship and competition, the things upon which communities are built. Fathers hand sons to neighbors they have cussed and embraced, so sons might learn from someone else, and not be ruined by fathers. In ranching culture, many young people find themselves by skipping generations. But family is formed by the land, that community of people who *know* Horse Creek, Lance Creek, or North Piney.

Intimacy with land is a cultural gift ranchers offer, but economic argument defines the image. When ranches sell and tears flow, salty water is ignorant of economic loss. Tears reflect loss of an intimate friend. This is the weight of stewardship.

I still walk to the very place I saw the first frog on this ranch, that place where the first salamander slid into the mud, the tree where young peregrines rest in wait of migration. I know ditches that seep, and those that cut, places once eroded and raw, now filled with silt and dense vegetation. I sit by holes where big fish hide and feed them grasshoppers.

My children have found places where warm water comes from under the land—places to swim, places ducks know in winter. Kids are cut from whole cloth, and they like to talk. They tell these stories to anyone who will listen. They bring notes home from school for talking too much.

The children are small. They still remember cattle—the Joe Cow, One Sixteen, Snake Horn, the Sweetheart Cow—and they remember wild things they see. Herons in the River Meadow. A sick deer in the brush behind the shop. Moose in the front yard. Rattlesnake on the porch. Lizards. In their eyes, these things go together. After all, in their youth they have seen most of the neighboring ranches turn into housing developments. They see these things more closely sometimes than the rest of society. Their bus that was nearly empty is now full. They see more dead rabbits on the well-traveled road—you can only outrun so many cars in a lifetime of rabbitry, it seems, or perhaps some people just don't watch for rabbits.

I am still a relatively young man. As such, I stand in awe of those the age of my father, men and women whose minds are sharp, memories intense, body and soul tied to the land on which they live. When my great-aunt was in her eighties, she lost her sight, and compensated by listening more clearly. She knew the day the bluebirds came home because she heard them. When she lost her hearing, she compensated by some other sense. When she told me there should be bluebirds at the window soon, I asked how she could possibly know such things. She said the day *felt* like bluebirds. A little less bite of snow on the breeze. Perhaps a bit of squish in the soil, a harbinger of frost coming out of the ground. Warmer sun on her face through the kitchen window. Mountain bluebirds danced at that window, busily checking crevices, gathering twigs, fluttering for her unseeing eyes, singing to her deaf ears. They were there. The bluebirds were *there*.

I have learned not to argue with these things. Instead I have found that buried in the culture of ranching lie observations and passions for all things on the land, and we can learn from them, whether statistically significant or not. At the dawn of the information age—first predicted, now reality—we have potential access to more than we ever imagined. The risk lies in becoming so infatuated with what is new that we let go of what is real. Our history and our future are one and the same. The trick lies in listening and learning from whence we have begun.

Things move slowly in ranching. This is a remnant of seeing too many schemes and instant solutions, all of them inconsistent with the pace of the land, none of them as patient as the grass. There is no fast money in ranching, just good and bad years, and lots of years in between. Those must be the normal years they talk about on the weather report. There are lots of moving parts—weather, markets, help, old neighbors, new neighbors, inventory of living things that never quit eating, equipment, parts, the latest rage in technology, quick fixes, and things that have worked for nearly a century. Perhaps the culture of ranching is merely a matter of sorting priorities. On normal days, you chase your tail, and parts, and cows. On a good day you count deer in the meadow, beaver in the creek, and new birds on the feeder.

I manage a ranch owned by The Nature Conservancy. Red Canyon Ranch is a jumbled landscape on the southeastern flank of the Wind River Mountains in central Wyoming. Six rare plants live here, one of them found nowhere else on the planet. Most of the wild creatures native to the region are present. The plants have been here longer than any of us. There are interlopers; the creeks are filled with fish from Europe, and we battle weeds imported for ornamental enhancement as well as species brought here to enhance the economic potential of the land. Apples are grown in an orchard more than a century old. White-tailed deer have worked their way from the East into these creek bottoms. Lilacs bloom and break harsh winter wind and snow. I did not make this place. Like the bluebirds or mule deer I love, I can only claim to live here. My care is limited by my understanding of the system—of time—of plants and animals that speak only in life and death. In caring for the land, I must try to hear silent calls for help, see invisible images of joy and pain, feel the immensity and nothingness of fog.

I am an advocate for wild creatures, rare plants, arrays of native vegetation, clean water, fish, stewardship of natural resources, and learning. I believe these things are compatible with ranching, sometimes lost without ranching. Some people call me a cowboy. A lot of good cowboys call me an environmentalist. I suppose there are lots of labels you can attach to me. There was a time when doing so was hurtful, so I threw back labels of my own. We throw a lot of anger at each other with words. It doesn't do much for the land, really.

As I wrote this essay, my oldest son read with some interest, and said nothing. A few days later we rode in the pickup, arms out the windows, dust in the mirror, red dirt caked on eyeballs, lips, and sticky necks. I finally asked him how he saw the culture of ranching, as eleven-year-olds see the world, and he offered a story that left me speechless.

"Did you know, Dad, that if you write the word 'red' in green and ask a small child to tell you the color, the answer will be 'green?' But if you show the same word to an adult, the answer will be red. Children see the color, not the word. Adults see the word, and not the color."

In a complex world of ecological mystery, we cannot allow words and images to limit the opportunity to learn from one another. We must respect the places from which we gain understanding. The world cannot be framed in contrast of black and white, in pure scientific light. Ranchers live in a gray world where subtle hues of green and blue gleam as vividly as neon, where the color of a bird can make a month seem right, and yet there is no incentive to speak of the color of birds. The time has come for all of us who care about the natural world, as well as our own communities, to think beyond labels, stereotypes, and misconceptions. There is no room for the language of hate and intolerance to supersede conservation on the land. Between eagle and cottontail, political solutions mean nothing.

The time has come to see colors, not words.

Chapter 4

No Place Like Home

L I N D A   M .   H A S S E L S T R O M

I moved to a western South Dakota ranch in 1952 at age nine when my mother married John Hasselstrom, youngest son of a Swedish cobbler who taught himself how to be a cattle rancher. For most of the next forty years, I lived and worked on that ranch. Our business was supervising 100 to 150 cows and their calves from birth through death or departure. Two stories, "Learning the Names of Cows" and "The Case of the Purloined Canoe," summarize some important principles of that business as I learned it. These parables emphasize elements that I consider particularly important as we approach the future of ranching west of the 100th meridian.

LEARNING THE NAMES OF COWS

I realized right away that my father could recount the family tree of every cow and every calf she'd produced. He could pick her current calf from a hundred of the same kind of Angus-Hereford crossbreds milling around the dusty corral.

Why, I asked, did a rancher have to know his cows so intimately? In order to have thrifty cows that raised strong calves, he said. We had to be able to identify and keep cows adapted to our native grasses, our dry summers and cold winters. Our best cows were often bony critters with prominent hipbones. The neighbors said they "looked like hell." My father said, "They put the kick in the chicken": raised a good calf every year.

"How do you tell them apart?" I asked.

"It'll come to you," he replied.

This was the man who, before my mother married him, asked me to choose either a nickel or a dime from his hand, and praised me for picking the dime because it was worth more. When he found out I didn't know the multiplication tables, he devised a unique teaching method. Each morning he'd open my bedroom door and shout something like, "What's nine times seven?" If I didn't holler the correct answer immediately, he kept yelling, yanking the covers off my bed. At dark, when I rode into the corral after a hundred-degree day moving cows, his first words might be, "What's six times eight?" Yet his only advice on recognizing cows was, "It'll come to you." When I protested, he added, "If you're going to raise cattle, you have to learn by experience."

Each fall at the home corrals, we sorted the year's calves. He always asked me what the steers weighed, and I was expected to remember my guess, as he did, when the weights flashed on the screen at the sale ring. Then we'd amble among the heifers while he talked about each calf's conformation and ancestry as he chose the best dozen for breeding cows. His final criterion was always "the look in her eye." We auctioned off most of the calves we raised at a sale ring, forced to accept whatever price the buyers paid that day. Most years my father tucked the check in his billfold murmuring, "Topped the market again." I knew that cash had to last a year, that most of my clothes were secondhand and we drove the oldest trucks and tractors in the neighborhood—but that's all I knew of ranching economics.

Ours was a single-family, cow-calf ranch, the most labor-intensive way to raise beef. We warmed new calves in the bathtub during March blizzards, and bought bulls from neighbors if we didn't raise our own. We harvested our own hay, and helped the neighbors fight fire. We didn't sell a good cow if she missed calving one year, so we had cows fifteen years old, named as we learned their personalities and idiosyncrasies: Whirlaway, named after a Kentucky Derby winner, could outrun most horses. We left broad strips of uncut hay along the edges of fields for deer forage because, my dad mumbled, "They have to hide those fawns someplace, and if we can't make a living without *that* hay, we better quit."

I was fourteen the first time my father told me to hold my horse in the open gate of our winter pasture and "count 'em in." Bawling cows, horns high, trotted down a rocky gully into the creek bottom and galloped toward the gate where I sat my horse, narrowing the entrance to force the cows into single file. They shoved and crowded, grinding my legs against the saddle and the gate post. I gritted my teeth and kept counting, mentally commenting on each cow. "Ugly's first again, granddaughter of the old Jersey who taught me to milk. Second in line—the cow that butted her baby around the rocks."

"A hundred and four," I said when my father drove up in the pickup, "and I knew every one of them!" After that, when he sent me to bring in "that cow that got fat while she starved her calf to death," I came back with the right one.

I'd gotten acquainted with the cows by pulling calves or driving them through gates—we'd shared some experience together. Our recognition was mutual, based on how we treated each other. I knew the cows because each of us had earned a particular place in the community of the ranch.

My father knew how many cows each pasture could support in a dry year without damage to the native grass. After a dry summer he might sell twenty or more older cows and keep only five heifers for replacement stock. I'd protest: What if we had a wet winter and plenty of spring grass? He'd shrug. "The cows we have left will raise better calves, and we'll tighten our belts. But I won't have to abuse my grass." Usually the neighbors were sacrificing cows cheaply or overgrazing by the middle of next summer, while he sat tight and smiled. Everything we did on that ranch depended on his knowledge of the details of that particular acreage in that time and place.

Moving to the ranch for me was finding a perfectly fitting life. My mother married as a wise investment in our future and believed she was sacrificing status and culture. She didn't like to get her hands or her shoes dirty and fought ferociously with my father as she tried to keep me inside the house learning to clean and cook. She scorned the experiences of our neighbors and never understood the qualities that balanced their faults. To her, cattle were creatures who lived just to provide new carpets.

She never joined the community my father and I found with the animals. Today she lives in a nursing home, pleased to be attended by people who help her dress and supervise her medications, and she loves to "drive out past the ranch."

Most of the people who are moving into my community these days are more like my mother than my father. For them, the ranch is merely a square on a map, scenery surrounding a home filled with the latest conveniences.

In spite of his wisdom, despite his knowledge of current events, against his lawyer's advice and my pleading, my father refused to create an estate plan. His simple will barely acknowledged me. He left everything to my mother, naming her executor. Following family and community tradition, he'd never told my mother how many acres or cows he owned. Since she'd never even balanced her own checkbook, I inherited the responsibility for carrying out my father's wishes. I sold his cows to a neighbor to pay his debts and start making repairs he'd neglected. Then I sold my own cows to the same neighbor to pay the taxes. Then I borrowed money, acquired title to the ranch, and leased the land to that same neighbor because I had no cattle left to run. Most of the cows my father and I raised are still on the land where they grew up. When I see them in a pasture, I know them by their history with me. The Cow That Bashed Her Baby Around the Limestone Outcrop in my stories may, to my neighbor, be The Cow That Kicked Him in the Head While He Tried to Milk Her.

"There's no place like home, there's no place like home, there's no place like home," Dorothy chanted in *The Wonderful Wizard of Oz*, clicking the heels of her ruby slippers together. L. Frank Baum wrote his book in and about South Dakota, but no matter how much I wanted to click my heels together and fix everything, nothing was quite so simple.

Eight years after my father's death, and nine months after the publication of *Feels Like Far*, in which I told most of the story of my father's decline, I'm convinced that most ranchers of his generation planned poorly for their family's future.

I have no children. I cannot write a book recording all my acquired wisdom about that land for some new owner, because some of the information requires a taste of soil, the scent of a blizzard in a particular wind. If I moved back to the ranch, found an apprentice, and worked there with her, or him, for the rest of my life, much of what my father and I have learned about that land might endure. That will not happen.

Whoever occupies the ranch after I die may not know its history. She won't know where to take shelter, walking home in chilly rain when the pickup's stuck in that nasty mud hole in the summer pasture. Or he won't understand that if he mows the willow patch below my house, he'll frighten away the old doe and her daughters, and lose the pleasure of watching them splash in the dam on moonlit nights. A new owner might learn how to raise cattle there in thirty or forty years, but his ownership may not last that long—after all, real estate prices are climbing in my district, along with taxes. Land is a "good investment."

Living with integrity on that land would require more than a new name on the deeds and appreciation of the scenery. Land is the basis of community, but creating a successful community means, I believe, learning all you can from previous inhabitants. No one can live ethically or intelligently in the West without exploring the history and knowledge of our forerunners. We remember little of the oral wisdom collected by the Native American people who lived there for thousands of years. We know too little about generations of plants and animals destroyed by homesteaders who foolishly plowed some of the ground. The American public will suffer a great loss if we conclude that ranchers have nothing to teach us. Men and women like that Swedish cobbler spent generations observing ecology in the West; they created ranching by adapting to a climate and landscape many people consider appalling.

Unfortunately, our record of learning from the past is poor. As Joseph Wood Krutch said, "If people destroy something replaceable made by mankind, they are called vandals; if they destroy something irreplaceable made by God, they are called developers."

Many of the new residents in my neighborhood have "ranchettes" and speak of cattle or buffalo as an "investment." By the time I learned to recognize all our cows, they were more than walking legal tender. In winter, when I walked among those cows, talking softly and patting shoulders and flanks, I knew I was safe because they recollected me by sight and smell. When roads drifted closed and telephone lines dropped, the cows were more family than job. Our relationship more closely resembled an exchange of amenities than ownership. Working with the cows helped me live more responsibly, to observe the human community more acutely, and to respect the human community less. When I ran to head a cow off at a gate, I judged her intent with the same measure I use to determine what a person will do: by her expression, by the look in her eye.

THE CASE OF THE PURLOINED CANOE

In May of 1992, four years after my husband, George, died, my father ordered me to stop writing or to leave the ranch. I moved to Cheyenne, Wyoming, five hours away. When my father died in August, I took up his responsibilities. The neighbor who leased the ranch hired a young couple who needed a home, so they moved into my parents' house.

Broke and jobless, fifty years old, living in a city for the first time in years, I raced back to the ranch nearly every weekend, thinking as I drove about the meaning of family and community. My family had fought fires, supported churches, bought quilts at the bazaars, and known everyone's name in that neighborhood for more than a hundred years. I felt responsible to the community as I tried to decide the future of the ranch, but I feared that my father's death might have annulled my place there. My childhood home was occupied by strangers, and I was looking for tenants for my own home. I believed I might no longer be part of my own community. Meanwhile, I spent most of my time on practical considerations: how to keep the place from falling down.

One day I noticed that the siding on both my mother's house and my own needed replacement. Following local custom, I gathered recommendations from neighbors and friends, and hired a contractor I hadn't met. With no income from the ranch, scrambling to meet expenses, I agreed to give several readings in the eastern part of the state while the siding was applied. I'd inspect the work on my way back to Wyoming. But a blizzard delayed me, and by the time I went back to the ranch, the job was done. Looking over the work, I was annoyed to find that the workers had scattered cigarette butts and empty soft drink cans everywhere. I accepted the mess as the price I paid for being absent.

Then I noticed that my husband's eighteen-foot Grumman canoe was no longer behind the garage where we'd stored it for fifteen years. Even the concrete block we used to hold it down in windstorms was gone. My tenants said no one but the construction workers had visited my house. I hadn't used the canoe since George died; I can't swim. Still, the whole county knew my house was empty, and I thought that unless I demonstrated that I was paying attention, the theft might be only the beginning of vandalism.

I dropped in for lunch with the senior citizens at the community hall. At first I wasn't sure how to answer their questions. For years, my family and the community had wondered why I wasted my time writing. Did I have a job in Cheyenne? someone asked. All I had to do was nod, and my move was suddenly understandable. It wasn't really a lie— I worked at writing every day. Then I chattered about the disappearance of my husband's canoe and told them I'd installed a security system. I mentioned how often I drove home to the ranch late at night, and reminded them I've carried a pistol for years, seeing as how a lone woman, and a widow at that, can't trust anybody these days. I added that besides my own guns, I'd inherited quite an arsenal from my husband, who had taught me how to shoot pretty well.

Most of the folks I talked to were men, and they all said if I caught anybody on my property I should skip the warning shots and shoot to kill. Several repeated the old maxim that nothing scares evildoers more than a nervous woman with a shotgun. I finally admitted, demurely, that I kept my husband's double-barrel, loaded, handy.

Later that afternoon, the contractor told me one of his workers had asked about buying the canoe. If he'd passed the message to me, I'd have sold the canoe cheaply and would now have no tale to tell.

Following three or four days of intensely casual chat with my neighbors, I knew the story: the two men spent a week working on my house without seeing me, and decided I am so rich I wouldn't miss the canoe. Local wisdom says absentee owners don't care about their own property, let alone anyone else's. They are not part of the community, and they hire strangers to do their work rather than trading work like normal people. By the time they'd reasoned all this out, the men were packing up. They dumped their garbage in my yard and used a rope from my garage to tie the canoe on top of their pickup. (More than a year later, I stumbled over the concrete anchor a hundred yards away among my windbreak trees.)

After a few more pleasant visits with helpful neighbors, I knew the men's names, tribal affiliations, and where they lived. One evening I stopped at a campground café a half-mile up the road, operated by a neighbor who never seems to make any money ranching even though his wife has three jobs. When this man was in my Sunday School class, he was a skinny, freckled kid with a runny nose. Now he's six foot two and weighs close to three hundred pounds, most of it muscle. A volunteer fireman, he is our sheriff's unofficial bodyguard. "Oh," he says, "I kinda ride along with him if he expects things to be tough, like for domestics and bar fights."

While he deftly spread cheese and pepperoni on my pizza, I told him about the canoe's disappearance. We chatted amiably about the illusion that one is alone in the country. Most folks who drive through don't know that strangers are usually watched. I told him that when I walk my dogs in the cemetery in Hartville, Wyoming, I feel the hair on the back of my neck rise and glance up to see a sentry on a hilltop, pretending to fix fence.

I even told him about the retreat I visited in New Mexico. A couple of female guests took a picnic to a hill above a nearby ranch, and doffed their clothes. The ranch woman noticed her pre-teenage boys gawking at the hillside, scanned it with binoculars, and then fired a few rounds over the women's heads. When they returned to the retreat, we explained to the women that country people can see further than most city folks, and assured them that the woman was merely expressing her opinion. If she'd meant to hit them, she would have.

Serving my pizza, my neighbor said the men had dropped in for lunch several times, and he'd heard them talking about how handy a canoe would be to fish the Missouri River on their reservation. He allowed as how the sheriff had been keeping an eye on them anyway, because they both had convictions for theft. He conveyed this information without mentioning names or committing himself to action. Finishing a slice, I remarked that he'd helped me make a decision. Since all I wanted was my canoe, I wouldn't report the theft to the sheriff or my insurance company for two weeks. Perhaps the canoe would reappear during that time, and I would forget it had been gone. If he knew anyone who was interested, he might repeat this information.

I reminded him of the time a few years back when several of us women who lived alone had started being disturbed by our dogs barking and growling at night. Mornings, we'd find cigarette butts near our windows. He'd heard how, one night, I jerked open the door to the deck, fired one round from the shotgun toward my woodpile twenty feet away, and the other in the air. Then I shoved in two more shells and slammed the door. None of us were disturbed after that. He nodded and observed that anyone who had borrowed a canoe for a little fishing trip might want to bring it back in daylight.

The next day I went back to Cheyenne. Two weeks later, I was composing a letter to the sheriff—trying to figure out how to explain why I hadn't reported the theft—when the phone rang. My tenant reported that a pickup had just driven toward my house carrying a canoe, and left without it.

Soon after the canoe returned, I arranged a traditional barter of the kind that has kept my community going for years. My cousin uses my canoe to take his children fishing. I keep his johnboat tied to a concrete anchor by the garage. I can paddle or pole the stable, flat-bottomed boat around the dam when I want to watch chorus frogs.

My politics and opinions are different than those of most of my neighbors. But I asked the community for help in the Case of the Purloined Canoe rather than calling outsiders—The Authorities. The canoe came back in a way that demonstrates what I believe: that people cooperating to solve problems form communities.

Sometimes I wish my neighbors knew less of my business, or I knew less of theirs, but we can rely on each other because our actions have proved we can. That's how community functions: give and you shall receive. You need not contribute for a hundred years, but you have to start the exchange: First you have to give.

My father's father, Charley Hasselstrom, like many immigrants, was smart enough to figure out how to run cattle in a hostile environment after being a cobbler—without agricultural colleges, federal experts, government subsidies, or participation in a global market. He taught his sons and daughters that hard work was the basis of a life well lived. He illustrated good husbandry, demonstrating that a ranch had to be a single, sustainable element in the native landscape. My father and his brother increased the size of the ranch, even though they divided it between them. They expanded their knowledge of that particular microclimate and their skill in raising cattle there. My father took great pains to pass those instructions on to me.

But my ranching ancestors made three mistakes: they didn't talk, they especially didn't talk about money, and they had no sons.

The fact that they didn't talk forced their children to learn by observation. I think paying attention is the most useful survival skill anyone
anywhere can learn. Because they didn't talk about money, strangers own
some fine ranches in my neighborhood. Or widows and daughters are
trying to hold on, fighting development and rising property taxes. My
father believed that his finances and his ranching methods were so private they were neither my mother's business nor mine. Each autumn,
when we took our calves to the sale ring for auction, buyers bought our
calves as cheaply as possible and shipped them to eastern feedlots where
they spent the rest of their lives jammed together, belly deep in mud,
eating corn and becoming cholesterol-laden American beef. When I
asked my father what he thought about that, he said, "It makes me sick."
Then he shrugged; our business was raising calves. What happened after
they left the ranch wasn't our business.

But the world is filled with people who have strong opinions about
feedlot runoff in rivers, manure on their hiking boots, and cattle standing belly-deep in mud. Because we've been stoic and silent, a lot of these
people think *all* cows are injected with hormones and live on corn.
These activities *are* our business if we really believe ranching can be sustainable and beneficial to the grasslands of the West.

It's time to break our western tradition of silence inside, as well as
outside, the family. Silence has encouraged myths and misinformation
that threaten not only our livelihood but the well-being of the land
we—and a lot of city folks—love. I get letters from wives, daughters,
mothers, and sisters of ranchers and farmers, long-time rural residents,
who made no attempt to teach anyone else in the family, especially the
women, about the business of running the place. What might be called
paranoia if it occurred in one man, or in one family, is creating turmoil
in western culture that's at least as threatening as the growth that is bury-
ing ranch land under asphalt and housing developments.

The good news is the women who succeeded many of the ranchers
who made those three little mistakes. A lot of these women are helping
each other, taking crash courses in economics, learning how to explain
sustainable ranching and the validity and importance of our knowledge
of western habitat. Our fathers respected and practiced the behavior that
created community in the neighborhood. We respect their wisdom, but

we have taken the next step: talking to each other, exchanging information. We have to practice the give and take of community within our own families. And we have to teach the people who are moving into our neighborhoods how a community works.

My uncle Harold told a story that sums up my hopes for the future of ranching. Two men he knew were riding horseback on the shortgrass prairies where our family ranch lies, between the Black Hills and the Badlands. A thunderstorm came up, and they saw lightning start a fire. They galloped toward it, hoping to put it out. But before they got there, the wind came up, spread the fire a half-mile wide, and blew it toward them. They turned their horses and raced away, trying to outrun the flames.

"Frank," hollered one cowboy. "Do you think we're gonna make it?"

"I dunno," Frank yelled back. "But I sure ain't gonna quit trying."

Chapter 5

An Intimate Look at the Heart of the Radical Center

PAGE LAMBERT

In 1996, I wrote a book about transplanting five generations of family ranching roots from Colorado north to Wyoming. This is how that book, *In Search of Kinship: Modern Pioneering on the Western Landscape,* begins:

> I am a woman—of French, Scotch-Irish, English, Dutch, and a small amount of Cherokee ancestry. Born in the suburbs of Denver, in the foothills of the Rockies, I now live on a small ranch near Sundance, Wyoming, with my husband Mark and our two children, Matt and Sarah. We have lived here since the mid-1980s with a few sheep, cows, horses, white-tail and mule deer, porcupines, coyotes, and an occasional curious fox. Our modest, hand-built log home sits at the base of the Bear Lodge Mountains, part of the Wyoming Black Hills. The history that is part of this land has slowly been permeating my spirit, molding it, awakening it.

Beginning with our migration north to Wyoming from Mark's family ranch in Colorado, the stories in *Kinship* became linked to the land by these transplanted roots—stories of aborted foals and beloved mares, of orphaned calves and bum lambs, of summer fawns in the meadow and their fathers, the bucks, in the fall. These stories chronicle a modern family's attempt to recreate a legacy of living on, and with, the land.

> Denver has spread like an oil slick in the last one hundred years, swallowing up grasslands and ranches and wildlife habitat. . . . The decision to leave our native Colorado was a hard and painful one, for we were leaving behind both good land and good people. But we were not the first to flee encroachment—man has been encroaching on man since Cain slew Abel, in varying degrees of holocaust.

Our family faces no genocide; we need not fear for the lives of our children. Yet, as others tried to re-mythologize our lives, we did fear the enemy within our own hearts—the disbelief—the doubts that we would be able to pass on this heritage to Matt and Sarah. We feared for the West; we feared the grazing decisions (on public and private lands) made by bureaucrats far removed from the land herself. These fears are abating as those of us in "the radical center" seek compromise and solution, but we *still* fear that many well-intentioned people do not yet understand the role of hoofed animals on the western grasslands—nor the role of the rural perspective in the nation's consciousness.

Many of the same questions I asked in 1996 I am still asking now in 2001:

> Who will be the caretakers of the future if there is no one left to remember the land as she once was? What tradition will guide us into the next century? The land is much more than a series of artificially drawn boundaries—sections and townships, Bureau of Land Management parcels and Forest Service allotments. The land is marshes and meadows, deep draws and dry gulches, streams that flow from neighbor to neighbor, from high country to harrowed field. . . .

I am still writing ranch stories of our transplanted life in Wyoming. We only have fifty cows, but that's fifty more than we brought with us, and we've raised them all. If the winter isn't too hard, there will be fifty calves born this spring. Our son Matt is off to college. Our daughter Sarah survives the turbulent high school years by finding solace at home, on the ranch. Mark works as a range technician with the U.S. Forest Service because a herd of fifty cows cannot pay even half the bills. Mark seeks solace where he is able: horseback up in the Bear Lodge checking riparian areas on different allotments, horseback at home moving cows from one pasture to the next. I seek solace in the land, and in the stories of life and death that spring forth from her abundance.

I bring you now, on these pages, a bit of this abundance, a wild bouquet plucked from the four seasons of Wyoming ranch life. You may not be able to discern where culture leaves off and ecology begins, for these things seem inseparable on a ranch—as elusive as the life at risk about which we write. Despite this elusiveness, I hope you will be able to smell the fragrance, see the colors, feel the wind on your face. I invite you onto our ranch, into a year of our life, one fleeting glimpse at a time.

JANUARY

Eighteen below zero when feeding the cows this morning, the air crisp and clear with four inches of fresh snow on the ground. The Bear Lodge appears black and white, snow layered on the branches of the stark oak trees. Despite my insulated boots, my toes grow numb as I watch the cows' breath rise in vapors. When I feed the horses, their long eyelashes are white with ice. Coyote tracks, traveling fast, try to outrun the cold, but Winter has everywhere marked his territory. Embrace me, or die trying, he seems to say. Finally, he claims Romie, my beloved old mare of thirty years.

A chinook breeze comes out of the west, ruffling the few dried leaves that still cling to the oaks. The thermometer reads forty-eight degrees *above* zero. Melting snow rushes from rain gutters and drips from overhanging banks. I snowshoe for two hours, carrying with me ski poles and a halved apple. The wind has blown the high ground nearly bare, while three- and four-foot drifts fold like waves into the draws and ravines. Deer tracks are plentiful, small groups of chickadees chatter with nasal voices while flitting from tree to tree; squirrels, cottontails, and wild turkeys leave hieroglyphics in the snow. I follow the bird tracks up to the water tank, then hike to the end of the draw. On a fallen log, staring straight at me, not moving a feather, perches a sharp-tailed grouse. The grouse, joined by five others, makes clacking noises—like tail feathers clicking together—as they take to the air. They land a few hundred feet away in the upper branches of a ponderosa. An hour later, five or six more flush out of the trees on a barren, southern-facing slope.

Before heading back to the barn, I leave an offering of apple near porcupine tracks circling the base of a tree.

Yesterday the veterinarian's assistant, a sheep rancher, struck a bald eagle with her car. The impact broke her windshield wiper and mangled, but did not kill, the eagle. Cautiously, she gathered up the injured bird. "I was being careful of the beak, but forgot about the damn claws," she later told Mark. "How'd you put the eagle in the car without him tearing things up?" Mark asked. "Put him in the trunk," she answered. "Took him to the game warden's. My husband couldn't understand why I wanted to save that dang bird," she said, rubbing the gashes on her arms. "We lost over a hundred lambs to eagles last spring."

Spectacular sunset tonight, blazon layers of changing shapes moving across a turquoise sky. Pink to lavender, then a deep plum. The clouds turn a stormy gray, the sky a foreboding slate.

We visit the Black Angus ranch of close friends. A. R. shows us a Lakota horse stick he has made from a single-bitted ax handle. He used a rasp for shaping, a Charolois tail for the mane, and a tail from a butchered steer for the horse's tail. Three raptor claws hang, with feathers attached, as decoration. The stick honors the Lakota tradition of honoring their warhorses, while ornately painted skulls speak to the transience of the flesh. He tells about rescuing a coyote from a trap (not his) that the animal had been dragging on one hind foot. The trap became snagged on a barbed wire fence, painfully tethering the coyote. A shovel kept the coyote's head pinned down while A. R. freed the animal's leg. "I had a long talk with that coyote," he tells us with dry humor while holding the horse stick. "I spun him around five times, then kicked him in the rear and said, 'Go get the neighbor's sheep, but don't let me see your ass back here.'"

Sarah and I make angels in the snow after doing chores. Big, gentle flakes fall from a fathomless universe. The air sifts warm and still in the soft, mountain evening. Dusk turns to dark—we go inside and turn on the television. We are bombarded by a different culture, where it is much harder to make angels in the snow with one's teenage daughter.

FEBRUARY

Twice a day when I feed the cows, I pass by Romie's frozen body. Deep snow and impenetrable drifts have prevented Mark from moving her.

The cows mill carefully around her. I stop, brush the snow from her face, stroke her nose, check for coyote tracks. I cut a strand of her mane and strands of her long black tail, and keep them safely tucked inside in a small box Mark's brother made of apple wood from the old ranch in Colorado.

While feeding cows this morning I notice two things about the snow. First, the snow forms waves—birthed by blizzard, sculpted by mountain wind, and left as a frozen reminder of the great sea that once sprawled across this Wyoming terra firma. These waves fold gently into draws, curl around haystacks, crests sparkling like the uplifted white wings of a snow bunting. Second, I notice the hollowness of my footsteps on the eviscerated carcass of Winter. His bone-white hide appears as fresh as fall's first flakes, but his flesh has become dry and hollow. Up from my footsteps echoes a hint of spring.

We've been in the throes of a wild blizzard for six days—everything's shut down. Mark wades through waist-high snow to get the livestock fed this morning; the drifts are ten feet deep in the draws. Mountain lion tracks have been found up the canyon.

Snowshoeing today I find a coyote's den dug into the snowdrift up at the boneyard. The coyote has started an early spring cleaning, kicking winter debris from the den. The entrance is covered with deer hair, bones, teeth, and hide. Duke, with his border collie hair standing on end, looks like a Rhodesian ridgeback.

Our longhorn cow calves two months early thanks to the neighbor's bull. The lone calf, with no playmates, wanders listlessly among the cows.

It is ten below zero; still, the land is my constant companion, my deepest yearning. I am connected to the land in all ways, at all times—to the coyotes who flush white-tails from the forest, to the flick of my horse's ears as he listens to the coyotes, to the wind that lifts our scent and swirls it among the barren branches of the oaks.

MARCH

At the library in town, Clara Lee, a sprightly ranch woman who has raised children and grandchildren in this gentle yet fierce country, asks, "Have you seen a bluebird yet?" She tosses her head of silver hair. "It's March 10—they always return on March 10." This ranch woman teaches me to honor the faithful shape of season in the Bear Lodge: round—like sun and moon, round like the gravid bellies of the ewes and cows.

I fly to California and spend five days beside my dying father. I stroke his body, speak softly to him, hold his hands. On the fifth day, the doctor disconnects his life support. I phone home and speak to Mark and Matt and Sarah. They are in the basement with a newborn calf. Birthed during a blizzard, the calf is hypothermic. They massage the calf's body, use hot water bottles and an electric blanket to warm him, speak softly to him. He dies within moments of my father, at high noon on the spring equinox. Despite the sorrow, I am grateful my children view death, not impersonally as filtered through the media, but as a vital part of their own lives.

The day after I return home, I'm alone in the barn with an old ewe. I pull two dead lambs from her birth canal. Despite two hours with my hand deep inside of her as I try to maneuver a third lamb into the proper position, the ewe dies with only the front legs of the third lamb visible. This is birth gone wrong. Legs and heads twisted and bent within a womb too old to unfurl itself. I hold the pain, and responsibility, for this dying in the palm of my hand. I am torn asunder and feel bits and pieces of myself strewn upon the earth. I regather myself, tiny red granules of earth cling to me. I begin to heal.

When Sarah and I go to feed the cows they are gathered in the corral on the east side of the barn, sheltered from the weather. The wind has died down; fog hangs over the ranch, enclosing the moment in quiet. We walk up to the stack yard. Gentle musical notes begin to fill the air. "Do you hear that, Mom?" Sarah asks. I listen. The lead cow appears, then another, until fifty cows trail out of the corral toward the haystack. From each placid cow hang slender slivers of ice—delicate percussion instruments that strike gently against each other, sending thousands of notes into the still afternoon. Mesmerized, we listen to the symphony, the cows as finely tuned as any philharmonic. The tinkling notes stretch out in an ethereal melody, a sublime contrast to the staunchly solid line of cows. What virtuosos! Such *delicato* and *dolce* notes. Such refinement! A barnyard duet of nature and culture.

A cow gives birth out in the middle of the hayfield—in the wind. I am irritated with the cow; her calf could be sheltered in the oak trees.

I head out to ear-tag him and iodine his umbilical cord. The longhorn's two-month-old calf catches sight of the new calf and runs eagerly toward him, tail held aloft. He spends the entire day bedded down next to the newborn—in the wind. Community. The cows cannot exist without it, nor can we.

Seven babies on the ground, we have to pull two. Our first heifer is having trouble calving. Matt is working in town; Sarah and I are home alone. We ease the heifer off the field and into the barn with an older cow to keep her calm. Mark arrives just in time to finish the final, hard pulling. He gives the stressed calf a dose of vitamins while Sarah rubs him down. The older cow moos softly, teaching the heifer. The heifer moos back and begins licking her calf. They teach Sarah lessons she could never learn at the mall.

It's night. Matt stands on the deck and howls at the coyotes. They howl back. In the morning, a brazen coyote follows the cows and calves in off the hay meadow. He is so brazen he doesn't run off when he sees Mark, just crouches in the grass and watches. Matt howls again that night, warning him off. We don't shoot the coyote, but we do claim the calving pasture. The ridges and ponderosas and grasslands we share.

APRIL

Spring thaws come and we are finally able to take Romie's body to the boneyard with the tractor. Mark drags her across the hayfield and I think of how, for nearly thirty years, this horse and I have hugged—her head pressed against my thigh, my arms draped around her neck.

I watch my children do chores and am grateful for the nagging calls of the animals; every human being *needs* to feel needed. Sarah's orphaned calf calls out eagerly to her each morning; Matt's piglets run in ecstatic circles whenever they hear him. These are *vital* needs, and fulfilling them fills the deepest part of one's identity.

Two Canada geese are visiting the stock dam. I walk across the field, notice a third, long-necked bird, a blue heron standing knee deep in the partly frozen pond. I walk back through the oaks to the sheep pasture and watch a ewe struggle with the last stages of hard labor. Her water breaks and she licks the salty fluid from the earth. Finally, three lambs are born—front hooves, tiny noses, foreheads pushing into daylight, hips struggling to free themselves. Matt drives into the yard and waves, then joins me. Together we watch the triplets take faltering steps on lanky legs. We watch the ewe eat her afterbirth, and out of these shared moments rise questions from Matt about human birth. I see within him a growing respect for women. The ewe turns from lamb to lamb and rumbles in a low voice. The lambs answer in tiny bleats. Later, out in the pasture, they will call out to each other and be recognized. The coyotes, and the red fox who lives in the draw east of the pasture, will hear the newborn calls as well.

Do most Americans any longer understand themselves within the parameters of the natural world, I wonder? Our dissociation from nature seems as dangerous to our children as the loss of moral compass to society. In fact, it may be because of this dissociation that we find ourselves struggling for spiritual and moral direction. Our urban children are losing their gritty connection to life, and thus don't understand the harsh reality of death. Our young boys shoot each other in their confusion—it is the only rite of passage they know.

The ewes are my link to the land. They are my Dreamtime. Through them I travel thousands of years backwards to that time when women tended the flocks and milked the ewes, combed and spun and wove the wool in a ceaseless circle of renewal. They are a manifestation of the Earth's femininity, sprouted from plants born of seeds buried in ancient soils.

The morning call of a crested blue jay queedles through the oak trees. My muscles strain as Matt, Sarah, and I pull a calf from a heifer. With each contraction of the heifer, we pull in unison on the leg chains that we've looped over the calf's front feet. The heifer moans as we struggle together. Finally, the calf's shoulders pull clear of the pelvis, the hips lock for a moment, we rotate the calf slightly, hips slide free and the calf falls to the ground. Matt lifts him by his hind legs, swinging his head from side to side. The calf sputters, coughs up mucus. Matt lays the calf down. The sunrise casts a glow on Matt's face, or maybe it is a flicker of pride shining through the confusion of adolescence. That night the evening news brings the tragedy of Columbine High School to the ranch. I want to gather up all the children I can find and bring them here, to this place, to this land.

MAY

A beautiful, blustery spring day. I'm arranging wild turkey feathers in an antique apple cider crock from the old ranch. Mark found the feathers out on the big hayfield. The turkey had tried unsuccessfully to outrun a bobcat. I hear the tractor and remember that Sarah is harrowing the small hayfield. I look out the window, see the tractor idling by the barn, see Sarah in her cap closing the gate behind her, capable and competent in this new role.

I hike today on the school section, land we lease from the state. I find blooming sand lilies next to the sage and pasqueflowers on the high ridge to the west. A low-growing, pale blue flower blooms in the red dirt of the washouts— not a phlox or flax, but a spring beauty. The box elder trees are leafing out, and the hawthorns explode in full bloom. Mallards ripple the pond while killdeer tiptoe among the sedges. Flushed by my presence, the ducks lift from the water, circle a few times, then return. I do not see the Canada geese, nor the blue heron.

In the pines, Oregon grape blossoms bright yellow. I sample the sharpness of a wild onion; avoid the death camas just beginning to bloom. The red-winged blackbirds return; robins and fox squirrels chase the blue jays with endless ambition. The cows and calves laze on the gently sloping hills, where bluebells drip color onto the prairie grasses.

JUNE

A hike reveals a newborn white-tail fawn, only a few days old, hidden in the grass on the top of our highest ridge, so small she could nestle in the crook of my arm. Watching from a discreet distance, I enter her world of wide-open eyes, quivering nostrils, breath held in abeyance, ears tuned to each whispered breeze, each ominous winged shadow. She vacillates between the instinct to be motionless and the need to sleep. The lids of her large and liquid eyes close, flutter slightly, then open again. The sweet, pungent scent of sage floats over the land. Five Merriam jakes strut across my path after I leave the fawn, red heads bobbing, tail feathers in full fan.

The coyotes are especially vociferous tonight. Like the fawn, I hold my breath, open my own eyes in the dark, pray the coyotes will direct their hunting ambitions toward the wild turkeys.

The Black Hills, transition zone between east and west, provide habitat for species that live on the fringe. An eastern kingbird flits by, then lands on the barbed-wire fence; two goldfinches fly through the trees so rapidly they are mere flashes of yellow among budding branches. Western meadowlarks grace us with their song, while the rarer and less melodic eastern meadowlarks remain but a promise.

I hike up to the boneyard and regather Romie's bones, which the coyotes have scattered, rib by rib, vertebra by vertebra. Mark has already taken her skull to the granary, where it will be safe from the rodents. Someday I will be courageous enough to paint her skull, to honor her as the Lakota honored their warhorses, honor them still.

JULY

The Bear Lodge offers a microcosm of the Black Hills—diverse landscape, diverse habitat, diverse people. A muskrat swims in the dam near the arroyos in the school section, a small canine skull thrusts itself nose down between a large rock and two slabs at the bottom of the drainage, washed clean by last night's torrential rain and fierce winds. I bring home a yellow and white spreading fleabane; an unidentified solid yellow, eight-petaled, bare-stemmed flower; an orange flowering sage; a blue flax; a purple flower like a cow vetch, only with broad, large leaves instead; and an unidentified, red-stemmed flowering bush. I expand my reference library—for neither montane, nor high plain, nor prairie fieldbooks seem inclusive enough for these hills.

I retrieve Romie's skull from the granary and place it on the south side of our log home so that the sun can bleach it white. I am not yet ready to paint it—the power of her death is too strong, the lessons not yet learned. Still, I save feathers from a fledgling red-tailed hawk who has fallen from his nest, tuck them away with eagle down and sage and bits of wool.

I attend the annual, on-site meeting of the Vore Buffalo Jump Foundation, collect barbecue tickets, then watch flint-knapping and Indian dancing. Willie LeClair, a Shoshone mixed-blood, speaks about his vision quests and sun dancing. He shares a story about the buffalo bull that came to him during his fasting, and about his white father and Shoshone mother. While his father was alive he honored his father's Anglo traditions. Then, fifteen years ago, he began searching for the roots of his Indian traditions, seeking the old ways. Here—at this bison-killing site used for the last five hundred years by the Crow, Kiowa, Kiowa-Apache, Arapaho, Shoshone, Cheyenne, and Lakota—bones dramatically layer the red earth. The remains of twenty thousand bison, along with arrow points and artifacts, lie buried beneath this gypsum soil. Within the first few feet of excavation, the archaeologists found a grouping of bison skulls placed in a sacred circle of thanksgiving. I am reminded of Matt's plea years ago, when the orphan steer he raised had to have an emergency ruminotomy and couldn't be sold at the 4-H livestock sale. "You can still sell Bright Eyes by private treaty," Mark suggested. "But don't *we* need beef this winter?" Matt asked. Mark and I stood in awe of this young, brave-hearted man. "If someone else is eating him," he went on, "how will we know if they're remembering to say a prayer?"

AUGUST

Fire season. Flames engulf the ranch of a close friend while I am out of town. "The fire started at 2:00 P.M. at the neighbors north of us," she tells me, "a hot spot in a week-old fire that exploded when the old man who lived there hit it with a hoe. Within twenty minutes, it was traveling out of control toward us. We evacuated all the horses twice, first down the road across I-90 and then back and over the hill. The kids and I stayed until the flames were caught in their own firestorm," she goes on. "When we came over the hill toward home, just before I-90 opened at 11:00 P.M., the burning trees on either side of the interstate looked like the lights of a thousand skyscrapers. It burned about two thousand acres, crossed the dirt road before it got to the cows, barely missed the shipping barns and house. We had the command post and food in the garage. The firefighters moved down the creek yesterday, and today we saw five cows lying in the middle of the meadow, not far from the fire camp. They came off the hill through the burned trees for water. We lost no buildings or livestock—nobody got hurt. The wildlife is still here and happy. We're praying the fires stay asleep till the snow flies." They didn't. A few weeks later, a second fire blazed to life, backed up a draw, and trapped a neighbor who was trying to help. He had ranched in the community for decades; he did not survive.

Today, I cook the crippled cow's heart. I cut away the tough white membranes and think of her, the damaged heifer we raised from birth. She was always the last to graze the high ridges, the last to water at the stock tank. I asked her once, in a private moment, if she lived her crippled life in vain. She answered me by pushing her slow-moving head beneath my arm and waiting patiently for me to massage her crooked spine. For more than a year her heart has resided in my freezer, alongside hand-raised pork and pasture-fed deer. I have resisted cooking it—have taken package after package of safer cuts from the freezer—rib steaks and rump roasts, flank steaks and tenderloin, soup bones fashioned from her tail, deformed at birth. But the heart I saved for last. Even yesterday, when I defrosted the freezer to make room for this year's pork, I did not think I would cook her heart. But I did, and we lit candles at dinner in her honor.

I find the limp body of a red-shafted flicker in the woods and carefully pluck one reddish-orange tail feather and one spotted breast feather and put them with the strands of Romie's hair.

New weanling colts are locked safely in the barn where they cannot cut themselves on barbed wire, or break a leg jumping a fence. They have been with us, and without their mothers, for three days. We leave the light on in the barn every night so they will not be frightened in this new place of strange smells and sounds. The barn cats, barn swallows, and band-tailed pigeons keep them company.

I push open the top half of the Dutch door and sun streams into the enclosed barn. The dun paint colt approaches the light, his eyes wide open, ears perked. He gazes out into the brilliance and the roan eases up next to him. From the distant ridge, a bull bellows. The colts flare their nostrils, taking in the mysterious horse-scent brought by the breeze, not their mothers' scent, nor the brood mares and colts to which they had grown accustomed, but the strange, curious horse-scent of our geldings, Tee, Black, Cisco, and Poco. The paint colt dances; the roan looks quietly on. The call of a crested blue jay mimicking a red-tailed hawk floats into the barn.

A thunderstorm darkens the sky and lightning cracks from the mountaintop: a bolt so close that it silences the storm, lights the sky, then crashes to earth, "Something's hit," Mark says. The next morning we find a black cow dead on the side of the hill, her live calf by her side. Four redheaded turkey vultures take up temporary residence. They gorge themselves on her carcass. Too heavy to fly, they walk flatfooted in the grass. When not quite so satiated, they spread their dark wings and lift themselves only as far as the branch of the closest ponderosa. All the while, the other cows mill around the dead cow, keeping her company, pondering this stiff-legged, bloated, and gutted comrade who will not get up and move on with the herd. The calf, like the herd's umbilical cord, keeps them tied, one to the other, all to the earth.

SEPTEMBER

A late summer storm howls outside. The staccato hammering of a red-headed woodpecker resounds through the trees. Wind sways the huge oaks, bending their massive burly trunks. They lean toward our log home, then away, into the draw, then back again, long branches heavy with wetness that seems to reach through the windows. Rain falls on the countryside, dripping from brittle pine needles. The cows do not seek shelter but stand hump-backed in the forty-degree weather. The giant trunks of the oaks groan as the wind buffets them and I hear the echo of a great tree falling somewhere in the forest.

We've harvested six pickup loads of dead oak out of the woods southwest of the hay meadow and hope to get a few more before the snow falls. We drive cautiously; this is the only time we allow vehicles on the land. We invite friends to come over and get firewood; the men do the sawing and the women and kids load the trucks. There is a skiff of snow on the ground but lots of sun and blue sky. We indulge in hot chocolate and peppermint schnapps, toasting the coming winter.

Horseback, we moved sixty pairs of cows that summer on our place back to milder winter pasture. Tee, the gelding I now ride, is walking sore-footed. I know it the minute I try to bridle him. He doesn't lower his head into the hackamore, and puts his ears back when I try to lead him. The others push the cows up the road, but I lead Tee into the barn and take off his hackamore, put on his halter, unsaddle him, get the curry-comb and brush. I get a hoof pick out of Mark's shoeing box and clean the red clay and embedded pebbles from his unshod hooves. I brush the mud away, rub him down with a towel, massage his shoulders and legs. Tee stands easy, eating grain, accepting my hugs, flicking his ears when the colts nicker. Outside, a steady rain falls and I think of Romie.

OCTOBER

Fifteen inches of heavy, wet snow fall on the still-leafed-out oaks, aspens, hawthorns, and box elders. Huge branches, torn from the trees, lie scattered about. This morning, after a glorious full moon, the sun shines in a cobalt blue sky. The temperature reaches sixty degrees. Sarah and I use brooms and shovels to knock the snow from the lower branches but even the ponderosas suffer.

Exotic members of the Mongolian Parliament visit our small community. Wyoming's remote landscapes remind them of their own steppes, deserts, and mountains. We become their sister province. In town, Sarah shakes the hand of Mr. Taukel Sultan and, with the help of his Mongolian interpreter, he asks, "Do you ride horses?" Her eyes light up. She smiles. "Ah," he smiles back, using both his hands now to shake hers. "In my country, every year, we hold a horse race for the children! Six-year-olds race bareback thirty-five kilometers! You should come see our horse races!" He goes on to tell her about the wrestling matches and the archery competitions. "Do you drink milk?" he asks. She nods her head. "Ah," he smiles again, "our yaks have the fattest milk!" he exclaims. "Our yaks, like your beef cows, graze the open grasslands and uplands of the mountains. . . ." Sarah is enthralled.

Up in the national forest with friends, we help gather cows out of their allotment. The north wind blows us wet, snowy kisses at fifty miles per hour, reducing the visibility to near nothing. Two mule deer and one coyote vanish through the trees. Vaporous puffs of breath come from the horses' nostrils, their hooves cut into the snow-packed ground—their steps dainty and cautious—crushing unseen deadfall beneath their hooves. Cold despite my winter snowpacks, leather riding skirt, down jacket, scarf, wool scotch cap, leather gloves, and heavy coat, I spend an hour holding the herd on a high, barren hill while the others gather in strays. The sun appears in patches, shining down through the storm, illuminating the yellow leaves on the aspen trees. These gilded leaves glitter against an indigo sky. Snow, like white ermine fur, drapes the deep green branches of the pines.

NOVEMBER

Sarah and I see two bald eagles a couple hundred feet from the road this morning—one perches on a small knoll close to the road, while the other eats carrion on the side of the hill just beyond the knoll. Crows, not brave enough to risk the eagle's wrath by snatching a morsel, mull around, venturing within a few feet of the carcass. A truck pulls up behind us. The eagles grow nervous and take to the air, flying to the pine trees a few hundred yards away. They turn their stark white tails to us, their wings black against the sky. Darkly feathered bodies blend into the forest greenness, the eagles' faces an incongruous white.

I hike up to the knoll where the two eagles were and find the crow tracks, but no eagle tracks. Urine marks a patch of pale yellow snow. I find the carrion: a yearling white-tail doe. The birds have scoured the flesh from one side—leaving the hide ripped back, bare ribs spiking into the air. I turn the yearling over by her legs, flipping the small, feminine head with my hands. This side, untouched by the eagles or crows, is still fully furred and unmarred, except for a touch of pinkish blood about midway along the deer's torso. I push the hair away, dig my finger beneath the thick winter guard hairs, and find a round hole—from either a bullet or arrow. I flip the yearling back over, leaving her picked-clean ribs protruding from her body like armor. Chilled by a sudden wind, I hear crows cawing from the distant cluster of pines, but can see no telltale patches of white perched in the uppermost branches. As I am about to leave, I notice a tiny bit of white eagle down. Tucking it close to my breast, I head off the knoll, feeling a storm riding in on the shirt-tails of the wind. By the time I arrive home, the snow is falling fast and hard.

I hike up the red-eroded draw in the northern pasture in search of the fox den. A weathered fox skull, with the spine and a small amount of hide still attached, lies in the draw twenty feet below one of the den's openings. The skull is too old to belong to the fox I often see trotting across the pasture. For this I am glad. I place the skull near the entrance of the den and whisper a truce into the tunneled darkness, wondering how it is that dead bones can be so full of life.

DECEMBER

Near the bald eagles' carrion, a slash pile from the neighbor's logging looms on the terrain like a giant corpse. Footprints in the melting snow reveal that the pile is providing early winter quarters for a number of four-leggeds. How long until the slash, like the deer, will work its way into the landscape and the trees become the soil from which they grew?

Scavengers have dragged the eagles' doe several hundred yards away; her carcass, spine, three legs, and head are all that are left. But even in this state of dismemberment, her face looks poignantly delicate and feminine—her teeth tiny and spirit-sharp. She, too, is quickly becoming the land from which she grew.

We make our annual trek in search of a Christmas tree. We hike across the pasture to the ridge, cold air in our lungs, snow beneath our feet. The wide-toed tracks of a snowshoe hare scatter among the lupine. We find this year's Christmas ponderosa growing from within a low-growing juniper; we leave the rare spruce to spread their seeds for the next generation. We hike down the hill, past the ponderosa, to pay homage to the old cedar tree that grows in a grass-covered crevice near a deep draw. We hike back up the hill, rest a moment, then begin our ritual.

Holding hands, we pray beside the young ponderosa, then take turns with the axe, smelling the piney white inner flesh. The tree falls gently to the ground, cradled by the juniper. We lug the ponderosa down the hill, half a mile back to the house, sharing her weight, finding handholds among the limbs. We put the tree down and rest, feel her branches rub against our legs, smell her sap, feel her stickiness on our gloves, our cheeks, our arms. Sarah and I hoist her awkwardly up and over the barbed-wire fence, carry her past the cows, past the barn, through the gate, and into the yard.

We measure her, admire her, mourn her. Mark trims her length, leans her excess against the woodpile. Sarah asks, "Is the tree dead, or still alive? She'll be thirsty, you know. Is she suffering?" The tree *is* thirsty; she drinks four quarts of water in twenty-four hours before becoming satiated. Sap runs down her pine needles and drips tiny amber jewels on the floor.

I look at the lodgepole walls of our log home and am reminded that other pines—planed, cut, and sanded—gather around us. Knotholes, like eyes, watch us. Swirls of grain, like fingerprints, reach out to us. We hang colored lights from the limbs of the ponderosa, dangle pairs of candles from her nubile buds, twirl glittering ornaments collected over the years from her branches. The scent of juniper rises from her trunk, mingling with pine and cinnamon and clove. One limb flings itself away from the rest of the limbs, as if the survival of the whole forest depends on just this one brave act.

I am finally ready now, I realize, to paint Romie's skull. I will choose the verdant green colors of renewal, the same colors that nature paints the land each spring. I think back to the day Mark drove in with the stock trailer from Colorado, bringing the horses here to their new home. My throat tightened as Romie backed out of the trailer. I led her away, holding one hand near her nostrils and speaking softly to her. She raised her head and took in the scent of this new place, then lowered her muzzle and sniffed my hand. I rubbed her nose and she nickered softly to me, pressing her head against my chest. I put my cheek on her neck and felt how small with age it had become. I wondered if there would be time for her to learn where the tender grasses grew, for Matt and Sarah to learn to ride upon her lean back.

There was time. Romie did learn where the tender grasses grew. Matt and Sarah did learn to ride upon her back. We have many lessons yet to learn about the tender grasses—about living on, and with, the land. Yet, as Romie once did, the land teaches us new lessons each day, and each day we become more eager to learn. Therein lies the hope; therein lies the color of the future.

Chapter 6

End of the Trail: Ranching Transformation on the Pacific Slope

LYNN HUNTSINGER

California is rangeland transformed and in transformation. Autumn rains bring dormant seeds to life, sparking a vibrant, glow-in-the-dark green that lights the understories of the oaks and the ridges of the hills. By spring this growth lengthens to a muted tangle of hundreds of species from places all across the globe, one of the most diverse grasslands on earth. Desiccation begins in late spring as patterns of brown creep across the hills, the dying annual grasses shadowing the variegated water-holding capacity of the soils and the canopies of the oaks. Within this sea of wild oats, bromegrasses, filarees, and clovers, where the land has not been acquainted with the plow, native bunchgrasses like purple needlegrass, California melic grass, and squirreltail remain, sentinels of California's past for those who recognize them. Ranching, similarly swamped in a diversifying ever-changing powerhouse economy, is beginning to signal a bygone era. How can it persist?

In the last two hundred years, California rangelands have been transformed by wave upon wave of exotic annual grasses and plants. Each species has a historical tale, journeying far to take permanent root in a familiar climate, from the shores of the Mediterranean Sea, from Africa, from Australia, from other places with dry summers and wet mild winters to the New World. Accompanying these physical tranformations have been vast cultural and economic changes. The range has been reinvented by cycles of human immigration and investment, by technological innovation, and by changing markets and connections to the rest of the world.

California's ecological diversity is matched by its large number of tribal groups and indigenous lifeways. Fire has traditionally been used for management, as has transplanting, cultivating, and harvesting of plants, fish, and game. Indigenous management shaped the California landscape, creating a rich environment for native life.

Starting in 1769, the Spanish brought in many of the grasses that cover the rangelands of today, as well as the cattle, sheep, and goats that flourish there. The Gold Rush of 1849 drew people from all over the world—from back East, from Europe, from China—all in search of elusive riches. New kinds of livestock, new plants, new types of ranching, all had their roots in this tumultuous time. The harvesting of timber for the mines transformed Sierran forests.

California became part of the Union in 1850. The Gold Rush receded like the outgoing waves on the Pacific tide—and in the latter part of the eighteenth century, people simply left the state. Those who remained settled in, and for a while agriculture reigned supreme in a land with lots of water, flat fertile bottomland, and little frost. The great Central Valley, now fingered with outgrowths of urban sprawl, remains one of the most productive farmland areas in the world.

As in much of the West, California's rangelands, kept open for decades after statehood to encourage settlement, were closed in the twentieth century. Natural, indigenous, and rural burning was suppressed, beginning a long cycle of fuel buildup and wildfire that has again transformed native range. Today about half the state is managed by the Forest Service and Bureau of Land Management (BLM). In general, the Forest Service controls the mountain and forest summer ranges, the BLM the desert and lowland ranges of the southern state. Annual grasslands and oak woodlands, the most productive and extensive rangelands and wildlife habitat in California, are overwhelmingly privately owned and belong to ranchers.

CALIFORNIA'S RANCH INDUSTRY

Livestock first served to support missions and converts under the Spanish, then gradually helped define the lifestyle of individuals granted extensive lands under the Spanish and Mexican governments. For a while, the Gold Rush created a livestock entrepreneur's paradise: Not only were cattle herded into the state to feed the booming population, but legal shenanigans favored the transfer of the large Mexican land grants to Anglo-Americans. When the people left, the market went with them, and millions of newly worthless cattle perished of starvation or from floods on the range.[1] As crop agriculture became more important, ranching retreated to the hills. When the Forest Service took control of mountain pastures in about 1906, allocating grazing permits to local cattle ranchers and outlawing tramp sheep grazing, livestock numbers declined and then stabilized. Today's westside ranchers either follow a transhumant cycle of grazing from the foothills to the high country of the Sierra or practice season-long grazing in the coast ranges, foothills, and valleys.

The 1930s and 1940s began a period of "improvement" in livestock production and marketing. Advisory agencies like the Department of Agriculture's Soil Conservation Service (now the Natural Resources Conservation Service), the University of California Cooperative Extension, and other agencies and programs worked with landowners under the premise that the rancher's primary goal was cash income. Such agencies introduced new forage species, subsidized oak removal and brush clearing, and encouraged upgrading and intensive management of herds. Irrigated pasture was developed to compensate for lost upland and lowland meadows. As agriculture expanded, hay and agricultural by-products became available to producers for feeding cattle. Cattle numbers could grow with the alternative sources of feed.

During this time the cattle industry began to fragment. Consumers were encouraged to buy grain-fed beef instead of leaner, different tasting, range-fed beef. Feedlots were a way to use underpriced grain and by-products to produce profitable meat. Investors supported the creation of large feedlots where yearling animals, purchased off the ranch, could be fed for market to the new specifications of a generation of consumers. This practice not only increased the number of cattle that could be produced for market every year but also linked livestock production to grain production in the Midwest and corporate investment.

The creation of more middlemen between rancher and consumer is often blamed for keeping cattle prices depressed. As feedlot, packer, and supermarket have become more vertically integrated, their ability to hold down prices has grown. It has also been argued that "hobby ranchers" keep prices down by producing cows as a lifestyle rather than strictly as a business. It seems that for those engaged in it, ranching is valued as much for the way of life as for the cash profits. A study of ranchers in several California counties found that only a quarter to a third of them made more than 75 percent of their income from the ranch. Trying to sort out who the "real" ranchers are would be a complex undertaking indeed. Even the iconographic family ranch has been viewed as a unit of consumption rather than production by prominent range economists.[2] In several surveys most ranchers reported that they choose to ranch because they like "feeling close to the earth" and being near natural beauty. They need income to survive, but it is not their primary reason for choosing to ranch.

A BIG CIRCLE GANDER AT THE CALIFORNIA RANCH

California, with $1.4 billion in sales in 1999, is the seventh-largest producer of cattle and calves in the United States. But California is the largest agricultural economy in the United States, as well, with $23 billion in sales in 1999. Trends in the industry have been universally downward over the last ten years: Beef cows have declined from 955,000 to 800,000 head; feedlot numbers have declined from 930,000 to 570,000 head; and the number of ewes has dropped, stunningly, from 620,000 to 330,000 head.[3] The range livestock industry is hard pressed by competing demands for land, both public and private. Recreationists and "nouveau rural" homeowners often see no reason to share the mountains with cattle, and land prices in many foothill and coastal range areas have skyrocketed while livestock profits, industry, and infrastructure have deteriorated.

The half of California's 35 million acres of rangeland that is privately owned produces about 90 percent of the forage on annual grasslands, oak savanna, and oak woodlands.[4] While the contribution of public range like that of the Forest Service may be small in absolute terms, it can be a critical source of otherwise hard to find summer grass. An array of other public entities also lease land to graziers, including the Department of Defense, water districts, state, regional, and local parks, and game refuges. Of ranchers surveyed in San Francisco Bay Area counties with virtually no federal range, slightly more than a third used some form of public range. These usually charge much higher fees than do the Forest Service and BLM, but they often have far more productive range-lands on a per acre basis. Of oak woodland in parcels larger than 20 acres throughout the state, 11 percent were subdivided between 1985 and 1995. During the same period, the proportion of landowners reporting they were less than 5 miles from the nearest subdivision increased from one-half to two-thirds.[5] Extrapolating from a number of data points about the extent of oak rangeland in California from studies spanning the period 1930 to 1992, an accelerating rate of decline is apparent.

Pressure for development means high land prices, high property taxes, and, eventually, high estate taxes. This problem has been some-what alleviated by a program, referred to as the Williamson Act, that allows landowners to keep their properties taxed on the basis of agricul-tural value. Conservation easements are also becoming increasingly pop-ular. Proposition 13, passed in 1978, limits the amount of tax increase that can be levied on property in continuous ownership to 2 percent annually. But without strong land-use controls such as an "urban limit line" or large parcel designations, these programs are either transitory, disappearing once land prices get high enough, or spectacularly expen-sive. In a survey of ranchers in three counties, more than three-fourths of the respondents believed that state and local land-use planning is a threat to ranching.[6] Ranchers often have most of their assets in land. In fact, one economic study in the Sierra found that ranchers make more money from land appreciation than ranch-based income sources.[7] Land-use planning may reduce these assets. Finally, a time-honored way of making ends meet in times of trouble is to calve off a few parcels and sell them for hard cash.

Land-use planning also runs up against core values of the ranching community—the right and privacy to do what you want on your land. Ranchers will tell you that one reason they chose ranching is because they can make their own decisions, and they are not interested in defer-ring that power to the government. More than 80 percent of ranchers in the three-county survey agreed that "overregulation is an important rea-son to quit ranching." A statewide survey of oak woodland landowners with more than 20 acres found that 88 percent of them agreed that state regulation means a loss of liberties and freedom, and 75 percent did not agree that the state should regulate private resources. (This number dropped to about half when compensation was offered.) A significant majority of ranchers in the three-county survey agreed that animal rights, the Endangered Species Act, and state or federal wilderness designations are a threat to the future of ranching.

RANCHERS AND THE OUTSIDE WORLD

Regulation runs counter to the nature of pastoral peoples worldwide: Ranchers prefer to police themselves. On a visit to Gray Davis Preserve, at the north end of the Central Valley, members of the environmental community and some cowhands who worked for the livestock leasee viewed the range and touched on the issue of a neighbor's cattle. The hands explained that they often found a neighboring rancher's cows in one particular canyon. When members of the group asked them what they did about it, they said: "We round them up and take them over to her place. Sometimes we call and ask her to come get them." Some of the guests were surprised, wondering why animal control or the sheriff weren't brought in to take care of the problem. The cowhands found this a totally alien idea.

From the time of the Spanish rancheros narratives of ranching tradition make it clear that building good relations with your neighbors, and helping each other out, are crucial.[8] Ranchers prefer to solve disputes, not with legal or outsider intervention, but by informal networks of peer pressure. Our three-county survey found that most California ranchers, when confronted with trespassing cows, would round them up and return them to the owner, or call and talk to the owner about it, rather than report the animals to any official entity. All twenty-two ranchers interviewed in the Central Sierra in a current study were adamant that they would not consider bringing in outside authorities to resolve a grazing dispute. An industry that is based on roaming animals and weak fences simply has to value mutual trust and respect— making land-use control efforts, and federal land management, a challenging task indeed.

Observations in public-range states suggest that at least some of the quarrels that arise between federal managers and permittees stem from cross-cultural misunderstandings. We accept this now when we work abroad: Professionals working in other countries are counseled and trained in cultural sensitivity. Yet the suggestion that a Forest Service land manager might benefit from training in the cultural mores of American ranchers would be met with derision—an example of agency "capture" or "going native." But the gulf between them is often deep: educationally, politically, and in life experience.

To relate a second story, a rancher and two guests are standing on the bank of a creek. The rancher explains that he thinks he could make better use of the water because so much of it is just being *wasted*—going right down the creek. The guests, visiting members of the conservation community, think this notion is pretty outrageous. But in fact the rancher was just expressing a common worldview in the ranching community, a view that goes all the way back to the settlement of the West and the ideas of John Locke: That which is not put to good use for the benefit of people is waste. A stock pond like those scattered through the San Francisco Bay foothills provides another example. A rancher viewing a stock pond will tell you about the history of the pond, how his grandfather or father dug out the pond, and how it keeps cows well distributed and watered into the dry season. He or she may even comment on the benefits deer and other wildlife are getting from it. An urbanite, by contrast, may find the stock pond an ecological travesty. Cows have walked in it! The native amphibious life is being stepped on! The grass around its edges is *eaten*. For the rancher, grass grazed is grass put to good use. For the environmentalist, missing grass is a sign of devastation. In general, then, it might be said that for many with an environmental perspective, to use a natural resource is to despoil it. For those with a more agricultural orientation, not to use it is a crime.

In 1989 I surveyed members of the local community, BLM employees, permittees, and members of an environmentalist organization called the Oregon Natural Resources Council about the conditions of rangeland in Malheur County, Oregon.[9] I found that two people looking at the same piece of ground can see vastly different things. Livestock permittees thought range conditions were pretty good in their county—evidence of overgrazing was scarce. Members of the environmental community looking at the same range thought rangeland conditions were poor. BLM employees and members of the local community fell somewhere between these two extremes.

THE SUBURBAN RANGE: TO RANCH OR NOT TO RANCH?

As a landscape becomes more residential and less rural, conflicts with neighbors may add to the costs and frustrations of ranching. Trespass by people and pets, complaints about agricultural activities, negative car/animal interactions—all can impinge on the rancher's livelihood.[10] Urbanization makes ranching more difficult, and it also affects the outlook of ranchers.

We surveyed ranchers in a rural setting, Tehama County in the northern part of the Central Valley, and in two urban counties adjacent to one another in the San Francisco Bay Area, Alameda and Contra Costa counties.[11] Ranchers in urban California counties were less concerned about the fate of their lands if sold than those in the rural county—and more willing to accept development of the land for housing. They were also more willing than rural ranchers to consider selling to a public agency or conservation organization. Ranchers in rural Tehama County showed a definite preference for their land remaining private grazing land, thinking of it as a productive land use. More than three-fourths of all the ranchers surveyed believed that urbanization is a threat to the future of ranching. In the urban counties, 82 percent of ranchers believed that local land-use planning is a serious threat to ranching; in the rural county, only 54 percent felt that way. In rural Tehama, ranchers believe that the local populace is more likely to share their views about planning, while ranchers in Alameda and Contra Costa counties see their viewpoints being overwhelmed by the tidal wave of urban and suburban residents.

About 60 percent of the ranchers surveyed were at least third-generation ranchers, and most had owned their land for decades. In both urban and rural areas, about half the ranchers want their children to continue in ranching. A third to a fourth of the ranchers reported that their kids do not want to ranch; about a fifth are so discouraged that they do not want their children to ranch. Not only is the estate tax situation complex, but the influence of conservation easements and Williamson Act designation on estate taxes is somewhat unclear. One thing, however, is certain: A vast majority of ranchers believe that estate taxes and heirship issues are major obstacles for ranching in the long term. In the comparative study of urban and rural ranchers, no new ranches had been started in the last ten years in the urban counties. Interestingly, some ranchers who had sold out in the urban area used their profits to buy a larger spread in rural California.

More than 90 percent of the California ranchers surveyed agreed that feeling close to the earth—and living in a decent place for family life—were good reasons to keep ranching despite the low returns and hard work. Ironically, though ranchers are committed to core environmental values like enjoying natural beauty and feeling close to the earth, they worry about hostile environmentalism. About 88 percent think that environmentalism is a "threat to ranching." More than two-thirds reported that "society's hostility to ranching" is a reason to quit.

THE MOTHER OF INVENTION

Necessity is said to be the mother of invention, and these are indeed times of necessity. Can the ranching community transform itself and survive? I think it can, and here are a few indicators:

• Despite the problems of urban ranching, many ranchers are deeply committed to it as a lifestyle and would remain if conditions permitted. One of the most exciting developments in the Bay Area is a group of ranchers and agriculturists who are working with planning departments to conserve agriculture in the urban counties. In other places, collaborative resource management and planning groups are beginning to include ranchers.

• Education works. California ranchers have shown themselves receptive to educational programs sensitive to the ranching community's mores and methods—and are beginning to demonstrate how such programs can help ranchers meet environmental goals. After the implementation of a Cooperative Extension program designed to educate ranchers and other landowners about the benefits of oaks and how to manage them, the cutting of oaks by California ranchers sharply declined.[12]

• Grazing reduces fire hazard. Fire hazard management in flammable California can in many cases be augmented with grazing. There has been a resurgence of goat herding in the Bay Area, for example, as landowning public agencies pay to have their shrublands mowed by goats. A city council in the Bay Area recently voted to keep ranching on its lands because the suburbanites want cattle there. They like seeing them, and they like the reduced fire hazard.

• Grazing is a tool. Grazing is a chemical-free way of manipulating vegetation for forestry and restoration projects. Some native species benefit when alien species are controlled by grazing. Conservation organizations have found that grazing can be used to meet management goals on some properties—encouraging native species that otherwise would be drowned out by competition with exotic grasses.

• Biodiversity matters. Recent research indicates that biodiversity is enhanced by intermediate grazing regimes in Mediterranean ecosystem.[13] The Nature Conservancy has conducted studies examining the utility of grazing for encouraging floristic diversity.

• Opportunities for income diversification abound. With a growing population comes problems but also opportunities to diversify income sources. More than a third of the ranchers surveyed agreed that diversifying their operations was an important goal for their ranch. One California rancher hosts tour groups from Japan, and hot-air balloon races, and sells honey and bay leaves from his ranch. Marketing range-fed beef and other products for specialty markets also offers opportunities. A diverse population demands diverse products—for example, a sheep rancher I know in the Central Valley markets lambs to meet the specifications of the nearby Sikh community.

• Ranch lands have been saved. Conservation easements—combined with rancher-friendly planning efforts based on mutual understanding—have helped maintain lands in agricultural use that clearly would have become city long ago without them. A hopeful development is the California Rangeland Trust, an organization supported by the California Cattlemen's Association that helps ranchers with estate planning, brokering the use of conservation easements, and land trust participation. About 4 percent of the ranchers surveyed in a three-county study had some sort of conservation easement on their land.[14]

• Concerns about water quality have often been put forward as a problem for ranchers—and in some areas they are. But well-managed rangeland grazing has far less impact than most other land uses. Evidence is mounting that ranch lands have a role in preserving healthy watersheds.

• California ranchers have shown themselves amenable to certain measures for protecting ranch lands. About two-thirds of ranchers have land enrolled in the Williamson Act—a ten-year rolling contract whereby, in exchange for a lowered tax rate, the rancher agrees not to subdivide land. Statewide about half of all oak woodland landowners with more than 20 acres have enrolled in the act.

• Ecosystem management demands it. The link between ranching and an ecosystem management approach—one that considers the role of private lands in conserving California ecosystems at a landscape scale—needs further examination. For example, considerable acreage in the Sierra foothills is privately owned by ranchers who to some degree rely on access to public forage. This land is largely foothill oak woodland, a type described in a recent Sierra Nevada ecosystem report commissioned by the federal government as "severely threatened by development."[15]

Ranching can be part of the solution to this crisis, but only if those concerned with rangeland conservation work together. This will require cooperation and, perhaps, the reinvention of ranching itself.

REINVENTION?

How can ranching be reinvented in ways that will help it persist? To survive in the overheated economic and political environment of today's California, ranching and grazing need to manifest ecological benefits. These can be at a local level (as in species restoration) or at a landscape scale (maintaining watersheds and open space). Elements of the environmentalist movement have shown a growing interest in ranching as a means of accomplishing conservation goals. The ranching community, in turn, had better meet the challenge of demonstrating that this trust is well placed. Putting faith in ranching has been a big step for some of these environmental groups. They have had to overcome an ideology which insists that every open space must be a vestige of pristine America as well as a belief that all will be well if land is simply left to itself. To take advantage of these opportunities for alliance, ranchers must meet environmentalists halfway.

Ranchers, in exchange, had better be able to glean economic benefits from these ecological services. The perpetually sordid state of ranch finances limits all efforts to protect ranching. In Spain today, national and European Union subsidies support the maintenance of the culturally and environmentally valuable oak woodlands. The European Union has provided large subsidies to farmers and ranchers to support culturally and environmentally significant land uses. In Wales, The Nature Conservancy has contracts with farmers to maintain farming and allow hikers to use trails crossing their property. One element of economic relief could be well-designed conservation easement programs and other efforts that help alleviate estate tax burdens and encourage people to remain in ranching. Land-use planning must be concerned with maintaining extensive agricultural areas intact with a critical mass of ranchers to preserve shared labor pools, packing plants, auction yards, and so forth.

Ranchers must overcome some of their own cherished mythology—total self-sufficiency and independence, for example. Ecologically, and economically, we are deeply interconnected. As the world grows smaller through globalization, the ranch is more connected to distant markets, to local people, to expanding cities, to nearby parks, reserves, and open space, to subdivisions and tourist outlets. But some ranchers are so determined to maintain a dogged illusion of total independence that they refuse to have anything to do with conservation easements, for example, that are publicly funded. They will not participate in land-use planning except to obstruct it, however possible. But ranches today, no matter how private or where they are, are already partly public space. They provide numerous public goods to which the public has staked a claim: clean water, clean air, wildlife habitat, scenery. The average citizen, driving down the highway, sees rangeland and thinks of it as "open space," not agricultural land. The very term conveys the public perception that this land has a public character. Asserting the ownership status certainly will not change the perception.

One key to ranching's future—and a big one—is recognizing the public's claim to private range and learning how to work with it to the benefit of both the ranching community and the public. If ranching is to survive, the public will foot part of the bill. Indeed there are those who say it is already during so, if not through subsidies, then through donations, tax breaks, and in-kind incentives. Ranching must extend the benefits of the ranching life to society at large and make sure that the resources it has the privilege of living with are well stewarded. By the same token, the public must recognize the needs of the ranching community. This will require trust, mutual understanding, and good lawyers and estate planners.

NOTES

1. L. Burcham, *California Range Land: A Historic-Ecological Study of the Range Resources of California* (Davis: University of California Press, 1982).
2. J. Workman, *Range Economics* (New York: Macmillan, 1986).
3. California Census of Agriculture, 1999.
4. R. Ewing et al., *California's Forests and Rangelands: Growing Conflict Over Changing Uses* (Sacramento: Anchor Press, 1988).
5. L. Huntsinger et al., "Ownership and Management Changes on California Hardwood Rangelands: 1985 to 1992," *Journal of Range Management* 50 (1997): 423–430.
6. R. Liffmann et al., "To Ranch or Not to Ranch: Home on the Urban Range?" *Journal of Range Management* 53 (2000): 362–371.
7. T. Hargrave, "The Impact of a Federal Grazing Fee Increase on Land Use in El Dorado County, California" (M.S. thesis, University of California, Berkeley, 1993).
8. T. Grigsby, "Buckaroo Ranchers: Sociocultural Factors Related to Economic Performance Among Range Livestock Operators of Southeastern Oregon" (Ph.D. dissertation, University of Oregon, Eugene, 1976).
9. L. Huntsinger and H. Heady, "Perceptions of the Vale Program" in *The Vale Rangeland Rehabilitation Program: An Evaluation*, ed. H. F. Heady, Resource Bulletin PNW-RB-157 (Portland: Pacific Northwest Research Station, Forest Service, U.S. Department of Agriculture; Bureau of Land Management, U.S. Department of the Interior, 1988), pp. 103–133.
10. R. Ellickson, *Order Without Law* (Cambridge, Mass: Harvard University Press, 1991).
11. Liffman et al., "To Ranch or Not to Ranch."

12. Huntsinger et al., "Ownership and Management Changes on California Hardwood Rangelands," 423–430.
13. A. Perevolotsky and N. Seligman, "Role of Grazing in Mediterranean Rangeland Ecosystems—Inversion of a Paradigm," *BioScience* 48 (1998): 1007–1017.
14. Liffman et al., "To Ranch or Not to Ranch," 362–371.
15. T. Duane, "Human Settlement 1850–2040," in *Sierra Nevada Ecosystem Project Final Report to Congress: Status of the Sierra Nevada,* ed. SNEP Science Team (Centers for Water and Wildland Resources, University of California, Davis), p. 246.

Chapter 7

Perceptions of Ranching: Public Views, Personal Reflections

MARK BRUNSON AND GEORGE WALLACE

Ranching has never been easy. Since the earliest days of the open range, western livestock producers have struggled to cope with daunting forces outside their personal control: flood and drought, blizzards and wild-fires, fluctuating feed costs and beef prices. But these days the job may seem even tougher, because ranchers face new but equally daunting forces whose origins are largely political and social rather than natural or economic: relentless and unparalleled population growth in the Inter-mountain West and the unresolved public debate about the future of livestock grazing on public lands.

These new forces may seem especially threatening because ranchers hear confusing and often contradictory messages from the various groups seeking to influence how ranching is done in the West. Government officials seem to make new demands weekly as they struggle to respond to an ever-widening array of advocacy groups. Meanwhile the news media report even the wildest accusations by grazing opponents and supporters as if they were unassailable fact. Adding to the confusion, academic experts can be found to support any side of the debate.[1]

It's no wonder, then, that ranchers may find it hard to tell where they stand with average Americans. On the one hand, it's clear that a signifi-cant number of politically active people see livestock grazing, especially on public lands, as an environmental evil. On the other, ranching remains a compelling national symbol—as evidenced by the TV commercials that use cowboy culture to sell everything from automobiles to ZIP drives; the tourists who annually visit western rangelands in search of an authentic American experience; and the popularity of rodeo, roping, riding, and other ranch-related pastimes that thrive across the United States and abroad.[2] So which is the true public image of ranching: unsustainable land use or cultural icon? Or is it a little of both?

In this essay we first try to clarify the public image question by describing results of some recent studies that have examined American attitudes about ranching and western rangeland management. Then we offer some of our own ideas, based on years of observation as university researchers and residents of farming and ranching communities, about how livestock producers and community leaders can work to reduce the polarization of the range management debate while improving ranchers' ability to address the concerns of new as well as traditional rangeland constituencies.

POSITIVE IN PRINCIPLE, VARIABLE IN PRACTICE

American attitudes toward western ranching tend to depend on whether one thinks of the principle or the actual practice. Overwhelmingly we feel positively toward ranching as an institution as well as the open landscapes that ranching provides. But many people find fault in the effects, real or perceived, of livestock grazing on western rangelands—especially when it occurs on lands managed by federal agencies such as the Forest Service or Bureau of Land Management.

Clearly western ranching holds a special place in the American psyche. What other outdoor occupation can claim to have an entire genre of literature, hundreds of motion pictures, and a highly popular spectator sport devoted to it? Yet the sense of tradition that surrounds ranching can work to its detriment as well as its benefit. Ranchers sometimes resist changes that could improve their public image, as well as their bottom line, because doing so wouldn't fit their long-held vision of the independent ranching lifestyle.[3] Meanwhile urban citizens who embrace the western frontier myth can become disillusioned when they see the modern ranching reality of ATV-riding cowboys, helicopter roundups, and real estate agents from "land and cattle companies" who sport Stetsons, boots, and big belt buckles.

Even so, the basic concept of ranching remains popular with Americans. Partly this is due to the continued importance of the pioneer ideal in modern society; partly it is because ranching basks in the positive light in which Americans view farming as a whole. Our veneration of agriculture is a cultural trait that dates to the earliest days of the republic when Thomas Jefferson called farmers "the most valuable citizens of all . . . the most vigorous, the most independent, the most virtuous . . . tied to their country and wedded to its liberty and interests by the most lasting bonds."[4] Evidence of this enduring positive view can be seen in the results of an August 1999 opinion poll commissioned by the American Farm Bureau Federation which found that 85 percent of citizens rated farmers as giving "a great deal of contribution" to society. This rating was on a par with teachers and firefighters (both 86 percent) and well ahead of the clergy (68 percent), business people (37 percent), bankers (29 percent), and politicians (13 percent).[5] Similarly, a 1996 study found that 80 percent of Colorado's residents believe agriculture is important for maintaining the quality of life, while an even larger percentage think it is important for the state to maintain land and water in agricultural production.[6]

In the 1999 Farm Bureau poll, two-thirds of consumers rated farmers as "very effective" at conserving natural resources and caring for the environment—well ahead of environmentalists (60 percent), scientists (58 percent), government officials (21 percent), and logging companies (19 percent). These ratings were even higher when the question asked about family farms rather than corporate farms. In the 1996 Colorado study, 60 percent believed agriculture "usually" or "almost always" has been responsible in protecting the environment, while 67 percent agreed to some extent that agriculture does a good job of providing wildlife habitat.

Just because some people feel positively about a concept overall doesn't necessarily mean they feel positively toward every aspect of it. It is entirely logical for someone to have a positive attitude toward pork as a food product for example, but a negative attitude about living next door to a large hog farm. This also is true for Americans' view of how agriculture treats the environment. The Farm Bureau poll found that while three out of four respondents rated farmers as being good at taking care of the land, fewer than half thought they do a good job taking care of water or using chemicals properly.

Even when people are critical of agriculture, they may prefer it to other land uses. Colorado residents in the 1996 survey favored agriculture as a land use over mining and suburban development—highly controversial enterprises in a state where concerns about urban sprawl, open space, and the loss of rural amenities are acute. In a 1994 study of visitors to Steamboat Springs, Colorado, researchers found that most visitors believed their enjoyment had been enhanced by attributes of ranch open space such as wildflower meadows, cattle, horses, corrals, ranch buildings, and cowboys. In fact, the study found that tourists would be willing to pay $15 to $25 per day to protect ranch open space.[7] Routt County, where Steamboat Springs is located, has subsequently begun purchasing conservation easements on ranches in the nearby valleys. A 1996 study of public attitudes toward land use and wildlife in southwestern Colorado's La Plata County found that three-fourths of those responding agreed that ranches should be protected despite pressures to subdivide and develop them.[8]

RANCHING ON THE PUBLIC'S LAND

One factor that affects how people feel about ranching is the ownership of the land where livestock grazing takes place. Americans feel strongly about their national forests and parks and other public lands, and they have definite ideas about what activities are appropriate there. Much of the negative attention given to western ranching applies specifically to livestock grazing on public land. Citizens feel they have a legitimate stake in what happens on these lands, and activists who oppose western livestock management have the political and legal leverage to force changes in management of public lands as opposed to private property.

Many visitors to public lands in the West are surprised to discover they may have to share their recreation site with cattle or sheep. We suspect these same visitors are unaware of how important grazing leases on public land are to the viability of western ranching operations; nor do they understand the history and patterns of land disposal and settlement that created this dependence.[9] For many people, the most accessible source of information about ranching has been top-rated TV series like *Bonanza* and *Dallas*, which feature atypically wealthy livestock operators whose ranches bear little relation to reality. Television ranchers don't talk about animal unit months, allotment management plans, or forage utilization monitoring over the dinner table. So it's little wonder that Americans may not realize that public-land forage keeps most western ranchers in business. When citizens do make this discovery, they usually feel they should get a say about how, or even whether, grazing should take place on public land.

While most Americans believe ranchers take good care of their own property, they're less sure that federal rangeland managers do the same for the public grazing lands. In spring 1993, a survey of U.S. attitudes toward federal rangeland management found that Americans generally believed livestock grazing had caused environmental damage to federal lands.[10] Sixty percent agreed with a statement that cattle and sheep had overgrazed most federal lands, for example, and 86 percent agreed that rangeland water quality had declined over the previous fifty years. Yet only 17 percent agreed with the demonstrably true statement that the extent of overgrazing had declined on federal lands in the previous half-century. Such negative beliefs don't necessarily lead to the conviction that livestock grazing should not occur on public lands. In fact, two-thirds of those surveyed said federal land policies should emphasize multiple uses of rangeland as opposed to either preservation or commodity production. But neither did the survey find a ringing endorsement of grazing on public land. In fact, 34 percent agreed with a statement that livestock grazing should be banned on all federal lands, while 45 percent said they were neutral or undecided. Similarly, a study in 1992 and 1993 found that two-thirds of recreation visitors to Colorado's Uncompaghre National Forest considered grazing at least conditionally acceptable on lands managed for multiple use. But 40 percent said grazing should be allowed only if range management were improved to ensure good range condition, protect riparian areas, and reduce conflicts with other users.[11]

Virtually all federal lands that are used for livestock grazing are also used for outdoor recreation—and the two activities do not always coexist easily. Thus people may feel negatively toward livestock grazing because of its interference with recreation. Before being told that the Uncompaghre study would be about grazing and recreation, respondents were asked if anything had interfered with their recreation experiences. Cattle were the most common source of interference mentioned, ahead of other people, road conditions, weather, insects, or all-terrain vehicles. This study also showed that the quality of visitors' experiences depended on *where* they encountered cattle and sheep during their visit. Encountering cattle in meadows for example, was seen as more favorable than finding them beside a stream. And while about a third of the recreationists surveyed said that the presence of cattle had detracted from their overall experience, the same percentage said it had added to their enjoyment. This finding lends support to a contention often made by ranchers: Removing livestock would diminish the "western feeling" many tourists seek from a visit to public rangelands.

It's important to note, however, that these findings were for a relatively moist, higher-elevation area that is managed for multiple use and visited mainly by in-state residents. Public support may be much weaker for livestock grazing on sensitive public lands where the management emphasis is on protecting ecological and other noncommercial values. A 1999 survey in the BLM's Grand Staircase–Escalante National Monument—where livestock grazing was specifically retained as a land use by the presidential proclamation establishing the monument—found that 68 percent of backcountry recreation visitors felt seeing cattle on the open range had detracted from their visit while just 8 percent thought it had added to their experience.[12]

Similarly, recreation visitors are less likely to support grazing in designated wilderness areas than in multiple-use lands. A 1994 survey of more than a thousand visitors to U.S. Forest Service wildernesses in Colorado and Utah reported that roughly equal numbers of people found livestock grazing acceptable and unacceptable.[13] But three-fourths of those who might accept grazing said they could do so only if there were proper management to protect rangeland ecosystems. A majority said livestock use had detracted from their wilderness experiences—even such innocuous encounters as seeing rustic fences and corrals or spotting cattle in the distance.

Visitors' perceptions of outdoor recreation settings are often influenced by their previous experiences at the same site or similar places. A Colorado study in 1997 and 1998 looked at national forest visitor perceptions using questions similar to previous studies—except that the number of cattle allowed to graze was reduced by 30 percent during the second year of the study.[14] This management change was apparently too subtle to be perceived by most visitors. They felt no differently about grazing in the second year than during the first year. Even though people say they would approve of grazing if ecological conditions were improved, such changes happen slowly and are hard for most visitors to detect without help from managers or producers in interpreting what they see.

Another factor that may influence public attitudes is the reason why grazing occurs. If the grazing is intended to achieve widely beneficial goals, such as reducing weed infestations or fire risks, it is likely to be seen positively. A 1994 Utah survey asked citizens how they felt about different means of achieving an environmentally desirable change in range vegetation on public lands. In this case respondents preferred grazing as a management tool over plowing, chaining, or herbicides. Only natural fire was rated as a better way to produce a change in plant species.[15]

Private economic benefit however, is seen as a less worthy goal of public land management. Americans are very sensitive to the suggestion—true or not—that some people benefit disproportionately from the use of common resources such as those found on public rangelands. Several participants in the 1999 Grand Staircase–Escalante survey commented that livestock grazing, recreation outfitting, and other commercial uses should not be allowed on lands owned by all Americans. In the 1993 national rangeland survey, two-thirds of the respondents thought ranchers should pay more to graze livestock on public lands. While there is much debate about whether ranchers are subsidized by the public to use federal lands, the perception persists. Moreover, this perception is exploited by advocacy groups who use economic arguments to marshal support against grazing. Ordinary citizens confuse cost with the *value* ranchers obtain. If grazing leases on private rangelands bring $8 to $10 per animal unit month (AUM), many people can't see why the same lease on public lands should be as low as $1.35 per AUM. Such claims rankle ranchers who argue that you can't compare public and private lease rates. They point to costs over and above grazing fees that have to be paid for while grazing on public lands and explain that on private lands these same costs are usually included in the grazing fee.

WHO BELIEVES WHAT—AND WHY?

Because attitudes flow from a lifetime of personal experience, people with different life experiences feel differently about ranching. It shouldn't surprise anyone to learn that our surveys have found more positive attitudes toward livestock grazing among rural citizens than urban residents. In Utah rural residents felt more positively toward traditional ranch practices such as grazing, chaining, or herbicide use; in Colorado they were more tolerant of grazing on public lands. In the 1994 Colorado Department of Agriculture study, residents of urban Front Range communities assigned less importance to agriculture as an economic force—as did those who had lived in Colorado for less than ten years. As we might expect, those who had lived on a farm or ranch were most likely to support agriculture.

Ranchers and rural politicians often blame easterners for any negative measure that affects grazing on public lands. It turns out this assumption may be unwarranted. At the same time as the 1993 national attitude study, two parallel surveys were done in the state of Oregon.[16] They found that attitudes in the more urban, western half of Oregon were closer to those in the rest of the country than to those of people in eastern Oregon, where ranching is economically and culturally significant. Nationally the most preservationist attitudes didn't come from the East but from urban areas in the Pacific Rim states of California, Oregon, and Washington.

While geography and personal experience do much to shape attitudes toward ranching and range management, an equally crucial influence is a person's environmental value system. This is especially true for people who have no specific knowledge about grazing but believe they have a stake in determining how grazing takes place in the West. If people lack specific knowledge about grazing, they may rely on their underlying environmental values to help them interpret and respond to a survey, support or oppose an issue, or vote. For example, the national survey showed that those who believe all species have an equal right to live on the earth are more likely to oppose grazing on public lands. And because people use their belief systems to help them filter and interpret conflicting information, those who held preservationist beliefs were not only more likely to support a ban on public lands grazing but also more likely to believe that environmental conditions are deteriorating on public rangelands. Conversely, people who hold utilitarian attitudes toward public land use overall were less likely to believe rangeland riparian areas are impaired (despite a wealth of scientific information which suggests that they are).

PUBLIC INFORMATION OR PUBLIC INDOCTRINATION?

If people only believe what they're predisposed to believe—as the findings presented in the previous section suggest—it might be easy to conclude that public education campaigns have no effect on attitudes toward ranching or range management. We're not so pessimistic. But we do think it's important to design public information efforts with specific and realistic goals in mind. We cannot expect a public relations campaign to succeed at boosting ranching's image if all it does is show livestock grazing in a good light. Instead the campaign must present specific and well-balanced messages that address people's knowledge levels and relate to both preservationist and utilitarian value systems.

One thing is clear from even a cursory study of the grazing debate: One person's information can be another's propaganda. It's only natural for ranchers and their supporters to want others to hear only "the truth"—by which we typically mean the positive benefits of grazing management for both urban and rural citizens as well as for the ecosystems and economies on which we depend. But there's danger in this approach. First of all, a one-sided Pollyanna-style public information strategy can backfire if people see through it—as they almost surely will. Second, "the truth" is nearly always more complex than we like to admit. The fact is that ranching has not been, and still isn't, a wholly positive activity for rangeland environments. While we can point to riparian areas that are healthier thanks to carefully managed livestock grazing, it is also true that the West offers many examples of overgrazed watersheds. Just as there are progressive ranchers at the forefront of range management innovation, there are ranchers who refuse to change harmful practices in the face of overwhelming evidence.

The best strategy for illuminating the public debate, as well as for sustaining a responsive form of range livestock management, is to embrace the whole truth. Our beliefs are informed by the messages we hear from a wide variety of interests. In a democracy there is no way to silence the voices of those with whom we disagree, whether those voices are insightful or ill informed. But a curious thing happens when we pay continued attention to those voices: We start to reject the black-and-white pronouncements of the propaganda purveyors ("Beef is the only real food!" "Cows are the spawn of the devil!") and the shades of gray come into sharp focus. Only when the complexities of the ranching debate are acknowledged and addressed can we have enlightened discussion of a sustainable future for western rangelands.

We have seen that many people will support public land grazing only if they are assured that the land remains healthy and ecological conditions are improving. Such changes are hard for the public to perceive in the field, however, so public land managers and ranchers alike must point out when improvements are made. Interpretive displays or talks at campgrounds, visitor centers, and trailheads, for example, can explain riparian restoration, livestock exclosures, changes in grazing rotations, stocking rates, techniques to move livestock away from sensitive areas, and range improvements for wildlife. Before-and-after photos are effective for highlighting recent improvements that might otherwise go undetected. Ranchers and cowboys can be powerful educators and role models if they take time to visit with hikers or motorists and talk about management actions or invite people to accompany them while they move livestock or monitor range conditions. If ranchers are to address claims that public rangelands are recovering too slowly or not at all, improved communication with the public is critical.

Visitors' expectations must match what they find on the ground. The Colorado studies showed that most wilderness visitors did not know that livestock grazing is permitted in U.S. wilderness areas wherever it existed prior to wilderness designation (let alone that this compromise was vital to passing the Wilderness Act and has greatly increased the amount of land eligible for wilderness designation). Those who did know grazing is permitted were more likely to expect livestock encounters and were more accepting of grazing in general. By providing consistent, easily accessible information about the location and nature of grazing activities in popular recreation settings, public land managers and ranchers can improve the public's understanding about multiple use while reducing the likelihood that livestock operations will detract from visitors' recreation experience. Posting notices before and during cattle drives or roundups, for example, can help visitors adjust their expectations before encountering large numbers of livestock on public land. By making an effort to keep cattle away from areas of concentrated recreation use, ranchers can reduce the encounters that upset visitors most: trampling near streams and shorelines as well as trampling, livestock, and manure in and around campgrounds and trailheads.

THE BENEFITS OF PARTNERSHIP

Ranchers sometimes have trouble accepting that Americans value many things produced by ranches, including those which go beyond food and fiber. Many ranchers prefer to see themselves as producing beef, mutton, wool, and hay rather than aesthetic, cultural, and ecological values—even when the public seems ready to pay for them. During the 1999 elections, 116 of 130 open space initiatives passed nationwide. At a time when tax increases are extremely unpopular, people nevertheless agreed to tax themselves to pay for land and easements in order to limit growth and maintain rural or natural areas near their homes.

Many communities are using these revenues to invest in "working landscapes" where ranchers and farmers are paid for their development rights but are encouraged to continue their agricultural operations. There's nothing wrong with acknowledging the years and hard work it takes to produce and maintain a beautiful landscape—especially one that also makes room for streams, hills, forests, and wildlife habitats. The public that is willing to pay a rancher for an easement is saying it places real value on well-groomed hay meadows, sturdy barns and corrals, weed control, pastoral views of livestock and horses, and visual relief from the clutter of urbanization and strip development. The first step in forming partnerships with a supportive public is to acknowledge that these noncommodity ranch products and services are real.

Another necessary adjustment is an end to knee-jerk opposition to community planning efforts that would minimize the loss of agricultural land, water, and open space. Even though such programs are de facto indicators of positive public attitudes toward agriculture, some agricultural organizations have labeled them as threats to private property rights. But very few agricultural land protection programs use zoning classifications to preclude other uses of the land. Nor do they often reduce property values without compensation. Most agricultural land protection programs use willing-seller/willing-buyer techniques that offer direct economic benefits and other incentives to landowners.

Progressive agricultural groups across the nation testify to the benefits of ranch and farmland conservation techniques such as transfers and purchases of development rights, clustering of rural residential development, rancher-directed land trusts, and voluntary agricultural districting approaches that offer property tax and other incentives for ranchers and farmers who agree not to develop their properties for a given period of time.[17] Yet many livestock producers remain wary of them and do little to make them work. Others simply accept the talk-show rhetoric common to the "wise use" movement—dismissing all land conservation programs as "more government regulation" or "trying to make a museum out of my ranch." While such flippant dismissal of conservation programs may come easy and feel good, in reality the hope of ranching in most intermountain valleys lies in locally grown planning efforts. By pooling their land and capital resources, landowners can create "defensible development" proposals designed to protect the best working lands and ecologically important areas from future development. In this way ranchers can free themselves from the power of outside land speculators. Instead they can take advantage of the positive light in which most Americans view grassroots agricultural protection.

PART OF THE PROBLEM—OR THE SOLUTION?

The ranching culture must become more inclusive. Ranchers have many new neighbors on lands that have been subdivided. These include small part-time producers with a longtime relationship with agriculture, as well as newcomers who seek a rural lifestyle. Much of the livestock produced in the West comes from part-time operators,[18] yet these producers are often excluded from discussions about ranching despite their importance to the ranching economy. As for the second group, we continue to oppose the haphazard suburbanization of range landscapes.[19] But we must also warn against the tendency to see all newcomers to western ranching communities as "part of the problem." If imitation is the sincerest form of flattery, then some of the surest evidence of public support for ranching can be seen in the increasing desire of urban Americans to move to western rangelands to enjoy a miniature version of the ranching lifestyle.

It is ironic therefore that one of the few things ranchers and environmentalists often agree on is that "hobby ranches" are a blight on the western landscape. Conservationists oppose the subdivision of ranches because they know that landscape fragmentation and increased human density can pose threats to rangeland plant and animal communities. Ranchers' opposition tends to be cultural and economic: Culturally, the influx of newcomers brings nonconforming values to rural communities; economically, small-scale livestock operators (who typically have better access to cash than full-time ranchers) often sell hay or animals at lower prices and are willing to pay more for labor, equipment, and supplies.

But open or restrained hostility toward these potential allies is likely to be counterproductive. Not only do many of these new rural landowners have considerable empathy with both ranching and the environment, but they can provide an infusion of financial and political resources. Thus ranchers and conservationists alike should find them more useful as allies than opponents. Furthermore, just as ranches may buffer national parks, forests, wilderness areas, and public rangelands from less compatible uses, the acreages maintained by ranchette owners and part-time producers can protect established ranches from even more intensive settlement patterns. Of course, we do not support any reduction of efforts to keep existing ranches in production or to guide the subdivision of land toward ecologically sensitive or agriculturally productive areas. We also recognize the need to teach newcomers how to live carefully on a piece of land or in a rural community without harming it.

Established livestock producers could make powerful friends by reaching out to new neighbors: helping them understand the area, showing them how to fit into a working landscape and the community. It is time to include part-time producers in discussions about policies that affect ranch incomes. Otherwise they'll have little opportunity to learn the importance of solidarity when it comes to prices and as well to understand the cumulative effects of their decisions on the viability of ranching.

Our message, then, is to encourage ranchers to adapt to changes in the West. Public perceptions of western ranching are still largely positive and supportive—especially toward ranchers who are also stewards of the land and who husband our food. People do want improved rangeland health in general and especially on public lands. They will support management that is sensitive of other on-site users, but they need help understanding how ongoing management improvements can benefit both the land and the people who depend on it. We hope ranchers begin to accept the full array of values and products they produce and take steps to realize the economic potential of programs to protect open landscapes and the long-term future of agriculture. And we urge all ranchers to reach out to potential allies and marginal participants—seeking new avenues of education and outreach that are responsive to public perceptions of the ranching enterprise, culture, and landscape.

NOTES

1. J. Briede, "Viewpoint: Perceptions of the Western Rangelands by Media, Environmentalists, and the Public," *Rangelands* 16 (1994): 4–6.
2. R. Walsh et al., "Recreation Value of Ranch Open Space," Department of Agricultural and Resource Economics and Routt County Extension Office, Cooperative Extension Publication XCM-167 (Fort Collins: Colorado State University, 1994).
3. Writers who have examined how the western ranching tradition and mythic lifestyle affect modern ranchers include P. Starrs, *Let the Cowboy Ride: Cattle Ranching in the American West* (Baltimore: Johns Hopkins University Press, 1988); J. Jorgensen, "Land Is Cultural, So Is a Commodity: The Locus of Differences Among Indians, Cowboys, Sodbusters, and Environmentalists," *Journal of Ethnic Studies* 12 (1984): 3–21; and T. Grigsby, "Buckaroo Ranchers: Sociocultural Factors Related to Economic Performance Among Range Livestock Operators of Southeastern Oregon" (Ph.D. dissertation, University of Oregon, Eugene, 1976).
4. A. Koch and W. Peden, eds., *The Life and Selected Writings of Thomas Jefferson* (New York: Dutton, 1943).
5. Marketing Horizons Inc., "1999 Farmer Image Consumer Poll," report to the American Farm Bureau Federation, St. Louis, Mo., 1999.
6. G. Wallace and D. DeRuiter, "Public Attitudes About Agriculture in Colorado," report to the Colorado Department of Agriculture, Ag Insights (Fort Collins: Colorado State University, 1996).
7. Walsh et al., "Recreation Value."
8. P. Layden and M. Manfredo, "Public Attitudes Towards Land Use and Wildlife in La Plata County," Human Dimensions in Natural Resources Unit, Project Report 30 (Fort Collins: Colorado State University, 1996).

9. See Starrs, *Let the Cowboy Ride*, for an extensive account of this history.
10. M. Brunson and B. Steel, "National Public Attitudes Toward Federal Rangeland Management," *Rangelands* 16 (1994): 77–81.
11. Results of the Uncompaghre study are discussed in J. Mitchell et al., "Visitor Perceptions About Cattle Grazing on National Forest Land," *Journal of Range Management* 49 (1996): 81–86; G. Wallace et al., "Visitor Perceptions About Grazing on a Forest Service Cattle Allotment," U.S. Forest Service Research Paper RM-321, Rocky Mountain Forest and Range Experiment Station, Fort Collins, 1996; and J. Mitchell and G. Wallace, "Managing Grazing and Recreation Across Boundaries in the Big Cimarron Watershed," in *Stewardship Across Boundaries*, ed. R. Knight and P. Landres (Washington, D.C.: Island Press, 1988), pp. 217–236.
12. L. Palmer and M. Brunson, "Grand Staircase–Escalante Backcountry Visitor Study," report to the Bureau of Land Management, May 2000.
13. L. Johnson et al., "Visitor Perceptions of Livestock Grazing in Five U.S. Wilderness Areas," *International Journal of Wilderness* 3 (1997): 14–20. See also N. Hall, "Perceptions of Livestock Grazing on Public Lands: A Comparison of Wilderness and Non-Wilderness Visitors" (M.S. thesis, Colorado State University, Fort Collins, 1999).
14. E. Mohr, "Visitor Perceptions About Various Management Issues on a National Forest Grazing Allotment in Southwestern Colorado" (M.S. thesis, Colorado State University, Fort Collins, 2000).
15. M. W. Brunson, G. A. Rasmussen, and K. J. Richardson, "Acceptability of Range Practices and Policies Among General and Ranching Publics," in *Proceedings, Fifth International Rangeland Congress*, vol. 1, ed. N. West (Denver: Society for Range Management, 1996), pp. 72–73.
16. M. W. Brunson and B. S. Steel, "Sources of Variation in Attitudes and Beliefs About Federal Rangeland Management," *Journal of Range Management* 49 (1996): 69–75.
17. For a look at both private and public land conservation techniques that can be applied to ranches see L. Rosen, M. C. Cupell, and D. Dagget, *Protecting Ranches with Private Land Options* (Tucson: Sonoran Institute, 1996); see also American Farmland Trust, *Saving American Farmland: What Works* (Washington, D.C.: American Farmland Trust, 1997).
18. Sonoran Institute, *The New Frontier of Ranching: Business Diversification and Ranch Stewardship* (Tucson: Sonoran Institute, 2000).
19. R. L. Knight, G. N. Wallace, and W. E. Riebsame, "Ranching the View: Subdivisions vs. Agriculture," *Conservation Biology* 9 (1994): 459–461.

Part Three

THE ECOLOGY
OF RANCHING

The Work
For Our Land and the People

DRUMMOND HADLEY

Old Earth we are gathering these borderlands together
Mesas arroyos and valleys as far as our eyes can see
Blue mountain range upon mountain range forever
Turning toward dawn light then into the evening west
As far as pale north sky circling south to where Roberto
Crosses horseback by the broken mesas in Mexico
There's a low light stretching from the sea of undulating cloud
Sky streaked down to touch Earth from heaven
Who are you who cross through that dusk light before us
Past old growth juniper cedar and mescal
Across this great sea of sky old singer
We hear your voice calling turn back toward me

Come back to Earth

Chapter 8
Shades of Gray

BOB BUDD

I am a child of the West. My blood runs neither red nor blue—it appears to me to be the pale green color of sagebrush. Seven species of sage are found where I live and work. Each smells different. Feels different. Red dust coats my hair, itself thinned by patches of gray. My border collie is black and pink. Smells of sage, sometimes skunk and decay. The hair nearest her body is white as snow. It snowed yesterday, soaked into the red soil, fed the sage, turned my children red. Pleased and nourished their souls. People take on the character of the land around them. Today the thermometer pushes seventy degrees. A chinook blows out of the north. Patches of gray appear on the landscape.

Patches of gray may best describe patterns of arid land ecology, of ranching, of life in this region. These patches are elegant and wonderful things. Subtle shades of gray define black sage, big sage, bitterbrush, and sumac. Blue-grays tint stands of wheatgrass more ancient than mankind. Green-gray paints Idaho fescue. Depth of color tells the story of organic matter on the ground. It differentiates species. Bright red is dogwood. Dark red, chokecherry. Coyote willow lies between this spectrum of reds. Other willows are yellow or white. Birch is black. Buffaloberry is silver gray.

Lack of startling color is the whole world in the ecology of ranching. In the hair of deer and humans, feathers of birds, leaves of plants, shades of gray differentiate. In these plain patches lie secrets of rangeland ecology, essential links and pieces of the frame that teach us to revere, and suspect extremes, whether dark, light, or color. Greens are verdant only when heat and water come together in proper fashion—before snow is totally gone, before sun takes over. Like the brief dance of the sage grouse, plants in my landscape find little time for splendor. This is a good thing. For only when you learn to discern shades of gray can you truly appreciate the brilliance of a goldfinch.

The western landscape in which I work has a harsh and violent history. It is a landscape ripped from its roots, stood on end, blasted by lightning, washed by torrents of rain, waterlogged by snow, baked by drought, frozen by cold. For thousands of years this landscape has been grazed, burned, rested, desiccated, flooded, and washed. Rangeland ecosystems are immense and intensely complex. Mere strides take us from hard, cold desert to lush, dense riparian habitats. Sometimes we can travel for hundreds of miles in an apparent sea of nothing but sagebrush and grass. It is a vulnerable thing, this land, and it can be transformed from lush wellspring to barren waste. But this is incredibly resilient land, and the processes that shape it make it rich in diversity of life. It can be transformed from barren waste to lush wellspring, too, and sometimes we forget that.

Natural systems build themselves up and tear themselves apart. Aldo Leopold tried to teach us to understand systems: to see ourselves as part of a greater world. We can't control the natural world. But we can try to live within the variations it throws our way. The same waters that allow willows to grow rip beaver dams from streams. The same animals that devastate plants prepare a world in which plants may grow. Browsing by animals affects chemical composition in plants, which attracts insects, which provide the food base for many of the world's birds. These are not simple things. They are the elegance of life we will never comprehend—the magical realities that mesmerize and remind us that we are not in charge of the world.

People make choices both spatially and temporally. We choose to maintain species of rare plants knowing full well they cannot grow in healthy, robust, riparian systems. We choose to maintain forests of pine as we lose aspen stands. We choose to convert rangeland to farmland and, after that, eliminate all biological choices for the land. We choose to manage for creatures and plants that rely upon things we do not understand. We have no idea whether some species are evolution-doomed or whether they are emerging and undeterred by our efforts on their behalf.

In landscapes where the single ecological truth is chaos and dynamic change, we seem obsessed with stability. Instead of relishing dynamic irregularities in nature, we absorb confusion and chaos into our own lives, then demand that natural systems be stable. We ask systems that evolved in geological time to respond and perform in our own lifetime. Instead of engaging right-brain ideas—and testing even the most hare-brained of them—we answer ideas with reasons why they will never work. We argue about math and dream little of process. We hide hatred in emotional debates about science. Science becomes political, evangelical, competing for limited dollars, pleasing masters of inquiry. Questions are built around dollars instead of ideas. Answers become churches of high divinity. Proof is in numbers, amalgamation of statistics, mathematical design, and, ultimately, interpretation of numbers. Every ecologist seems to have a separate take on what the numbers say. We are a fast-food society. We want answers *now*. If the answers are incorrect or incomplete, so be it. Ecological inquiry is relegated to courtrooms and political chambers for instant determination.

The fate of landscapes ultimately lies in the hands of people on the land. Are we really content with the notion that butterflies and bears will do well in a landscape where they cannot compete? It seems incongruous, incomprehensible, that we would turn the fate of the land over to those who cannot hear snipe feathers slicing wind overhead, whose sense of feel is immune to frostbite in winter. Only when we strive to learn and share, rather than lecture and control, will we find our ability to care for land enhanced and expanded. We may even find our sense of touch. In doing so, we will find questions unanswered. But we will rejoice that we can pass them to others anxious to learn.

Rivers run. Soils wash. Grasses grow. Rarely do we speak of what we desire the land to provide. As a result, our measurement of progress is skewed at best. Have we lost the vital connection between the questioner who lives on the land and the scientist who can analyze questions built on decades of observation? The person who watches a bright blue bird without counting the bird is blessed for life by the meeting. The person who counts birds without seeing their color does no more than move blue beads on an abacus. Those who see the bird, and drop their work to follow it, and fly with it in their dreams, will see the land from the keen eye of the bird.

Late in April 1999, nearly a quarter-mile of rock face fell from the Red Canyon rim to the valley below. Six feet of snow combined with temperatures below zero—then into the upper seventies—cleaved tons of ancient ocean bed from its mooring above an eroded basin and tossed it aside as casually as a grizzly ladles spent salmon from a receding stream. Boulders larger than trophy homes bounced and tore forest from the earth, guided by nothing but gravity and terrain, luck of bounce, shape of fragments. Some boulders reshaped the creek below. Others left scars as large as coal mines on the face of the hillside. Laws prohibit such things, but they happen. Sometimes these little things should remind us we are not in charge of everything—including time, rain, and the wonderfully imperfect tilt of this planet in its irregular loop about the sun.

Landscapes of the West were shaped by plant/animal interactions, by fire, and by natural processes we are incapable of managing, or "manhandling." The level of herbivory was as varied as the landscapes themselves. In the Great Plains, there is little question that bison, elk, prairie dogs, and other mammals shaped the environment. We still see evidence of these species in wallows, trails, life, and vegetation that defines the region. In subarctic rangelands, caribou, moose, and hares drive systems physically and chemically. Big mammals, in systems devoid of cattle or sheep, with a full complement of native predators, influence plant chemistry, affecting insect preference, providing food for birds. They also have an impact on vegetation, one that we might not accept if the alterations were done by livestock.

In the northern Rockies, bison may not have been the keeper of the grassland, but other animals were equally integral to the web of life. The oldest data—art on rock—remind us that wild sheep, elk, deer, a complement of insects, disease, drought, fire, and erosion were essential to systems we try now to understand and control. Some landscapes evolved without large herds of animals. Some evolved with no large animals at all. Not all of these are arid lands. Some are lush systems where large grazers simply didn't have either presence or influence. There is a wide variation in landscapes, and a wild variation within landscapes. Without doubt, domestic livestock have had an influence on many of these. And some may never recover from the experience. Others may recover slowly, but it will not be ecological limitations that swing the balance. Instead the reality of world economics may have a greater influence on many ecosystems than our current ability to understand land.

Ask children what the word "grazing" means, and their answers will rarely be the same. Most will get around to eating of grass in the end, though their paths may wander from goose to moose, grasshopper to sparrow. Ask an adult, and the answer will almost certainly involve cattle, sheep, or horses—and, depending on political opinion, the word will be shrouded in black or white with few shades of gray to stimulate the eye. Extending the point, some are now engaged in a debate over the simple word "rangeland," certain that it means cow or sheep. To me the word means openness, a sea of vegetation, a vastness found in native lands of the western reaches of this continent. It may seem odd that so many ranchers end up at the edge of oceans—unless you have sailed the pale green sea of sage and grass. There is a magnetic pull to the unseen: to living things beneath the surface. It is a curious wonder, never sated, a childish yearning to learn, a hard lesson that we are not nearly as smart as we think we are.

As we entered the twentieth century, the word "fire" was equally incendiary. In fact, fire was virtually removed from the landscape. In its absence, homes and other refinements that now limit our ability to replace this essential natural process were born. Now we wonder how we might be able to bring fire back—not as a symbol of process lost but as a *real* influence on landscapes. In 1988, much of our largest and oldest national park burned in savage fashion. While we convinced ourselves it was the right thing, the natural way of the world, we knew better. For eighty years we had extinguished fires from cigar, campfire, and lightning with the same zeal, until suddenly we were no match for fire. Patch burns gave way to massive, complex fires that would likely have not occurred with the same intensity or scale.

We've grown up with two notions—one learned from a cartoon bear with a pointed hat, the other saying "fight fire with fire." Now we find natural fire impossible to mimic in most settings. Grass and trees that used to burn regularly have accumulated for decades. Fuels that never existed are now abundant. Habitats once maintained by fire are altered and overrun. And when they burn, they don't burn with "natural" intensity. We know in our hearts that fire in springtime is symbolic more than natural, but it is "safe" and rarely burns up summer cabins. Perhaps it'll do. But lightning and dry grass marry on hot summer days, and human presence is naught but fuel to a real fire.

Full agencies were created to eliminate erosion—to halt this menace in the same manner we taught fire to behave. At the same time, lands created by erosion were jealously guarded as prime farmland, and we built levees and dams to protect these lands from change. Countless national parks and landmarks were created, monuments to erosion: Grand Canyon, Bryce Canyon, Badlands, Colorado National Monument, Zion. There are more, every one a spectacular example of soil erosion running unchecked, even as we frown and allocate funds to control erosion upstream and downstream. We admire on the one hand, we control on the other, even as we know we are but one massive spring thaw, one torrential rain, one earthquake or eruption away from what will be. Despite our efforts, the Mississippi will one day spill itself into the Atchafalaya Basin.

Like fire, erosion, and drought, grazing is a natural process that can be stark and ugly. And, like fire, erosion, and drought, grazing is essential to the maintenance of many natural systems in the West. Bison were an integral influence on western ecosystems, but bison were not the only large herbivore on the landscape. Elk were common from desert to mountain. Wild sheep dominated enough of the landscape that Shoshones were referred to as "sheepeaters" by other tribes. Caribou and rabbits shaped the rangelands of the Arctic regions. And because adults tend to overlook other grazing creatures, we forget the impact of grasshoppers, rodents, birds, and other organisms that have long shaped the West.

Only recently have we begun to understand the cyclical nature of grasshopper outbreaks, though the "devastation" has long been noted. Like many creatures of the arid West, these rise and fall in response, not only to climatic conditions, but their own voracity. Grasshoppers require bare ground on south-facing slopes to flourish. And when their eggs hatch, little grasshoppers create an environment for succeeding generations. Before we fell in love with technology and sprays, grasshoppers may have defined the environment in a manner equal to the customary grazing animals named by adults. Late frost, heavy rain, and lush grass could contend with these insects that grazed the West, but these elements were not common. Grasshoppers were common.

Prairie dogs are now seen as an essential species in some western landscapes. In the absence of other grazing animals, they mow and remow grass, even pile it without eating. Prairie dogs even harvest shrubs, maybe to protect against predators. It has been theorized that the interaction between these small mammals and bison hinges on the ability of each to modify a world of grass that, in their absence, would burn. The interaction between prairie dogs, bison, and other grazing animals suggests that these species depend not only on one another but on extreme levels of herbivory some would decry as "overgrazing." Other species, burrowing owls, dung beetles, and many plants now rare, rely on the same interactions.

Some species now petitioned as "threatened" or "endangered" have a vital need for grazing animals. Species as common as the bluebird, as rare as the black-footed ferret, as unknown as the mountain plover, are tied to grazed lands. The edge between grazed riparian areas and lesser-grazed sagebrush steppe may mean the difference in survival for species like sage grouse and swift fox. Mule deer require a world of brush and deciduous trees—both dependent on a regime of fire and grazing. These are not species endemic to the Great Plains. They evolved and flourished in the Rocky Mountain West. These creatures and plants thrive on chaos and confusion. They revel in the results of fire, herbivory, and open space.

If my blood runs sagebrush green, it manifests itself in passion for species that define my world. A mule deer makes my blood rush. Sage grouse, standing tall and strutting, booming, make me smile. Bluebirds most often return to this ranch on the day of my mother's birth, in a snowstorm, bringing light to a world that sorely needs illumination. There are other species, but they are not the message. Children who see color instead of words are the message.

If we hope to carry a full complement of biodiversity beyond our own meager time, we must begin to manage for chaos and confusion—for the full range of successional states that allow birds to hide in tall grass and forage in open meadows. We have to think not of species, not of isolated populations of rarity, but of systems that allow these species to survive. Large landscapes offer not only large opportunity but a greater margin of error and a chance to learn about connections we simply cannot see. When I think of land, I remember the song of a meadowlark—in the dead of February winter—in a marketplace in Guadalajara, in a cage: a song as common as sunrise. Through metal mesh I stared at a bird that was hatched thousands of miles north, maybe even on the ranch where I work. We think too small. We have to learn to think and understand at levels we have never comprehended. Mathematics may explain that yellow-breasted bird in a Mexican market, but numbers won't give it a place to live and reproduce. A ranch can offer that.

If we choose to allow future generations a chance to make mistakes of their own, and correct some of ours, we must think and work on scales uncomfortable to science. Last fall I followed a peregrine falcon for the better part of a day—a young male resplendent in slate overcoat and auburn cummerbund. He rested in a juniper tree on private land, rose as if lifted until he was airborne high above red cliffs, then rocketed down to follow the creek bottom for two miles in a dive that made my blood rush. Up in spirals, then hugging sagebrush as it followed a mountain a mile west. In the space of minutes, he covered ten sections of ground, some of it private, some federally owned, some state. The night before, he left the place where he was fledged, a canyon wall further west, on Forest Service land. It is through these eyes that we must learn to see.

If we wish to maintain intact systems, we must learn to manage and inquire on a scale that recognizes biological lines rather than lines of property ownership. What is best for the landscape will only be realized when it can be accomplished in a manner that follows the flight of the falcon. We cannot demand fire, or rest, or surgical applications of grazing, if we cannot sustain the link between wetland silt and its parent rock. The scale on which we choose to think is critical. Choose too small, and we could find ourselves managing fleas while forgetting the dog. We cannot begin to reinstate fire on the scale of times past without a base of forage upon which we can build alternatives. The grass-banking concept used at the Malpai and Valle Grande projects is a solid model for incorporation of natural process in an economic world shaken to its core. We may choose to use this approach to achieve rest, to rebuild precious riparian areas and wetlands, to restore fire in a natural sense. But it will require an approach that incorporates economic stability with ecosystem integrity. There are no quick answers.

There are only a handful of natural processes that humans can affect. Fire has been suppressed to such a degree that we now have pine trees growing in areas once rich sources of winter forage, ensiled leaves of deciduous trees and shrubs. Grasslands and sagebrush steppe have become "stable states" of brush that now defy succession either forward or back. Where fire does occur, it is often with a vengeance born of decades of silence. And the result is not fire of the frequency and magnitude once necessary to maintain natural process on the landscape. Fed by years of suppression, fire is a furious storm that takes all in its path. Not long ago, fires in the same place would have left islands of brush and grass untouched, a patchwork of time sewn into a cloth of diversity.

Of the other natural processes we can affect, most are related to grazing animals. Resting the landscape may seem logical to humans in need of same, but rest was never the norm. It was the exception. Animals used the landscape as conditions dictated. In springtime riparian areas and wetlands were flooded with herds of elk, bison, sheep, and other species seeking the essential nourishment that would allow them to give birth, make milk, breed, and find strength to move higher as the sun did the same. Predators might have moved some animals, but they were few. Many predators we now revere made their *real* living, not by chasing the strong across the landscape to prevent overgrazing, but by eating things that died because they were old, or weak, or left behind. Grazing animals did not move in response to predation—they formed herds in response to predation. They moved when they were out of feed or water.

Grazing animals do more than just eat plants. Their movement, individually or as herds, their resting sites, their defecation and urination—all are interactions between animals and plants. Different animals eat different things. The same animals eat different things on different days, driven by seasonality, weather, and plant physiology. Some animals break down plant material. Others gain from the remains. Excited animals churn the soil; contented animals may compact it. In the northern Rockies, freeze and thaw equalize both. In other landscapes, where freeze and thaw are not a regulator, native plants have found other means of survival and perpetuation. Grazing animals, whether bird, cow, or wild sheep, have interacted with plants that anchor sky to soil, rain to river. Even in areas now declared unsuited to livestock (often rightly so), adaptations of plants are cause for question. If there is no history of grazing animals, why are plants so elegantly armored against herbivory?

Other living organisms are crucial, too, but often ignored in debates over ecosystem management. Some insects pollinate plants. Others incorporate dung into soil. Tiny mammals take organic matter beneath the surface and offer up soft, rich dirt in which seeds might grow. Birds seek the fleshy fruit of trees and shrubs, drop the seeds, and perpetuate the stand. Beaver cut down the stand, slow water, store eroded soil, and add woody debris to the stream. There is an intricate web of interaction we sometimes comprehend but dimly. In many cases, ecological systems have advanced to a point where sameness, not diversity, is reality. A forest without fire, grassland without grazing, may look lovely. But it may also be next to sterile for the full range of species that rely on a mosaic of habitat types.

In the past half-century, humans have wittingly and unwittingly removed the natural effects of fire and grazing from much of the western landscape. At one time, removal of fire was supplanted by aggressive harvest of trees for lumber and pulp. The removal of grazing animals has been more subtle, but some of the effects may now be showing scars. To salvage ranges from overuse and overstocking, the number of animals was reduced—a logical and correct analysis of the "tragedy of the commons" in Europe. It didn't take long for people to see that western ranges could not sustain a cornucopian view of natural resource extraction, and in some areas the impact of unregulated grazing by livestock led to irreversible changes on the landscape. So if livestock numbers were to be reduced, it meant that somehow the rangelands of the West would have to be regulated.

By altering the behavior of animals—mainly by stringing wire—and altering people's behavior—by subdividing management from a landscape scale to one of individual allotments cut from the whole—impacts became more focused. Some portions of the landscape began to recover from abuse. The notion that a reduction in numbers was equivalent to good management became a virtual law of natural resource management. Rest-rotation grazing was implemented. While this fix worked in the immediate term, it did not completely resolve problems, and economic margins got tighter. As the land available for grazing, or fire, or rest got smaller, the notes at the banks loomed larger.

Our greatest challenge in ecology, and in conservation, will be our ability to think, study, fail, and learn at scales that don't lend themselves to scientific tidiness. We are living Leopold's fear: his distrust of science. We have reduced natural science to a level where simple process is more important than systems. We keep asking the wrong questions. An answer may be statistically correct but biologically wrong. Science is seen, not as question and wonder, but as certainty spoken in code.

As a rancher, or land manager, I am an insatiable consumer of science. Should I choose to know the heart rate of a three-day-old calf, how to manage three or four acres with two steers, or four, or eight, a library might be available. Should I choose to know what happens to a stretch of water when a precise amount of cow dung is dumped from a bucket, there are answers. If I want to know the DNA patterns of four cutthroat trout that look the same, the information is available. But if I want to know how to manage cow, moose, or goose to give those trout an edge, there is damn little help.

Our understanding of systems ecology isn't limited by answers. It is limited by questions. Our ability to see the future through the eyes of the bird is limited by our demand for satisfaction here and now. If we really care about life common as bluebunch wheatgrass, mysterious as wolverines, rare as black-footed ferret, we can only try to keep the systems they need intact. And intact systems are ranches—an integration of land ownership that has precluded irreversible habitat loss. To paraphrase Wes Jackson, a poorly managed ranch is far superior to land turned by the plow. To paraphrase an ardent environmentalist, a really lousy ranch is a whole lot better than a really good subdivision.

Chapter 9

The Ecology of Ranching

RICHARD L. KNIGHT

Listen to this: "Livestock grazing has profound ecological costs. . . . Studies have confirmed that native ecosystems pay a steep price for the presence of livestock." Now this: "The trend of U.S. public rangelands has been upwards over a number of decades and the land is in the best ecological condition of this [twentieth] century."[1]

Could both statements be right? Or wrong? In 1994, the research arm of America's most august group of scientists reported that inadequate monitoring standards prevented them from determining whether livestock grazing had degraded rangelands in the West. Importantly they concluded: "Many reports depend on the opinion and judgment of both field personnel and authors rather than on current data. The reports cited above [this report] attempted to combine these data into a national-level assessment of rangelands, but the results have been inconclusive."[2]

The future of western ranching and the role of science in shaping public policy regarding ranching are topics still very much under discussion. What gives added urgency to this issue is the rapid conversion of ranch lands to rural housing developments in much of the West. As ranches fold and reappear in ranchettes, 20 miles from town and covering hillsides, people of the West and beyond increasingly wonder what this New West will look like. For with the end of ranching and the beginning of rural sprawl comes the question most central to conservationists: Can we support our region's natural heritage on a landscape, half public and half private, where the private land is fractured, settled, and developed?

Some people might think it is a far stretch to connect livestock grazing with former-city-people-now-living-country, but I see it differently. Ranching and exurban development are part of a single spectrum of land use in the West representing the principal alternative uses of rangeland in much of the mountainous New West. This is so because the protection of open space, wildlife habitat, and the aesthetics of rural areas runs right through agriculture: At one end stands a rancher, at the other a developer. As we transform the West, seemingly overnight, we see the region's private lands reincarnated as ranchettes, ubiquitous estates, ranging from mobile homes to mansions, that are covering hillsides faster than Herefords can exit. We have arrived at a point in western history where conversations about western lands and land health, grazing and ranchettes, are entwined and cannot be separated. They must be dealt with simultaneously when discussing the future of our Next West.[3] The science needs to be accurate, not value driven, and the conversations about cultural and natural histories need to be honest, not mythologized. Science is important in these discussions. But to be useful, the science must be done carefully so that the answers are the best we can get. Ranchers and scientists and environmentalists need to look more sharply and listen more carefully.

CHANGE ON THE RANGE

Can ranching be done badly? Yes. Was it done wrong in the past? Most certainly. There is little doubt among plant and animal ecologists, as well as environmental historians, that the history of livestock grazing west of the 100th meridian has, in many instances and periods, been a story of overstocking: too many animals on rangelands for too long with too little rest. To travel through the American Southwest today is to see untold thousands of acres of former semiarid grasslands that are now in mesquite and creosote, to name just a few of the shrubs that have replaced perennial native grasses. Too many cattle, sheep, goats, burros, and, yes, even pigs, on lands coupled with little or no rest and dry years have altered soil properties and created plant communities that are quite different from those that once existed. Visit America's basins, the Columbia, the Great, and the Great Divide, and you may read the legacy left behind by misguided grazing practices. Vast stretches of bajadas, valleys, and canyons display signs of grazing done wrong, with cheat grass, rabbitbrush, juniper, and piñon serving as billboards of rangeland misuse.

What has been the response to this? Decades-long reform that is ongoing. The Taylor Grazing Act of 1934 authorized the government to create grazing districts, formulate rules and regulations to restore the ranges, set grazing seasons, authorize range improvements, and charge fees for grazing privileges. The chief advocates of the Taylor Grazing Act were ranchers who realized that sustainable use of grass was impossible until access to grass was allocated. The alternative was continued overuse by tramp herders and wildcat ranchers who had no tenure and therefore used land as they could and got everything they were able out of it.[4] The Taylor Grazing Act, and earlier efforts by the U.S. Forest Service, were a beginning best described as compromises controlled by western livestock associations. Only in recent history have the efforts by stockgrowers' associations been subservient to other interests concerned with western public lands.[5] Despite the entrenched and self-defeating attitudes of some western grazing associations, ranchers are increasingly acknowledging that grazing public lands is a privilege, not a right, and that these lands have to be stewarded.

Range science is not the discipline today it was in the early twentieth century. Ranchers and rangeland ecologists have grown up together and learned by trying different things on private and public ranges: putting fewer cows on public lands with shorter periods of grazing and longer times of rest; moving cows out of riparian areas by herding; developing water sources away from streams; placing salt and minerals strategically to distribute cows better; and monitoring changes in plant communities and rangeland health. The national forest adjacent to the valley where I live has seen the retirement of more than sixty permits in recent years. The remaining permits allow fewer cows to graze for fewer days. My friend and neighbor Al Johnson is a permittee on the Elkhorn Creek allotment. In the 1950s the Forest Service allowed 150 mother cows and their calves on this land; today the Forest Service allows but 63 animals. And the cows come off earlier. When you walk the Elkhorn permit today, it is becoming increasingly difficult to see any signs of grazing, let alone too much grazing. Indeed, a sharp-eyed person might instead worry about increased trampling of vegetation by off-highway vehicles and expanding bare spots along Elkhorn Creek from campers and anglers. Wallace Stegner had it about right when he said: "The worst thing that can happen to any piece of land, short of coming under the control of an unscrupulous professional developer, is to be opened to the unmanaged public."[6] Have we arrived at a time in this New West where "the unmanaged public" means hordes of recreationists rather than herds of cows?[7]

A Wyoming rancher recently stood before an audience of nonranchers and apologized for what his parents, grandparents, and great-grand-parents did to the land. He said, approximately, "I am sorry for what my ancestors did to this land. They abused it, they were hard on it during dry years, and they kept too many animals on it for too long during lows in the beef business. I know that they taught me much about the land. They also spoke of what they had to do to make a living during the hard times. I cannot change how my relations lived on the land before I came, but I can work to make the land better for my children. If what you want is an apology from me when I was just a gleam in my daddy's eye, I apologize. Now can we move on?"

There are obvious implications to this story. But for the present, we might think hard about what he asked. In forgiving him the destructive land management practices, albeit unintentional, of his forebears, perhaps we can acknowledge our own limited understanding, even today, of what constitutes good land management practices. Perhaps we can appreciate that our knowledge of good grazing practices is evolving and that we are learning, adaptively, as we try to unravel the interplay of wind, soil, plants, water, and drought that make up the principal plant communities of the arid West: its grass and shrub lands. If we are able to recognize the incontestable fact that we harmed western lands in the past, perhaps we can refocus our energy toward working together to put right what was once torn asunder.

COWS: AIDING OR ABETTING RANGE HEALTH?

Have we learned anything at all about how to use livestock to enhance and maintain the health and vitality of grass and shrub lands? Ranchers and agency officials, who tend to be optimists and measure progress in decades rather than calendar years, believe that rangelands today are more nearly approximating historical conditions.

But what about rest—the hope that rangelands will improve by removing livestock? This belief is nearly a century old, and many environmentalists and natural resource agency personnel still cling to it as their shortcut to rangeland salvation. Rest has seldom proved to be the solution, however, even over decades of time. The emerging consensus from ecologists is, amazingly, premised on the belief that functioning plant and animal communities are the product of periodic disturbance, not pure rest. Although we no longer doubt that riparian areas require flooding to promote the health of our streams and rivers and that forests need fires to ensure forest health, we have been slow to acknowledge that rangelands are only healthy if fire and herbivory occur—within the historic range of natural variability.

In other words: Just as we can overgraze lands, we can overrest them. Rangelands are disturbance-prone ecosystems that evolved with natural regimes of fire and grazing. These regimes themselves have been altered in response to human activity, climate change, species arrivals, extinctions, and other factors. We would do well to learn from the historic patterns of these disturbance regimes and try to reinstate them through active management. How long will we persist in believing in simple fixes for ecosystems such as rangelands? This issue is particularly relevant as our understanding of rangeland function evolves—reflecting a level of maturity that no longer makes them the victim of simple thinking.[8]

One of the most thorough analyses of the ecological effects of rest compared twenty-six long-term grazing exclosures with similar ungrazed areas in Colorado, Wyoming, Montana, and South Dakota.[9] The exclosures varied from seven to sixty years; the average was more than thirty years without livestock (once more proving the benefit of having national parks, refuges, and other protected areas across the western mosaic of landscapes). Scientists found no differences between the grazed and ungrazed areas in a number of respects: species diversity; cover by grasses, forbs, and shrubs; soil texture; and percentage of nitrogen and carbon in the soil. The study furthermore concluded:

(1) Grazing probably has little effect on native species rich-

ness at landscape scales; (2) grazing probably has little effect on the accelerated spread of most exotic plant species at landscape scales; (3) grazing affects local plant species and life-form composition and cover, but spatial variation is considerable; (4) soil characteristics, climate, and disturbances may have a greater effect on plant species diversity than do current levels of grazing; and (5) few plant species show consistent, directional responses to grazing or cessation of grazing.

A word of warning about these results: The West is not one place but many places that grade into each other. In southeastern Arizona, for example, there is a subtle transition between the Chihuahuan and Sonoran deserts. They have different biological histories and different ecological structures and functions—upon which cultural histories and landscape have been superimposed. These regional and local differences in the ecology of the West have implications for grazing by large domestic ungulates. Slope matters—as do elevation and aspect and local rainfall. Taking a longer view, so does the post-Pleistocene environment in the presence of large, social ungulates: bison, elk, pronghorn. As a first approximation, then, some places are more compatible with grazing by large, social, *domestic* ungulates than others.

Grass and shrubs coevolved with herbivores, species that grazed and browsed their new growth. The West has always been defined by large populations of herbivores, although their identity has changed over the centuries. Whether it was mastodons and sloths, or bison and pronghorn, or grasshoppers and rodents, grass and shrubs need the stimulating disturbance brought about by large, blunt-ended incisors clipping their aboveground biomass. Not to mention the dung and urine incorporated by hoof action facilitating more efficient nutrient cycling. Today the mastodons are gone and there are fewer bison and pronghorn. And there are cattle, though not as many as we saw in the nineteenth century. But we have learned that grazing by livestock, when appropriately done, contributes to the disturbance that rangelands require. Perhaps we have come to the point where we measure land health premised on disturbance rather than just rest and realize there is no "balance of nature" but only a "flux of nature." Getting the disturbance patterns right is the challenge.

RAINFALL, GRAZING, AND FIRE

As though to confirm the dangers of incomplete thinking and to empha-size one of the conclusions listed in the exclosure study described earlier ("soil characteristics, climate, and disturbances may have a greater effect on plant species diversity than do current levels of grazing"), recent stud-ies have begun to untangle the complex interactions among precipita-tion, livestock grazing, and fire in arid rangelands. We are, according to an ever increasing body of evidence, in the midst of a global warming trend. Ecologists predict that as North America heats up a couple of degrees over this century, plant communities, from forests to grasslands, will shift to the north and upward in elevation. Less appreciated perhaps is the impact that changes in storm frequency—and the droughts and heavier rains and snows these changes bring—may have on rangelands.

It turns out that some ecosystems respond more strongly than others to pulses in rainfall. And, importantly, these pulses of rainfall, with or without herbivory and fire, may determine the type of plant community that occurs in an area. Although scientists had long suspected that fluc-tuations in rainfall could alter plant productivity, such effects have only recently been confirmed at the ecosystem scale.[10] Because they are adapted to dry conditions, grassland and desert ecosystems show extreme responses to fluctuations in precipitation. In fact, wet years have a much greater effect on plant growth than do dry years. This is largely due to the ability of certain plants to resist drought and sprout new growth when well watered.

How does this relate to arid rangelands and the effects of historic overstocking? Understanding the effects of rain pulses, it now seems, is essential to understanding how herbivory and fire may reverse the effects of past desertification (increases in shrubs and declines in grasses) that have ravaged so much of the American West. Recent studies in New Mexico and Arizona have discovered a threefold increase in woody veg-etation across a gradient of different elevations. These changes, however, have occurred in both grazed and ungrazed (rested) sites. Importantly, these indicators of desertification appear to be the result, not of grazing, but of high levels of winter rain coupled with dry summers—all of which favor shrubs over grasses.

Work by scientists in the Malpai borderlands of Mexico, New Mex-ico, and Arizona using historical photographs dating back to the 1880s indicates an earlier period of desertification but also a second epoch of vegetation change early in the twentieth century. Their findings suggest that these vegetation changes are climatically driven, cyclical in nature, and apparently a pervasive feature of rangelands throughout the Southwest.[11] Examination of tree rings indicates that the area's presently high levels of rainfall have not occurred in nearly two thousand years. The upshot has been an increase in shrubs and trees expanding into grasslands.

Even if these changes, as now suggested, are not brought about just by overstocking, the question remains: How do we reverse the effects of desertification and bring back the grasslands? This is where our understanding of herbivory and fire comes into play, at least for those determined to restore ecosystems. Work now being done by Charles Curtin and his colleagues in the Malpai Borderlands has begun to document substantial increases in grass cover in what had been a degraded Chihuahuan Desert grassland only weeks after spring fires and extensive summer rains.[12] Importantly, this has occurred in an area that had not been grazed for nearly seven years. It took fire, followed by heavy rains, to accelerate the recovery of grass in this desertified rangeland. These results stand in stark contrast to those at a nearby area where drought followed fire. There grasses did not replace shrubs; indeed, in some plots vegetation actually decreased. Again these results suggest that climate, as expressed in pulses of rainfall, often has a greater impact than either grazing or fire.

Borderland studies have also documented the effects of herbivory by cattle and native species such as small mammals. The noted desert ecologist Jim Brown and his associates have found that small mammals may play a critical role in reversing the effects of climatically driven increases in woody vegetation. In long-term study plots near Portal, Arizona, they found that shrubs were more abundant in plots from which they had excluded small mammals. If small mammals can suppress shrub growth, Brown and colleagues hypothesized, livestock grazing might serve a similar purpose. They compared woody vegetation between grazed and adjacent ungrazed areas and, as expected, found that shrubs had increased sixfold in the ungrazed area and only twofold in the grazed site.[13]

What are we to make of these recent findings? They certainly do not fit our tidy stereotype: cows → overgrazing → desertification → rest → recovery.[14] Instead these discoveries reinforce what some might think is obvious: Nature is more complex than we can understand. Ecologists are continuing to learn about the interrelatedness of climate, fire, and grazing—not to mention the importance of time and space scales—in understanding ecosystems. Perhaps we should be humbled by this. After all, it was a similar appreciation of the nonlinear behavior of semiarid southwestern ecosystems that first prompted Aldo Leopold to consider the need for a land ethic.[15] To heal unhealthy lands we should seek counsel not only from ecologists but from those whose connections to the land are long and deep. Maybe research, management, and husbanding of cows along the Malpai borders of the Southwest have something important to teach us about how ecosystems function.

RANCHING, RANCHETTES, AND BIODIVERSITY

Earlier I suggested that ranching and ranchettes belong on the same continuum of western land use. Although some have denied this, their arguments betray a strong reluctance to confront reality. For ranchette development is not only a more lucrative use of ranchland, it is also the fastest-growing use.[16] Reconsider the statistics given in Chapter 2 by Martha Sullins and her colleagues. Nine of the ten fastest-growing states are western and have been so for over a decade. In Colorado, the loss of agricultural land is accelerating sharply. From 1987 to 1997, the average annual rate of ranch and farm land loss was 141,000 acres per year. Between 1992 and 1997, in fact, the rate of conversion nearly doubled this ten-year average, rising to 270,000 acres a year.[17] And most of this formerly agricultural land has gone straight into residential and commercial development.

Some claim that the conversion of ranch lands to rural housing developments occurs only in "pretty places"—Sun Valley, Taos, Bozeman, Aspen—but not in the Real West. In some respects this is true. Much of what has come to be called "the buffalo commons" is not booming, and ranches are not being avidly sought by speculators and developers. But a demographer recently declared that, given enough time, there is no place in the West so remote, so poor, with such bad weather and poor roads, that it can hide from the boomers—those who appreciate the easiest way to make money is to buy ranch land cheap and sell it high for houses and commercial development.[18] And I have seen it. When you visit the outback—the West away from interstates, airports, and blue-ribbon trout streams—you can sniff it in the air: newcomers prowling, looking for a deal on land, or a place to escape from, or to live a life that has animals and land in it. We are deceiving ourselves if we think parts of the West will be spared just by isolation and poverty. What is saved will come about from conscientious hard work involving local communities and good land-use planning.

To appreciate the real cost of converting ranch land to ranchettes, remember what Martha Sullins and her coauthors pointed out in Chapter 2: Growth in population results in a disproportionately greater conversion of land. New Westerners are not living in cities so much as on sprawling ranchettes. Look at her Figure 2.1 and consider her words: "From 1960 to 1990 . . . annual rates of land consumption reached 7.2 percent—far surpassing the 2.8 percent annual population growth rate." To deny that the conversion of ranch land to ranchettes has no connection to the maintenance of our natural heritage assumes that biodiversity is no different on ranches than on ranchettes. Consider Figure 9.1 for a second. This ranch in Colorado near where I live was sold in the 1950s. Over the years you can track the increase in homes and the spread of roads that allow access to these homes. The question relating to biodiversity comes down to this: Is there a house effect? Is the wildlife near these homes the same wildlife that occupied this ground before the homes arrived? If it's not, and if homes like these are becoming ubiquitous across the New West, then it is likely that our region's biodiversity is changing to something quite different from what it was.

E. Odell and I addressed this question by studying the birds and carnivores that occurred near ranchettes and asking whether they differed from those that occurred away from rural homes.[19] We found that the birds that lived near these homes were very similar to the birds you find near homes in cities, but not in rural landscapes. Robins, black-billed magpies, and brown-headed cowbirds, for example, were among the species most abundant near ranchettes. In terms of carnivores we found that domestic dogs and cats were most numerous near homes, whereas

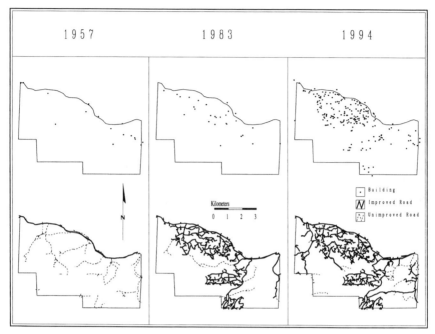

FIGURE 9.1. Changes in numbers of ranchettes and roads after a ranch was sold. This rural housing development is adjacent to the Roosevelt National Forest, Colorado, and is representative of many across the West.

coyotes and foxes were not. Indeed they only became numerous once you were a considerable distance away from homes. Prized songbirds, such as blue-gray gnatcatchers, orange-crowned warblers, and dusky fly-catchers, were nearly absent near homes and their numbers did not increase until you were in undeveloped areas hundreds of yards away from the homes.

Does this matter? Conservation biologists would say yes. The species that thrive near ranchettes—the cowbirds, robins, magpies, cats, and dogs—are exactly the species that result in depressed populations of other songbirds, raptors, and small and medium-sized mammals, many of great conservation concern. This happens because these human-adapted species are superior competitors for nesting sites and food or are skilled predators of other species. Even worse, the cowbird doesn't even build its own nest. It locates nests of other songbirds, dumps its eggs in their nests, and flies away leaving its young to be raised by the host species. Although these other songbirds are willing to be "adoptive parents," the young cowbirds grow faster—resulting in the starvation of the host's young.

We took our studies one step further. Northern Larimer County, Colorado, where I live, is a blend of protected areas, ranches, and ranchettes. Jeremy Maestas, Wendell Gilgert, and I are examining the bird, carnivore, and plant communities across these three different land uses. If ranchettes indeed attract generalist species and repulse species sensitive to elevated human densities—as we found in the study just described—we hypothesized that biodiversity would be more similar in protected areas and ranches than on ranchettes. And that is what we have found.[20] Generalist bird species such as magpies showed increased populations across the ranchette category while species subject to conservation concern, like towhees and grassland sparrows, were common only in protected areas and on private ranches. We found similar trends for native plants compared to exotic and invasive weeds and for dogs and cats compared to native carnivores.

Apparently The Nature Conservancy is doing the right thing when it promotes ranching as a compatible land use in the New West. When ranches support viable populations of species sensitive to urbanization, they serve much the same role as protected areas because they represent sources of sensitive plant and animal species. If ranchettes represent sinks (places where death rates exceed birth rates) for species of conservation value, populations in these areas are kept afloat by the addition of surplus individuals dispersing from nearby protected areas and ranch lands. The value of ranches becomes even more obvious when you compare the productivity of these lands. Public lands, by and large, occur at higher elevations and on the least productive soils. Private ranches, however, generally occur at lower elevations and on much more productive soils.[21] This is why conservation groups concerned with the maintenance of native biodiversity see ranches as critical components in their protection strategies. Perhaps not surprisingly, results similar to ours have been reported from Europe and Latin America.[22]

The upshot of the biological changes associated with the conversion of ranch land to ranchettes is an altered natural heritage. In the years to come, as the West gradually transforms itself from rural ranches with low human densities to increasingly sprawl-riddled landscapes with more people, more dogs and cats, more cars and fences, more night lights perforating the once-black night sky, the rich natural diversity that once characterized the rural West will be altered forever. We will have more generalist species—those that thrive in association with humans—and fewer specialist species—those whose evolutionary histories failed to prepare them for our high population densities and our advanced technology.[23] Rather than lark buntings and bobcats, we will have starlings and striped skunks. Rather than rattlesnakes and warblers, we will have garter snakes and robins. Is that the West we want? It will be the West we get if we do not slow down, get to know the human and natural histories of our region better, and then act to conserve them.

RANCHING: THE VIEW FROM HERE

The West is a region of diverse ecosystems, cultures, and economies. Ranching as a land use, and ranchers as a culture, have been with us for more than four hundred years, dating back to the early Spanish colonists who struggled northward over El Paso del Norte and found a home for their livestock near present-day Espanola, New Mexico. Today, more so than at any time in its history, the ranching culture is under assault. If what I have presented in this essay is true—that ranch lands are compatible with our region's natural heritage and that herbivory is a necessary ecological process in the restoration and maintenance of healthy rangelands—then why are ranchers and livestock grazing so vilified? Why have scores of environmental groups banded together for "a prompt end to public lands grazing"?[24]

Could it be a difference in values? I began this essay by reporting how a conservation biologist wrote a review of livestock grazing that universally condemned it as a land use incompatible with biodiversity. In trying to understand how his review differed from what other scientists have reported, ranging from the National Academy of Sciences to noted plant ecologists, I began to wonder if it was just a difference in values. Might some westerners want the public and private lands free of manure, cows, sheep, and fences because they want them for their own uses—such as mountain biking and river rafting? Do some want ranchers and their livestock off the western ranges because they believe what others have told them—that cows and sheep sandblast land and that cattle barons are arrogant bastards intolerant of any but their own kind? Certainly differing values and distorted mythology can obscure facts; at the end of the day, emotion may trump judgment. Would it make any difference if we found that ranchers are stewards of the land, that cows are being used as a tool in the recovery of arid ecosystems, that open space, biodiversity, and county coffers are enriched more from ranching than from the rapidly eclipsing alternative, ranchettes? Perhaps.

What about the Far Right—the New Federalists who are obsessed with spreading their private-property rights hysteria? When it comes to community-based conservation efforts in the New West that bring ranchers, scientists, and environmentalists together, the Far Right is as intolerant as the Far Left. These powerful players in the West—seldom are any of them actually ranchers—throw out incendiary remarks about wildland protection and government land grabs as easily as their counterparts reflexively oppose grazing. Thank goodness for those in the radical center who strive to build links across landscapes—connections that run through human and natural communities and cross sociopolitical chasms. Perhaps the wing nuts at either end of this human spectrum stir up dissent because they find it easier to simplify, divide, demean, and demonize.

There are those who say the only difference between ranchers and realtors is a rancher is someone who hasn't sold his ranch yet. Do ranchers really care for the land? Or are they developers in sheep's clothing? Certainly there are quite a few who see their ranch as their last cash crop, their private 401(k) account. Yet mounting evidence suggests that ranchers care for the West's geography every bit as much as those of us in the cities and suburbs. In Colorado the state livestock association has formed a land trust. To date some forty-seven conservation easements, totaling over 100,000 acres, have been entrusted to it from ranch families. Indeed, in Colorado the cattlemen's land trust is second only to The Nature Conservancy in acres protected under conservation easements.[25] Considering the economics of western ranching, it is clear that today's ranchers are in it more for the lifestyle than as a way to reap great profits.[26]

I once overheard a conversation between an environmentalist and a rancher. The environmentalist was laying it on pretty thick about the woes of cows and sheep on the western range. In a near fit of exasperation, the rancher blurted out, "You're treating us the same way we treated the Indians! You'd have us off our land and relegated to the worst places the West has to offer." The rancher, perhaps unknowingly, was raising a comparison made by others. Wallace Stegner was one who saw similarities between the First Americans and today's ranchers. In one of his most heartrending and evocative essays, "Crow Country," he observed a "cosmic irony" that connects ranchers and Indians:

> Out on the plains, the tamer country onto which the Crows were forced in the 1880s turns out to contain six billion tons of strippable low-sulfur coal. An equal amount lies under the grass of the Northern Cheyenne reservation next door. . . . The modern Crows can grow rich, if they choose to adopt white styles of exploitation and destroy their traditional way of life and forget their mystical reverence for the earth. Meanwhile the whites who now live in the heart of the old Crow country, as well as many who own or lease range within the present reservation, fight against the strip mines and power plants of the energy boom, and in the face of rising land costs, high money costs, high machinery costs, high labor costs, and uncertain beef prices work their heads off to remain pastoral. . . . There is a true union of interest here, but it is also a union of feeling: ranchers and Indians cherish land, miners and energy companies tear it up and shove it around and leave it dead behind them.[27]

Stegner's point resonates. After all, western ranching has spanned the time scale from the First Americans to the astronauts, avoiding the moving-on mandate of the get-rich-quick industries of mining and logging. Charles Wilkinson, among the most distinguished of our region's scholars, has exhorted us to "extend an honest respect to the ranching community—virtually an indigenous society in the West."[28]

In the heated argument between rancher and environmentalist, I will admit coming to the rancher's defense. Watching him squirm uncomfortably before an audience of urban, suburban, and recently exurban westerners, it dawned on me that perhaps we could settle the New West better than we conquered the Old West if we listened to the cultures that were here before us (and endure still). Might we have made a better place of this region if we had slowed down enough to listen to the First Americans? Did they have something to teach us about the region's wildlife, rivers and streams, grass and forests? In our haste to remake ourselves into the Next West, might we avoid some big mistakes if we showed a little respect to the ranching culture? My gut says yes. Going slow and getting to know your human and natural history is essential to living well on a place.

Perhaps it all comes down to values—of the rancher, the urban environmentalist, the scientist, the government employee. Each of us is in love with the West, its punctuated geography, its rich cultures, its wildlife, its heartrending beauty that stretches sometimes further than our imaginings. Ranchers will have to change; they will have to change more than any of us. They can do that. You only need to look at their history. They have changed in the past, they have adapted, and now they are evolving to fit a land whose demographics, whose economics, and, yes, even whose environment is different from what it was. But we must change as well. Other than those of us with extremely narrow ideologies—the Far Right and Far Left—the rest of us should meet the ranchers halfway or nearly so. The need of the moment is to find common ground on which to work for a common good. Good-faith efforts, and a retreat from demonization and demagoguery, are what we need today.

If it makes what I have written any more palatable, let me admit where my values come from. My wife and I live in a valley along the northern end of the Colorado Front Range. Our neighbors and friends are ranching families and those who live on ranchettes. Over the years we have come together to dance, eat, neighbor, and chart a common ground. Whether working together in our weed cooperative, developing a place-based education program in the valley school, or fencing out overgrazed riparian areas, we are working together to be known more as a place where people cooperate, collaborate, and show communitarian tendencies than as a place where they engage in combat, litigation, and confrontation. We are home, we have our hands in the soil, we have our eyes on the hills that comfort us. In our imperfect lives, we work together to build a community that will sustain us and our children. For we understand that we belong to the land far more than we will ever own it.

NOTES

1. These opposing views are perhaps best captured by reading two articles. One is by T. Fleischner, "Ecological Costs of Livestock Grazing in Western North America," *Conservation Biology* 8 (1994): 629–644; the other by is T. Bock, "Rangelands," in *Natural Resources for the 21st Century*, ed. R. Sampson and D. Hair (Washington, D.C.: Island Press, 1990), pp. 101–120.

2. The report is *Rangeland Health: New Methods to Classify, Inventory, and Monitor Rangelands* (Washington, D.C.: National Academy Press, 1994), which concludes: "All national assessments [of rangeland health] suffer from the lack of current, comprehensive, and statistically representative data obtained in the field. No data collected using the same methods over time or using a sampling design that enables aggregation of the data at the national level are available for assessing both federal and nonfederal rangelands. Many reports depend on the opinion and judgment of both field personnel and authors rather than on current data. The reports cited above attempted to combine these data into a national-level assessment of rangelands, but the results have been inconclusive" (p. 26).

3. The single best account, written in an accessible and enjoyable format, is P. Starrs, *Let the Cowboy Ride: Cattle Ranching in the American West* (Baltimore: Johns Hopkins University Press, 1998). For anyone interested in western land use and its associated human and economic endeavors, this book belongs at the top of your list to study.

4. There is a wealth of literature documenting this point, including E. Wentworth, *America's Sheep Trails* (Ames: Iowa State University Press, 1948), W. Calef, *Private Grazing on Public Lands: Studies of the Local Management of the Taylor Grazing Act* (Chicago: University of Chicago Press, 1960), and F. Carpenter, *Confessions of a Maverick* (Denver: Colorado Historical Society, 1984).

5. One of the most thoughtful writers on western law, policy, and reform is C. Wilkinson. See his *American West: A Narrative Bibliography and a Study in Regionalism* (Niwot: University Press of Colorado, 1989); *The Eagle Bird: Mapping a New West* (New York: Vintage Press, 1993); *Crossing the Next Meridian: Land, Water, and the Future of the West* (Washington, D.C.: Island Press, 1992); and *Fire on the Plateau: Conflict and Endurance in the American Southwest* (Washington, D.C.: Island Press, 1999).

6. W. Stegner and P. Stegner, *American Places* (New York: Crown, 1987), p. 216.

7. Alarmingly, outdoor recreation is the fourth leading cause for the decline of federally threatened and endangered species in the United States on all lands both private and public; see B. Czech et al., "Economic Associations Among Causes of Species Endangerment in the United States," *BioScience* 50 (2000): 593–601. On public lands, outdoor recreation is second only to water development as the chief culprit for their decline; see E. Losos et al., "Taxpayer-Subsidized Resource Extraction Harms Species," *BioScience* 45 (1995): 446–455. For more information on wildlife and recreation see R. Knight, *Wildlife and Recreationists* (Washington, D.C.: Island Press, 1995).

8. Early beliefs were based on the equilibrium theory of degradation caused by overgrazing and by secondary succession to a stable climax following the removal of grazing. Today, however, the emerging consensus by ecologists on how ecosystems, like rangelands, actually function is now a nonequilibrium theory of vegetation dynamics based on natural disturbances such as fire and herbivory. The seminal paper on this idea is by M. Westoby et al., "Opportunistic Management for Rangelands Not at Equilibrium," *Journal of Range Management* 43 (1989): 266–274. For the story of this transition in thinking—from belief in a stable state without disturbance to a dynamic vision that incorporates disturbance processes—see L. Joyce, "The Life Cycle of the Range Condition Concept," *Journal of Range Management* 46 (1993): 132–138.

9. This definitive study was written by T. Stohlgren and colleagues, "How Grazing and Soil Quality Affect Native and Exotic Plant Diversity in Rocky Mountain Grasslands," *Ecological Applications* 9 (1999): 45–64. Importantly Stohlgren et al. varied the size of their sampling plots and found that plot size could give different results. They also concluded that most exclosure studies have used poor sampling techniques, particularly with respect to plant diversity (p. 46).

10. These startling results are presented by A. Knapp and M. Smith, "Variation Among Biomes in Temporal Dynamics of Aboveground Primary Production," *Science* 291 (2001): 481–484.

11. A variety of scientists have contributed to these emerging generalizations. For especially fine work see J. Brown et al., "Reorganization of an Arid Ecosystem in Response to Recent Climate Change," *Proceedings of the National Academy of Science* 94 (1997): 9,729–9,733; C. Curtin, "Analysis of Vegetation Change Through Repeat Photography, Chiricahua Mountains, Ari-

zona," *Southwestern Naturalist* (in review); C. Curtin and J. Brown, "Climate and Herbivory in Structuring the Vegetation of the Malpai Borderlands," in *Changing Plant Life of La Frontera: Observations of Vegetation Change in the United States/Mexico Borderlands*, ed. C. Bahre and G. Webster (Albuquerque: University of New Mexico Press, 2000); R. Neilson, "High-Resolution Climatic Analysis of Southwestern Biogeography," *Science* 232 (1986): 27–34; T. Swetnam and J. Betancourt, "Mesoscale Disturbance and Ecological Response to Decadal Climatic Variability in the American Southwest," *Journal of Climate* 11 (1998): 3,128–3,147; and R. Turner et al. *The Changing Mile* (Tucson: University of Arizona Press, 2001).

12. For an excellent summary of these findings see C. Curtin, "Integration of Science and Community-Based Conservation in the Mexico/U.S. Borderlands," *Conservation Biology* (2001): In press.

13. C. Curtin et al., "On the Role of Small Mammals in Mediating Climatically Driven Vegetation Change," *Ecology Letters* 3 (2000): 309–317. See also Curtin and Brown, "Climate and Herbivory."

14. If the research findings from other scientists I have presented here are indeed correct, they further discredit the polemic work of D. Donahue's *The Western Range Revisited: Removing Livestock from Public Lands to Conserve Native Biodiversity* (Norman: University of Oklahoma Press, 1999). In any case Donahue's ecological reporting has been evaluated and found inadequate by two distinguished grassland ecologists. See F. Knopf, "The Western Range Revisited," *Journal of Wildlife Management* 64 (2000): 1,095–1,097, and S. McNaughton, "Rethinking the Old Range Wars for New Reasons," *Conservation Biology* 14 (2000): 1,558–1,559.

15. Leopold was strongly influenced by his years in Arizona and New Mexico, where he first encountered the complications imposed by aridity, soil erosion, grazing, fire, and the dilemma of past cultures that had not persisted. An understanding of Leopold's path in developing his land ethic can be gleaned by studying his writings. See for example *A Sand County Almanac and Sketches Here and There* (New York: Oxford University Press, 1949). See also B. Callicott, *Companion to A Sand County Almanac: Interpretive and Critical Essays* (Madison: University of Wisconsin Press, 1987); C. Meine, *Aldo Leopold: His Life and Work* (Madison: University of Wisconsin Press, 1988); R. Knight, "Aldo Leopold: Blending Conversations About Public and Private Lands," *Wildlife Society Bulletin* 26 (1998): 725–731.

16. A most amazing statement to this effect appeared in *Conservation Biology*: "Agriculture—both livestock production and farming—rather than being 'compatible with environmental protection' has had a far greater impact on the western landscape than all the subdivisions, malls, highways, and urban centers combined." See G. Wuerthner, "Subdivisions versus Agriculture," *Conservation Biology* 8 (1994): 905–908. Yet suburbanization is second only to invasive species as the leading cause for the decline of federally threatened and endangered species on all land, private and public, in the United States. See Czech et al., "Economic associations."

17. To track the loss of agricultural land in Colorado, visit the Colorado Department of Agriculture's web site [www.ag.state.co.us].

18. Look on p. 57 and scan the other figures in *The Atlas of the New West* (New York: Norton, 1997) to see how little land is indeed safe from developers' eyes. For a more empirical analysis of growth in America and the West consult papers by K. Johnson, including "Renewed Population Growth in Rural America," *Rural Sociology and Development* 7 (1998): 23–45, and "The Identification of Recreational Counties in Nonmetropolitan Areas of the USA," *Population Research and Policy Review* 17 (1998): 37–53 (with C. Beale).

19. E. Odell and R. Knight, "Songbird and Medium-Sized Mammal Communities Associated with Exurban Development in Pitkin County, Colorado," *Conservation Biology* 15 (2001): 1,143–1,150.

20. This study is being conducted by Jeremy Maestas, Wendell Gilgert, and myself. In the second field season we are comparing plant, songbird, and carnivore communities across three different land uses: protected areas, ranches, and ranchette development. Our study sites occur on the same soil and vegetation type and at the same elevation.

21. That private landowners will be the key to achieving an effective conservation reserve system in the United States is abundantly clear from the data in a remarkable article by M. Scott et al., "What Are We Protecting?" *Conservation Biology in Practice* 2 (2001): 18–19.

22. For studies demonstrating the importance of ranch lands in maintaining regional biodiversity see A. Hansen and J. Rotella, "Regional Source-Sink Dynamics and the Vulnerability of Species to Extinction in Nature Reserves," *Conservation Biology* (2002): In press; and G. Daily et al., "Countryside Biogeography: Use of Human-Dominated Habitats by the

Avifauna of Southern Costa Rica," *Ecological Applications* 11 (2001): 1–13. As Americans we are sometimes parochial in our thinking and might benefit from the infusion of ideas from places where humans, agriculture, and biodiversity have struggled for coexistence far longer than in our nascent West. See J. Pykälä, "Mitigating Human Effects on European Biodiversity Through Traditional Animal Husbandry," *Conservation Biology* 14 (2000): 705–712, and listen to his caution: "Traditional livestock grazing and mowing are widely used to maintain high biodiversity or rare species. Their similarities to natural processes are rarely recognized, however, so the importance of traditional animal husbandry as a conservation tool is underrated. . . .Because of the similarities between the effects of natural disturbances and animal husbandry, traditionally managed habitats can harbor many features of pristine habitats" (p. 105).

23. For field studies conducted in the West that confirm this generalization see W. Vogel, "Response of Deer to Density and Distribution of Housing in Montana," *Wildlife Society Bulletin* 17 (1989): 406–414; R. Blair, "Land Use and Avian Species Diversity Along an Urban Gradient," *Ecological Applications* 6 (1996): 506–519; S. Torres et al., "Mountain Lion and Human Activity in California: Testing Speculations," *Wildlife Society Bulletin* 24 (1996): 451–460; R. Harrison, "A Comparison of Gray Fox Ecology Between Residential and Undeveloped Rural Landscapes," *Journal of Wildlife Management* 61 (1997): 112–122; J. Boren et al., "Land Use Change Effects on Breeding Bird Community Composition," *Journal of Range Management* 52 (1999): 420–430; and K. Crooks and M. Soulé, "Mesopredator Release and Avifaunal Extinctions in a Fragmented System," *Nature* 400 (1999): 563–566.

24. Called the RangeNet 2000 Symposium, about a hundred lawyers, scientists, and activists gathered in Reno, Nevada, in November 2000 to develop an action plan to end all public-land livestock grazing west of the Rocky Mountains.

25. For a review of ranchers who care about keeping ranches as part of a working landscape see stories in the Summer 2000 issue of *Orion Afield*. Included is a story on the Colorado Cattlemen's Agricultural Land Trust.

26. By far the most convincing evidence of this statement emerges after reading P. Starrs, *Let the Cowboy Ride*.

27. Stegner and Stegner, *American Places*, pp. 111 and 115–116.

28. Wilkinson, *The Eagle Bird*, p. 150. Further scholarly evidence that ranching is a distinct culture worthy of our consideration can be found in the archives and activities of the Western Folklife Center [www.westernfolklife.org].

Chapter 10

Cows and Creeks:
Can They Get Along?

STEVE LEONARD AND WAYNE ELMORE

Will the livestock industry survive as we now know it in the New West? Ranching can indeed survive, but not as we know it today. The western livestock industry's survival depends on immediate, broad-scale demonstration of riparian restoration with the presence of livestock (primarily cattle and sheep)—and simultaneous education of a doubting public. We believe that, in most cases, livestock grazing is compatible with the restoration of watersheds and streamside areas. The restoration and maintenance of watersheds is imperative if we are going to sustain grazing while at the same time preserve ecological and aesthetic values. Restoration of riparian areas is a cornerstone to the restoration of an entire watershed. No other landscape feature connects ecosystems or reflects watershed conditions as effectively as streams and their associated riparian zones. Healthy riparian areas connect plant and animal communities and are critical for diversity, recovery after floods, long-term stability, and resource production.

WHAT DO YOU MEAN "RESTORATION"?

There are many definitions of watershed restoration. To some it implies a return to conditions that existed before the presence of Europeans. To others it is an engineering approach to minimize damage to life and property caused by erosion and floods. Our perception of restoration is based on the physical process of how streams and rivers function, not the presence or absence of humans and our associated infrastructure. The physical process is simply the way that water runs naturally over the land. As it moves, it connects a network of ecological processes. If we can approximate the natural retention of "water on the landscape" and the associated flow patterns, we should be able to maintain the natural stream conditions. Most of the undesirable impacts associated with water arise from landscapes shedding it faster than they originally evolved to hold and store it—thus creating accelerated erosion and higher floods. This would seem to make them good water *sheds*. But keeping water on the land longer should be a primary objective, so we prefer the term "water catchment" instead of "watershed." Perhaps we should be discussing "catchment recovery" rather than "watershed restoration."

Many factors, both natural and human, alter a landscape's ability to retain and release water from natural catchments. A certain amount of natural disturbance, followed by recovery, is necessary to achieve a dynamic equilibrium of ecological processes. Some of our human alterations adjacent to rivers and streams—such as highways, shopping malls, and houses—can permanently alter the amount of water that stays on the land. Dispersed uses such as recreation, timber harvest, and livestock grazing also have a direct impact on the landscape but can be managed in a manner compatible with stream health.

STREAM RECOVERY WITH GRAZING?

Improper grazing has been associated with several impacts on the retention and flow of water across a landscape. Reducing vegetation can increase the impact of raindrops, thereby accelerating erosion. Disturbing the surface can increase erosion and lead to compaction, which reduces the penetration of water. Changes in the types of plants influence how water stays on the land. As runoff and erosion increase, the increased energy often changes flow patterns, increasing erosion even more. These effects are often observed in riparian areas and streams in the form of excessive buildup of sediment. The absence of the right types of vegetation—such as deep-rooted sedges, rushes, and willows—to buffer and slow flood events has led to downcutting and widening of stream channels, resulting in water leaving the land faster than it should.

As the water table is lowered, plants that hold streambanks together are lost because the land is no longer irrigated naturally. Loss of soil can permanently alter a site. And if downcutting occurs, adjacent areas can also be lost.

Early attempts in the 1960s and 1970s to demonstrate the effects of grazing on streams resulted in the construction of exclosures—fenced areas within grass and shrub land that eliminate grazing in small plots that can then be compared with adjacent sites. Although livestock exclusion on uplands has resulted in mixed responses, exclusion of riparian areas has generally resulted in dramatic comparisons of no grazing versus inappropriate grazing. In the last two decades, positive recovery comparable to cattle exclusion has been demonstrated on thousands of miles of riparian areas and millions of acres of upland rangeland throughout the western United States—with the presence of grazing. Once the problem is recognized, grazing strategies can often be devised that restore the catchment functions of the landscape with little or no reduction in total number of animals. Many ranchers have reported increased economic income at the same time.

Figures 10.1 and 10.2 show photographs of Bear Creek taken from the same location. In 1977, the trees in the foreground (Figure 10.1) were removed in a range improvement experiment. Prior to 1977 the Bear Creek area was a single pasture grazed with only twenty-four animals through the summer. Continual grazing depleted streamside vegetation and deepened the channel, causing it to be unstable and actively eroding. Summer streamflow was often intermittent and of low quality. In 1977, however, the Bureau of Land Management decided to rest the pasture in hopes of restoring the riparian area. Cows were put back on the area for one week in September 1979 and in 1980. In 1983, juniper trees were removed from the uplands to improve range condition and watershed health. In 1985, a grazing treatment was designed to use the area from the time of spring runoff (mid-February) until 15 April in a three-pasture rotation system. By allowing adequate time for the vegetation to recover after grazing, the amount of forage had increased fivefold by 1988 and the area continues to improve (Figure 10.2). Furthermore, the rancher has reportedly cut his hay bill by $15,000 a year. The resulting improvement in water quality and quantity has also allowed the reestablishment of rainbow trout. Though this early-season riparian

FIGURE 10.1. Bear Creek: BLM land in central Oregon in 1977.
(Photograph by Wayne Elmore)

grazing treatment works well on this site's sandy loam soils, it might not be so successful on finer-textured soils with high moisture content or areas of considerable snow accumulation.

Other studies have shown results similar to Bear Creek using a variety of different grazing strategies. Each success is unique because each is a different landscape with different grazing animals and, most important, different people. Although there are no simple formulas for riparian recovery, there are some common elements. Each success required a change in one or more of the following: timing (when livestock begin grazing), intensity (the amount of vegetation removed), frequency (how often livestock are allowed access), or duration (how long livestock are allowed to graze). Some changes are minor—shifting a pasture season of use forward or backward, for example, to accommodate a longer period of growth for a certain plant species. Other grazing strategies called for

FIGURE 10.2. Bear Creek: BLM land in central Oregon in 1996.
(Photograph by Wayne Elmore)

substantial modification of the entire ranch operation including investment in facilities or changes in livestock breeds or handling practices. Most operations required some form of adaptive management: the ability to change in order to meet objectives. When uncertainty involves your livelihood, it's more scary than exciting. But we can't improve conditions by continuing the same practices that degraded the stream in the first place.

One common thread of all successful strategies is the rancher's commitment to implement changes despite the uncertainty. A commitment from other interest groups or government agencies to support these changes is important, too, especially on public lands. Despite our so-called science base for resource management and new technologies, success still seems to depend on the hard work and determination of the people who move the animals. But it's also essential to have achievable objectives and a monitoring program that allows you to determine whether the changes are working. With few exceptions, then, we believe that the recovery of streams and rivers can be attained even with livestock grazing.

WHY IS RECOVERY WITH GRAZING SO RARE?

We believe that catchment recovery is frustrated by social factors even though many people profess to want the same results. Regardless of background, most people want clean water as well as ecological and economic sustainability. Most battles are being fought over past and future uses, however, with little thought to catchment sustainability. Although ecological or economic conditions are often touted as the rationale for one stance or another, arguments tend to degenerate into quarrels over types of use or rights of use.

On one side of the grazing issue are ranchers who in many cases have been on the land for generations. Few of them wish to jeopardize their livelihood by harming the land. In fact, most ranchers pride themselves on their conservation practices. But changes in resources tend to be imperceptibly slow. It's sort of like watching your kids grow up. They don't change much day to day, but suddenly they've grown up and are gone. Moreover, many of our watersheds were already degraded when these ranchers first saw them. Although some of them have tried to reverse a past legacy of exploitation, far too many deny that a problem exists.

On the other side are the environmentalists. Many are well informed about the impact of improper grazing and look upon their battle with the livestock industry as a way to restore ecological conditions for the enjoyment of generations to come. Some recognize that people are part of the environment and too, that improving ecological conditions will be a continuous process. Many also believe that if grazing caused the problem, then removing domestic livestock or drastically reducing their numbers should lead to recovery.

Unfortunately, some ranchers and environmental groups take sides simply for personal gain or gratification. Many potentially viable cattle operations have been subdivided so many times that they have become hobby ranches whose owners haven't the time, knowledge, or desire to graze livestock in a manner conducive to catchment recovery. Some so-called environmentalists view livestock as an impediment to their own recreational uses of the land but object vehemently when people suggest that these uses might also be degrading streams and rivers. Both sides feel obligated to seek the support of organizations that provide information and legal support for their views. The ongoing controversies over grazing or recreation in riparian areas has spawned the formation of even more of these organizations. Fear of the opposing side builds membership, so there is no incentive for these organizations to promote solutions. In this atmosphere, resolvable issues have become quagmires of bigotry and intolerance ultimately to be relegated to the courts.

The Bureau of Land Management and U.S. Forest Service are mandated to manage grazing in a sustainable manner in conjunction with other uses. Although it might appear that these agencies are merely caught in the middle of extremist views on both sides of the grazing issue, they have in fact exacerbated the conflict. In most cases where catchment recovery is still frustrated by improper grazing practices, the agencies continue to renew permits without modification. Essentially they have condoned the perpetuation of marginal grazing practices despite laws to the contrary. Many reasons are given for the continuation of these practices: personnel, budget, lack of adequate information, political influence, priorities. None of these reasons are valid. These agencies already have the expertise to make sound natural resource decisions. Money often seems to be wrapped in red tape and is spent inefficiently. Agencies continue to focus money and time on the worst areas— those with the least chance of recovery—just because they look bad. The solutions proposed are often the most contentious to both sides, and resolution must again be decided by the courts.

One might think the legal system would allow for the efficient resolution of resource problems. We doubt it. Certainly this approach doesn't work for recovery in any reasonable time frame at the watershed or catchment scale. The best way to ensure that nothing changes is for an issue to get tied up in a long legal proceeding and subsequent appeals process. Once in court, nothing changes until a final decision is rendered—often after several years. Most judges and lawyers are not knowledgeable about ecological issues and thus make poor resource managers. They can only assess the facts as presented by the letter of the law, not decide on the best resource option. Indeed many cases are finally decided on legal procedure that bears little relation to what will enhance stream restoration.

Arguments over livestock numbers still prevail in the courts because the term "overgrazing" almost always implies "too many." Reducing the number of livestock must seem an appropriate "punitive action" if resource problems can be traced to grazing. But in most cases neither the problem nor the solution is simply a matter of numbers of livestock. We have observed many problems that could have been corrected with adjustments in timing, duration, frequency, or distribution of grazing, rather than with reductions, but these actions are more complex than cutting the number of animals. Yet when only the numbers are cut, the resource problem usually remains unresolved and the conflict is perpetuated. Most legal decisions are inflexible too, and future options may again need to go through a burdensome and expensive court review just to be considered.

In the rare instances where stream health is improved on lands involved in litigation, the gains are quite meager in light of the social, economic, and even off-site ecological costs. Whichever side wins a court decision, the result is often bitter antagonism between opposing groups. Intolerance of others' opinions escalates, and the political and legal battles continue at great economic and social cost. And the average cost of litigation in these matters is considerable. Surely more could be accomplished if the same amount of time and money were dedicated to practical and feasible grazing alternatives. In management by litigation, we see no ecological opportunity to convert watersheds to "water catchments," at least in areas of mixed public and private ownership. Streams don't just run through properties, they connect properties. To restore degraded riparian areas, we have to work on the entire watershed.

When environmental groups win in court, the rancher's economic losses are often followed by his attempts to maintain short-term solvency on private lands—thus shifting the loss in one part of the catchment to a different area. Ultimately the rancher's failure will replace a manageable grazing solution with urbanization and subdivision. If the rancher wins, there is no longer an incentive to make improvements—in fact the court battle frequently reduces his ability to make necessary investments. What is legally right is not necessarily ecologically right.

COOPERATION WORKS

We are not trying to search out the guilty, a favorite American pastime, but merely to point out where we are. The question now is: Where do we go from here? If we continue to do the same things while expecting a different result, progress will be a long time coming. But what if:

- People could agree on some basic objectives—independent of their emotions—tied to their values and preferences for land use?

- Enough people were willing to work together—through education and the formation of partnerships—that solutions could be developed collaboratively and implemented at the local level by those most affected by the results?

- Priority for funding and technical assistance was given to those who were genuinely interested in implementing change?

- Effort could be refocused toward effective management strategies rather than scattered special-interest projects?

Sound far-fetched? Possibly. But we have seen enough successful efforts incorporating these principles to convince us that it not only could happen, but it must happen to prevent eventual gridlock. True progress will require the formation of partnerships, not the continuation of conflict.

Two well-known groups, in particular, seem to be trying a different approach to grazing and environmental issues. Both the Quivera Coalition and the Malpai Borderlands Group have pulled ranchers, environmentalists, and land management agencies together to work toward common-sense solutions to sustaining the land and the people on it. Amidst cries of compromise by outside extremists, these two groups seek no compromise of their basic beliefs, only communication and new ideas that may lead to mutual benefits. There must be a lot of give and take at each step, but embarking on the journey has led them much closer to their destination than those who cannot even agree on the direction.

Many less publicized watershed coalitions and watershed councils are attempting to work together on restoration with varying degrees of success. The less successful are still trying to identify the values they want to enhance, then trying to make the catchment systems produce these values. Consequently much time is spent fighting over the differences. Although conflict over values often precludes the development of a common vision and perpetuates mistrust, conflict itself is neither bad nor unhealthy. Properly managed, it can be the stimulus for learning and coming together that enables groups to solve problems.

Development of a common vocabulary and an assessment procedure that focuses on the physical processes of riparian areas allows people with different backgrounds to agree on restoration while sidestepping disagreements over different values. The National Riparian Service Team and an expanding Riparian Coordination Network have used the interagency Proper Functioning Condition Assessment procedure to accomplish these ends. When people can agree on what is limiting stream restoration, it is easier to talk about objectives and strategies to restore them. Ranchers and environmentalists alike agree that sustainable uses and ecological values depend on restoring the physical function of the catchment. Commitment to this common goal can transform an unlikely partnership into a successful collaborative effort. And successful partnerships lead to the following:

• Increased trust among partners due to shared decisions

• Pride in ownership

• Solutions that are likely to last

• Preservation of the integrity of the participants' lifestyles

Moreover, successful partnerships between ranchers, environmental groups, and others at the local level can produce a critical mass of people who establish reasonable priorities, influence the focus of government agencies, and insulate themselves from frivolous litigation.

Einstein said: "We cannot solve the problems of today with the same thinking that created them." Gridlock, management by litigation, failed land management practices—all must be changed. Our legacy for future generations need not be ruined by a legion of missed opportunities. It can be passed down as a heritage of cooperation, conviction, and conservation.

Chapter 11

Re-Creating the West . . . One Decision at a Time

A LLAN S AVORY

Sit back and imagine healthy rangelands, rich in biological diversity, healthy wildlife populations, and clear-running streams alive with fish. Soils would be covered with living plants and between them a layer of mulch and litter acting as a sponge for precipitation. Water that formerly flowed off in flood would now percolate down to replenish aquifers and nourish perennial rivers. Droughts would be rare, even in low-rainfall years. Vast amounts of carbon would be sequestered within the soil, enabling us to better combat global climate change. Unimaginable quantities of lean, healthy meat from wildlife and livestock, as well as other products, could be produced to help feed a hungry world. Rural families, communities, and towns would be prosperous. If our western rangelands were in such condition, would residential and commercial development even be a problem? (What rancher would consider selling out?) Would there be much conflict over public lands?

That our western rangelands were once in such condition is certain. What, then, has brought about the change we see today where so much of the life in our soils has been lost, ranch families survive on razor-thin profit margins in the best of times, and flooding has become the leading weather-related cause of death? I hope to show you that the underlying cause of this deterioration is in the way humans make decisions—something that hasn't changed fundamentally since we gained the ability to reason, make tools, and light fires. And I also hope to convince you that if we change the way we make decisions—whether we're ranchers, farmers, developers, academics, extension agents, politicians, or urban dwellers—we can begin to restore much of what we have lost in the West beyond the 100th meridian.

If we indeed make decisions with our own self-interest in mind, how have we gone so wrong? To understand, we need to go back to the rangelands of prehistoric times, well before the development of modern humans. Although there are a great many problems associated with croplands, forests, and urban centers in the American West, I concentrate here on the rangelands for two reasons. First, the rangelands make up the bulk of the land area in the West and thus serve as the largest water catchment area, ultimately controlling the fate of our water supplies. Second, when we do not understand the ecological processes at work in rangeland environments—and how they deteriorate in the absence of large herbivores—we use fire excessively to try to maintain grassland, a practice that can exacerbate desertification and atmospheric pollution.

A QUESTION OF COEVOLUTION

Soils, plants, and animals in the rangelands of America coevolved over millions of years. Over these vast aeons of time, massive fluctuations in life forms took place—periodic extinctions were often followed by periods of even greater speciation. Then, following the arrival of skilled human hunters some twenty thousand years ago, approximately three-quarters of the large-mammal genera in North America became extinct, most likely at the hands of these hunters. The loss of these animals, most of which were herbivores, and the increased incidence of fire, dramatically altered the American landscape in a geologically brief time span.

What was so different about *human* hunters as opposed to the myriad predators that had hunted the same large herbivores for aeons? Most of the large herbivores evolved in seasonal-rainfall environments, which characterize the American West, and they did so in association with pack-hunting predators. A standard defense of most herbivores against pack hunters is to drop all their young over a compressed time period—thus overwhelming their predators by sheer numbers. But their primary defense is to form into tightly bunched herds. Predators, fearing the large massed herd, had for millions of years been forced to isolate an animal to kill it, following which the whole pack fed on the one animal. Predators rarely killed their prey en masse because they would then starve en masse. When prey decreased, so did predators.

When humans became large-animal *hunters*, as opposed to mere scavengers, things were suddenly different. The large herbivores were now faced with something entirely new: an omnivorous primate that had acquired the use of fire, weapons, language, and organizational skills and learned it could hunt large prey in packs. This new pack hunter was able to drive whole herds over cliffs or into boggy areas, killing vast numbers, but feeding on few. The waste of meat was often enormous. Because the human pack hunter was an omnivore, human numbers were not limited by the numbers of their prey. When prey decreased, they could supplement their diet with nonanimal foods.

The impressive herds of bison, elk, pronghorn, and deer recorded by early European explorers were but a remnant of past diversity and numbers. Western rangelands had been in decline since the arrival of those first human hunters. And the rangelands have continued to decline ever since, going into an even steeper dive with the destruction of the last of the large wild herds (except for those in Alaska). The replacement of bison herds with scattered livestock—followed by the introduction of regulations based on the premise that large numbers of livestock cause destruction but fire does not—has brought us to where we are today. But why would the removal of vast herbivore numbers, or the livestock that remain, and the increased use of fire cause such a major disruption? To understand, we need to compare the vegetation life cycle—birth, growth, death, and decay—in two types of environment.

BRITTLE AND NONBRITTLE ENVIRONMENTS

All rangelands experience seasonal rainfall. Total rainfall can be high or low, but it is limited to a relatively brief period, as is the humidity. In these "brittle" environments the bulk of the aboveground vegetation (leaves, stems) dies over a period of a few months every year when the growing season ends. In the perennially humid ("nonbrittle") environments of the world, by contrast, where total rainfall can also be high or low but occurs throughout the year, aboveground vegetation dies throughout the year. A look at the types of herbivore that developed in both environments reveals a marked difference. In the brittle, seasonal-rainfall environments, although insect herbivores are plentiful, the main herbivores—those consuming the bulk of the vegetation—are large mammals. In perennially humid, or nonbrittle, environments, the main herbivores are insects.

In both types of environment, the main agents of decay, itself a living process, are small organisms of many forms. In nonbrittle environments, massive populations of microorganisms quickly decay whatever plant material dies during the year. Resting such environments, or "leaving them to nature," even when severely damaged, helps restore them because the life cycle (birth, growth, death, decay) remains unimpeded. Where ancient civilizations in nonbrittle environments failed, their ruins were quickly covered with vegetation. In *brittle* environments, where most aboveground vegetation dies at the end of the growing season, the insect and microorganism populations responsible for biological decay die down as well. The dead vegetation, unable to decay, begins to oxidize, a much slower breakdown process. It is here that the large herbivore's role becomes so apparent. Large herbivores cannot digest coarse plant material on their own. But over the aeons they developed a symbiotic relationship with microorganisms that thrive in the moist environment of their digestive tracts and complete the breakdown. It was—and still is—essential to have millions of large herbivores grazing, digesting/ruminating, and contributing to the cycling of vegetation by enabling biological decay to occur. Without these animals, biological decay shifts to the much slower breakdown process of oxidation, which eventually kills most perennial grass plants, those great soil stabilizers of the rangelands. Where ancient civilizations were abandoned in these environments, their ruins are today covered in desert sands.

Bunched perennial grasses have adapted to severe-grazing animals, as most large herbivores are, by moving their growth points, or buds, close to the ground, below the grazing height of the animal. These plants weaken and eventually die if not grazed because sunlight cannot filter through the gray, oxidizing leaves to reach these growth points. As the grass plants die, tap-rooted herbaceous or woody species often establish in their place. New grass plants have difficulty establishing if there are no herbivores to chip soil surfaces sealed by rainfall, trample in seeds, and compact soil around them.

Some brittle-environment grasses adapted to the absence of herbi-vores can survive for prolonged periods, although not necessarily in a healthy state. These grasses are sparse in form, such as the *Aristida* species, or have growing points above ground level, such as tobosa. Because of their structure, these grasses are not easily killed by the accu-mulation of oxidizing material that occurs when biological decay is impeded. Reproduction tends to be asexual—by runners or stolons—or by seed forms adapted to drilling into bare, crusted soil.

LEAVING IT TO NATURE

The destruction caused by resting rangelands either totally (no large her-bivores) or partially (too few large herbivores) is evident in the many experimental plots established by government agencies throughout the western states over fifty years ago to demonstrate the beneficial effects of livestock removal. Though these plots did improve initially, they have since deteriorated substantially. In most of them now, anywhere up to 90 percent or more of the soil is bare but for remnant algae/lichen com-munities that have encrusted the soil surface. In some plots, 100 percent of the perennial grass plants have died out. In other plots a sparse pop-ulation of "rest-tolerant" perennial grasses exists, reproducing asexually through stolons or runners. On a larger scale, several long-rested areas exhibit the same degree of deterioration as the experimental plots: Chaco Canyon National Park in New Mexico, Canyonlands' Virginia Park and Natural Bridges National Monument in Utah, and the Rio Grande Nature Preserve alongside my home in Albuquerque.

Perhaps the most striking revelation provided by these experimental plots is that, no matter what their annual precipitation, the deterioration is essentially the same both inside and outside the fences. In other words: Partial rest (too few herbivores) has about the same effect, but not quite so damaging, as total rest in the long run. Initially the experi-mental plots showed improvement simply because formerly overgrazed plants were free to grow unimpeded. The contrast with the land outside their fences would have been dramatic. Given a few years, however, the effects of rest would have become apparent. In the absence of large her-bivores, plant material would not be breaking down rapidly through biological decay, but very slowly through oxidation, and new grass plants would not be establishing. When this happens elsewhere, we prescribe a burn to remove the standing dead plant material and thus invigorate the grasses. But we also expose the soil—making it more prone to erosion, less able to absorb and retain moisture, and less hospitable to the establishment of new seedlings.

WHAT ABOUT OVERGRAZING?

If our commonly held belief is correct—that overgrazing is due to overstocking—then surely western rangelands must have been terribly overgrazed before humans saved them by eliminating most of the large animals. Not quite. Remember what I was saying about the primary defense that herding herbivores use to protect themselves from predators—bunching tightly into large herds? Well this behavior also discourages overgrazing. A plant can only be overgrazed if exposed to severe grazing for too long or reexposed to the animals before it has recovered. Animals in high concentration spread dung and urine all over their food, and no animals normally will feed on their own feces. Fouling of their feed would have obliged herds to keep moving onto fresh feed—unlikely to return until the fouling effect of the dung and urine had weathered and worn off.

Research conducted by Andre Voisin in the 1950s confirmed that the overgrazing of each individual plant was a function of time, not animal numbers.[1] Damage from trampling is also a function of time. If two cows spend 365 days on a piece of land, for example, it would result in 730 cow-days of grazing and trampling (2×365). And if 2,000 cows spend one day on the same land, it would result in 2,000 cow-days of grazing and trampling ($1 \times 2,000$)—nearly three times the amount. The effects on the land are quite different. While two cows grazing over a year cause damage—because they repeatedly bite the same plants (and thus overgraze them) and trample the same ground (and thus pulverize the soil surface while excessively compacting it below)—2,000 cows for a day do the opposite. They are not there long enough to overgraze plants or pulverize soil. But they've done the grass plants a favor by removing leaves that will become a liability if they don't decay rapidly; they've broken the soil surface so that air and moisture can penetrate; and they've compacted the soil enough to provide good seed-to-soil contact so that new plants can establish.

Now we can see why vast herds of millions or more large herbivores did not overgraze or overtrample the western rangelands as so few animals might do today. Tragically, for centuries, humans missed the vital difference between numbers of animals versus their time on and off the land—and failed to note that this was affected by the way the animals behaved in the presence of pack-hunting predators. And we missed, and generally continue to resist, the idea that only large herbivores can reverse desertification in the brittle environments of the world. It should come as no surprise that as recently as 1994 an international conference was convened in Tucson, Arizona, by a large group of scientists representing diverse institutions to answer the question "Desertification in the Developed Countries: Why Can't We Control It?"

TWO NEW TOOLS FOR OUR TOOLBOX

If you accept these ideas about the evolution of our rangelands and the essential role played by large herbivores, then you probably agree that we need to add some new tools to our land and wildlife management toolbox. Over the last million years or so humans have limited their tools to three: *technology* in some form (from the first primitive hand tools to modern genetic engineering), *fire*, and in recent centuries *rest*. To this day no other tool has been acceptable in mainstream thinking. In developing the concept of "holistic management" we have added two tools: *grazing*, using any animal that can digest (with the help of the microorganisms it hosts) and convert plant material into dung and urine, and *animal impact*, the trampling, chipping, dunging, digging, rubbing, and so on provided by concentrated herbivores.[2]

A growing number of people are beginning to acknowledge the need for these two tools and are using livestock to help restore damaged rangelands and, in some instances, even abandoned mine dumps. And this is a heartening development because neither fire nor any human technology can promote biological decay or carbon cycling (fire spews carbon directly into the atmosphere) and thus sustain healthy rangelands. If desertification can only be reversed with the help of large herbivores, in most situations we must now rely on livestock to do what is needed.

REST, FIRE, AND DESERTIFICATION

Desertification is initiated by soil exposure. Exposed soil—even if all the rainfall it receives soaks in—leads to droughts in low-rainfall years, as most of the water is lost to surface evaporation. Research by the Desert Research Foundation in Namibia shows that up to 83 percent of the water that soaks into exposed soil surfaces is subsequently lost to surface evaporation.[3] In high-rainfall years, exposed soil leads to high runoff and thus flooding.

The soil exposure that really matters is that which occurs between plants when litter or mulch is missing. This condition is vastly more common than large areas of ground devoid of all plant life, but not so obvious. You won't spot it while driving by or looking across a piece of land. It is, however, readily seen if you walk on any piece of range and look down. Only two things cause soil exposure between the plants over millions of acres of rangeland: rest (too few or no large herbivores present) and fire. In the absence of herbivores, the dead vegetation, remember, remains standing and oxidizing rather than being eaten or trampled to the ground where it provides a covering of litter that decays rapidly. Fire removes both standing material and litter. When rest and fire are combined, as they often are, soil exposure is magnified, as these two tools *promote* soil exposure. Soils dry out even more rapidly, and the reduction in plant roots and organic matter is substantial. As a result, even less carbon is sequestered in the soil.

Fire, by itself, has additional detrimental effects. We've long known that carbon in gaseous form is released through biomass burning. But recently researchers at Germany's Max Planck Institute have discovered that rangeland fires in the United States and Africa are also releasing methyl bromide—which has forty times the ozone-destroying power of CFCs.[4] Many people justify the use of fire today by likening human-set fires to the lightning fires that have been a natural feature of rangeland environments for a very long time. This false parallel ignores the fact that human-set fires are now more frequent and, moreover, that even lightning fires have become more frequent due to human management. In the brittle-environment rangelands of the past where truly large herds of herbivores roamed, there would have been less old material and little oxidizing matter on the plants at any time—but particularly at the end of the dormant season when most lightning occurs. Now, due to the paucity of large herbivores, both wild and domestic, there is not only more old material but also more of it that is oxidizing and thus more combustible.

I am not saying that all fire is bad. Fire is a useful management tool that has long played a role in maintaining diversity through the disturbance it provides. But burned areas that are then rested (from large-animal impact) generally suffer an increase in bare soil. This practice, which is widespread, is neither wise nor natural. Fire, like all tools, should only be used when it passes the tests, described later in this chapter, to ensure it is socially, environmentally, and economically the right tool to use at that point in time. Much of today's prescribed burning would not pass these tests since it only accomplishes what animals, properly handled, would do routinely—without soil exposure or pollution. Until the role of rest and fire in desertification is understood and accepted it will simply not be possible to reverse the desertification process. The challenge we face in restoring our rangelands, however, goes beyond even this.

When I first realized that large-animal impact was essential to reversing desertification, I did what many people today are doing—bunched animals and moved them. When I advised clients to do this, they quickly fell flat on their faces. Initially I believed this was because we could not handle the many variables involved—the complexities inherent in a rangeland environment, the differing seasons, livestock requirements, wildlife needs, and other factors—with any form of grazing rotation or set system. Thus I developed "short-duration grazing" (eventually called the "Savory grazing method") based on a military planning procedure that enabled us to address all these variables. Hundreds of ranchers in southern Africa and South America used this new planning process in the 1960s with promising results. Then in the late 1970s I introduced the process to ranchers in the United States and it took off.

SUCCESS, FAILURE, AND LESSONS

How successful was it? All the projects I had under my guidance in southern Africa failed in the end, including two "advanced projects" where I was pushing animal numbers to extremes in high and low rainfall with nothing but good results. The low-rainfall advanced project lay in a very erratic 10- to 12-inch rainfall area. Here we had taken thousands of acres of severely degraded annual grassland—not a single perennial grass plant even in the best of years—and restored it to full perennial grass cover at a total cost of $1.80 per acre. We had done this by trebling the stocking rate, bunching the animals, and planning the grazing. For over eight years we quintupled the meat per acre, and impala, zebra, giraffe, wildebeest, kudu, and other species of wildlife were drawn to the area. Then it collapsed completely. The cattle had to be removed, as there was nothing left to eat. At the same time, the advanced project in the high-rainfall area (35 inches) suffered a similar fate. In the United States we put over 10,000 people through training, but I doubt 10 percent succeeded more than modestly. Clearly something was still missing.

I had expected all grazing systems and rotations to break down in brittle environments at some stage because none of them catered for the many variables cited earlier. But why was the planning process I had promoted so strongly, which overcame this weakness, also breaking down? After studying hundreds of cases on three continents, I began to understand the breakdowns were not the result of anything in the planning process per se. They were due to other factors and complexities that could never be covered in a grazing plan: poor financial planning, social strife (divorce, family disagreement, business succession), government regulations, the allure of reverting to the old familiar ways of doing things (the cause of both advanced project failures), and so forth.[5]

In short, while each failure could be pinned on a financial, social, or other factor, there was more to it than that. I had begun to recognize that the inconsistency in results—some succeeded, but most didn't—was somehow connected to what was driving the people in each situation. Why, for instance, does a person give up so easily on a fitness program? We know that more exercise will lead to greater health, but millions of people buy running shoes and exercise machines and fail to use them for more than a month or so. Why would the same managers who had experienced success with planned grazing for eight years in southern Africa drop the planning in favor of something that was more familiar, and thus easier, and watch the collapse without doing something about it?

THE BEGINNINGS OF AN ANSWER

We found what appears to be an answer. Originally people began practicing holistic management by analyzing ecological processes in an attempt to improve their functioning and thus restore the land to health. I had developed a number of management guidelines to help people accomplish this, as well as a few simple tests they could perform mentally to ensure their actions were appropriate for the situation. With experience we began to recognize the futility of manipulating ecological processes without some idea of what we wanted to produce. Thus a production goal was defined. Soon after, we encountered the problem that afflicts so many other businesses: production goals achieved at the expense of the environment that supports them.

Including a landscape goal was a major step forward. But still the people involved often argued to a standstill over production goals—and thus the desired landscape. Some time passed before it appeared that this conflict could only be resolved by finding a common vision, in terms of quality of life, from which to proceed. By including a quality of life statement in the goal—a statement that reflected what the people valued most, what they lived for, what made them want to get out of bed each morning—we gained the personal commitment needed to achieve whatever else had to be achieved.

We subsequently realized the three goals—the production goal, the landscape goal, and quality of life—had to be combined into one comprehensive, holistic goal. Otherwise decisions could be made in support of one aspect while damaging another. Once the people expressed what they wanted in terms of quality of life, they would know what they had to produce to create the outcome envisioned. Once they knew what they had to produce, they could begin to envision the sort of landscape that would sustain what they produced. "Production" in the holistic goal became "*forms* of production" when we saw that people were only including products that could be sold or consumed—forgetting to include things like "meaningful work" or "an aesthetic environment," which would have to be produced to create the quality of life they envisioned. Landscape became the *future* landscape when we found that people were describing the land as it was—not as it had to be if it was to sustain them several generations hence. And it became the *future resource base* when we realized we needed to include reference to the people who would be resources to us in achieving the holistic goal. The future resource base still encompassed the idea of a future landscape. But the land manager now had to describe the land in terms of how the basic processes at work in any ecosystem—water and mineral cycles, energy flow, community dynamics—would have to function.

The holistic goal brought order to the ideas I've covered to this point, resulting eventually in a new framework for management that outlined a process we could use for making the decisions so critical to management. All the decisions we made in planning how to reach the holistic goal, or in addressing problems or opportunities that arose along the way, were evaluated according to the same criteria we'd always used. In addition, however, we now asked seven simple questions (the tests I referred to earlier) to ensure our decisions were socially, environmentally, and economically sound and would lead us toward the holistic goal. In other words: Any action taken to deal with a problem, to reach an objective, or to meet a basic need should not only accomplish what was required but should also enhance progress toward the holistic goal. To ensure that this happened, a feedback loop was established. Thus if monitoring showed the decision was not taking us where we wanted to go, we could act immediately to correct it. This process is beginning to produce consistent results at last—so long as people share a deep commitment to achieving their holistic goal. Our successes have been most notable in three areas: conflict resolution, profitability, and measurable land improvement.

OLD VS. NEW

It only dawned on me much later that the way we make decisions—have always made them—was ultimately responsible for the land deterioration we had been striving to reverse. It was the root cause of my many failures and explained the lack of success so many others had experienced. A summary of the essential differences between holistic decision making and conventional decision making should help you see what I finally saw.

In the conventional pattern, our decisions usually emanate from the desire to meet a variety of goals. We only accept the use of three tools with which to manage land: technology, fire, and rest. To make sure our decisions about these tools (or any other actions contemplated) are in line with our goals, we consider various criteria: past experience, expert opinion, research results, intuition, laws and regulations, cultural norms, political expediency, fear, peer pressure, cost effectiveness, profitability, compromise, and so on. If we are convinced the action we are contemplating will achieve the expected outcome, we go ahead with it.

Generally we assume we have made the right decision, although we can't be sure until we see what actually happens.

When we manage holistically, however, we first determine the extent of what we're managing: the whole. This whole always includes the decision makers (anyone who makes decisions affecting management, including those with veto power over any decisions), the physical resources available (including people), and the money available. The decision makers then form a holistic goal and, subsequently, any number of short-term objectives. If they are managing land, particularly in brittle environments, they add two more tools to their toolbox: grazing and animal impact. They base their decisions regarding tools, as well as any other management options, on all the criteria they might have used conventionally. But now they include an additional step. They will run any action proposed in the pursuit of an immediate objective through seven tests to ensure their decision is socially, environmentally, and economically sound, both short and long term, in light of the holistic goal. Finally, they monitor the results for early signs of warning so they can make a correction before damage is done. In other words: They don't wait to see what happens, they make happen what they want to happen.

The process may sound complex, but no more so than if I were attempting to describe how to ride a bicycle. Once the idea is grasped, making decisions this way is no more time-consuming than before. Everyone now has a common focal point (the holistic goal) and a sense of direction. They know how decisions will be evaluated and can see for themselves whether the resulting actions are likely to lead to the mutually desired outcome.

The holistic management decision-making process, under development for close to forty years, coincides with the thinking of many scientists and others today who are publicly acknowledging the need for humans to think and manage more holistically.

ONE DECISION AT A TIME

I believe we can create rangelands in the West that once again support a vast array of life, healthy soils, and stable water systems. But we can only do it one decision at a time. Two requirements have to be met. First people at the grassroots must be empowered—through education, training, and community support—to manage holistically in each situation, as all situations (or wholes) are unique. And second, because these people are compelled to operate under policies emanating from various institutions that prescribe what they can and cannot do on the land, these policies must be holistically sound. Sound policies, involving a decentralization of decision making, education, and training, would enhance the ability of people at the grassroots level to make socially, environmentally, and economically sound decisions. Today, far too many policies preclude this.

Research and experience however, indicate that it is always a very long time before new thinking becomes mainstream enough for institutions headed by democratically elected leaders, and supported by a bureaucracy, to adopt the new thinking. In fact, it can run to hundreds of years. This slow pace of adoption is understandable. Standing in the way of any democratic bureaucracy to adopt new thinking is a minefield of conflicting views, institutional and private egos, deep beliefs, traditions, differing objectives and goals, feelings and fears, as well as personal and institutional agendas. Only when the new thinking has stepped through that minefield successfully and recovered from every false step and attack does it become mainstream and thus accepted by institutions.

SPEEDING ACCEPTANCE

That we can ill afford this slow and tortuous pace when it comes to the need to manage holistically is highlighted by the state of the soils on our rangelands, as well as in our forests and croplands. Despite the greatest concentration of scientists ever known in one nation, eroding soil is America's greatest annual export—greater in weight and value than all grain, timber, meat, weapons, and commercial and intellectual property exports. How can we, faced with these alarming facts, adopt new ideas more speedily?

When every ranch, farm, forest, piece of public land, and community is unique—when there are so many variables and such a cacophony of views, goals, objectives, environments, and community needs—there clearly is no single answer. No people will forever accept a solution imposed on their community through laws, regulations, or the views of single-issue pressure groups. Our innate compulsion to make decisions in our own self-interest preclude such a solution for more than a short period of time.

Holistic management provides a framework that recognizes the uniqueness of each situation. It enables people to find the solutions appropriate to their needs at any given moment, as they must, because today's solution is often not tomorrow's. Centralized planning and regulation can never do this.[6] As much as our institutions must change, they cannot lead a change to holistic decision making. By definition, democratically elected leaders cannot lead, other than in crisis or war, but must always follow the will of the majority. Thus the change to holistic decision making has to start at the grassroots.

The deterioration of America's rangelands that has occurred over the last ten thousand years is so extensive it is beyond the power of any institution to handle. So great is the challenge of restoring them now that only ordinary people can do it: ranchers, farmers, foresters, range managers, teachers, parents, businesspeople, or whatever we are outside our institutional or social identities. Until each of us begins to change the way we make decisions, there won't be a sufficient groundswell of opinion to make it safe for elected leaders to change the way *they* make decisions. Fortunately, that groundswell is beginning to build.

NOTES

1. The fact that overgrazing is a function of time of exposure and re-exposure of grass plants to animals is discussed at length in Voisin's book. Andre Voisin, *Grass Productivity* (London: Crosby Lockwood & Son, 1959) (republished in 1988 by Island Press).

2. Holistic management is a specific process for decision-making, management and policy formation that addresses the underlying cause of problems associated with biodiversity loss, desertification, poverty, and social breakdown. It is described in Allan Savory with Jody Butterfield, *Holistic Management: A New Framework for Decision Making*, 2d ed. (Washington, D.C.: Island Press, 1999).

3. Figures quoted appear in a booklet produced for villagers in Namibia. *Rainfall in Namibia: What is Normal?* (Windhoek, Namibia: Desert Research Foundation of Namibia, 1993), p. 9.

4. Mano, Stein, and Meinrat O. Andreae, "Emission of Methyl Bromide from Biomass Burning," *Science* 263 (1994): 1,255–1,256.

5. The long story of my effort to track down the causes of the breakdowns in each case so we could avoid them in the future is recounted in Allan Savory, *Holistic Management: A New Framework for Decision Making* (Washington, D.C.: Island Press, 1999).

6. As James Scott so tellingly points out in *Seeing Like a State* (New Haven: Yale University Press, 1998).

Part Four

THE ECONOMICS
OF RANCHING

Our Land in the Belly of the Beast
Businessmen Overheard in the Palm Court Restaurant Plaza Hotel New York City America

DRUMMOND HADLEY

Take them invite them out to lunch don't get attached
It's money it's property it's real estate it's things
You say do you want to sell
What do you want to pay me to sell it for you
We made 50 or 60 million he died penniless
His children asked us for 1,000 dollars for the funeral
It was tax deductible of course we gave it to them
Is it legal the government pays lip service
But the competition is fierce you will have no license
You will be seen as a mortgage consultant a foreigner
Your English will not be like theirs
The property will be worth more
Than eight to ten times what we pay for it
You will ask them for three or four
But before they know it you will get 10 million
When I am going to foreclose
I pay the lawyers maybe $50,000 4%, 3%, 5%
The poor man never wants to pay the lawyers
So you know the poor man will lose
These companies are like candy stores
Make all the dough you can buy today sell 'em short
Take them invite them out to lunch
Subdivisions in mountain valleys
Wild running rivers country ways of livelihood
Deer cowboys mountain lions javelina
Don't get attached it's money it's property
It's real estate it's things
Take them invite them out to lunch

Chapter 12

Blue Birds and Black Cows

BOB BUDD

At one time I might have harbored illusions of owning a ranch. My father's father was raised out of rock and water, third generation on the same piece of land, near a town that bears our family name on Main Street. My mother's father came west in 1931, with wife and new daughter, a dream, and precious cash. He nurtured a ranch out of glacial till, boulder fields, and red hills that ran more clay than water when it rained. When I entered high school, both ranches were still in the family. By the time I was sixteen, both ranches were in other hands. And though we never spoke of it much at the dinner table, we knew our parents could never go home again. From that point on, we didn't visit those places as often, then not at all. Mom and Dad still spoke of their roots, strangely in past tense, and when they did, their remembrances came down to two simple things: land and people.

Thirty years later, I point those places out to my children as we pass by. The kids look out the windows and say little. I too am quiet, for I know exactly what they are thinking. My wife, always quick with a smile, support, encouragement, and optimism, chokes on her own question: "Am I teaching my children to love something they can never have?"

The ranches and homes lost to my parents went away for different reasons. In one case, it was a matter of scale and poor decisions. Poor decisions aside, the ranch would never have sustained the single family that tried to make it work through the 1970s. It was sold to the neighbors for enough money to pay off the note at the bank, build a new house up the lane, and allow the neighbors to keep their own kids on their own ranch. Today, despite acquisitions made in the late 1960s and early 1970s, these families are facing the same questions of scale a single family encountered three decades past.

The math of ranching is hard-core new math, made harder to figure when you always knew the home place as a ranch built out of six ranches. Three generations ago, it was split in half between brother and sister when parents died. Now half of the whole is only a piece of one ranch. Follow the math. Six ranches were established in the 1900s, became one in the 1940s, turned into two in the 1960s, part of one in the 1980s. They have fared well. Down the road, there is a place that went from eight ranches to one, then divided into four, and, ultimately, became more than a hundred parcels on the market. The parcels sold. The ranch disappeared. I used to hunt sage grouse there, stealing them from circling falcons. There is no room for any of us now, let alone the cows that dotted the flat for a brief time in spring and fall.

The fate of the other ranch is still unknown. My grandfather sold it to his sons, an early inheritance, more or less. In retrospect, it was an amazing choice: to leave a piece of ground he nurtured from nothing into something, at the age of fifty-five, to his own young sons. He knew their strengths and their weaknesses. Brothers fight sometimes. Suddenly a ranch that was home and profit to one family had to be home and profit to two families. A ranch that would buy a new truck for the price of five calves had to buy two trucks, and new trucks were twelve calves each. Within a few years, a new pickup was twenty calves; nights in the calving barn were still twelve long hours. In the end, one brother became a judge, the other a realtor and public relations specialist. They were good at what they did, and they were happier. After all of the hard times, sweat and fret, they had a little money in the bank, a "stake," as the old cowboys said, and they made the most of it. The ranch was loved by a man who lived in the old family house and worked for a man who had lots of money and visited rarely. Not long after the ranch was sold, the new owner told the realtor he would really like to have one more piece of ground he had seen, a really pretty place, with lots of aspen and grass.

"Buy it," he told the realtor, who doubled as a brand inspector, confessor, card dealer, and rancher himself.

"It's yours," the multitalented realtor smiled.

"Dandy," said the buyer. "Tell me how much to make the check for."

"I mean, it's yours *already*," the realtor said, "but I guess you can write a check to yourself. My commission is seven percent."

Today that same ranch is the subject of daily rumor. One day it will be subdivided, sold to Japanese golfing aficionados, or lost to foreclosure. The land is now an appreciated asset, not a source of income. What are the choices for this portion of the ecosystem? It may be "saved" by some conservation organization, or by a caring soul who can afford to own land that doesn't produce the standard rate of return, a place that eats money for fixing fence, moving water, and paying taxes. More than likely, this ranch will become a series of houses, each with lane, horse, septic tank, well, and partial water right that is misunderstood. The houses will be nice, the wine old and red, the view spectacular, unless you saw it once as a place to raise twin fawns, or build a nest, or let out a deep, rasping croak that would attract a sleek, stylish, green mate. One rumor does not persist . . . the cows are gone . . . and no one would believe for a minute that a working ranch will reemerge from this dream.

Not long ago, agricultural lending was founded on the same premise, allowing debt to pile up, patient that markets would cycle as they always had, that there would be periods of gain and periods of loss, and that they would even out over time. Interest rates would sustain that ebb and flow, and while land sold back and forth it was priced according to its productive ability. As long as the value of the note was in line with the value of the land, it was a safe investment.

There was a cultural phenomenon buried within this economic world: a premise that some families would grow, others shrink, and that family business was a thing to be valued. Access to land was fiscally possible because people built legacy at the same time others retired. It was the same ebb and flow bankers saw in commodity markets. Values were consistent, and it was possible to build a place up, cash in and retire, and leave the new owner with a better piece of ground.

Only recently has access to forage, or access to land and water, become the limiting factor, both culturally and economically. In the Sandhills of Nebraska, families have grown and declined for nearly two centuries. People there tell of working for an older couple, getting a chance to buy the place where they worked, raise a family, and see their own children sell it back to the great-grandchildren of the original owners. Now land values are driven higher than reasonable economic sense allows, and yet the ranches sell to ranchers. The buyers are people frustrated by lack of access to forage on public lands in the West, suddenly able to cash out the scenic value of their private lands one home at a time, and get the heck out of Dodge. Everything comes down to economics, and economics comes down to access to grass and water. For every permit reduced to economic uselessness, you can find a nearby riparian area converted to houses. For every millionaire made by selling the creek bottom to newcomers, there is a young person outbid in his own backyard. Perhaps it is just "survival of the fittest," but it may be time to wonder if that ecological premise really fits the economic world. Maybe it fits Wall Street, but does it truly fit the Flint Hills of Kansas, Shortgrass Prairie of Colorado, or what is left of the Palouse Prairie in Washington?

Sometimes, what is owned and what is known are far apart. In the world of Daniel Quinn's *Ishmael*, leavers owned little and cared much for land that bound them together. Takers owned much but knew little about the land that was forced to sustain them. They never shared strawberries with a bear, fed grasshoppers to fish just to see them rise, or sat and looked at land without boundaries. If there weren't enough dollars in the calves, there were plenty in the land. Just as long as it was flat enough to roll a golf ball, set a foundation, or see mountains from a picture window.

Ranches go through their own path of succession, just as plants occupy land. At one time land might have been land, but it was fought over as forcefully as dogs mark territory, bears claw trees, or eagles kill falcons. Natives fought for certain places that offered opportunity for survival—the greatest shelter, most food, best water. Right or wrong, these were the same lands snatched up as the nation grew. Color aside, people could easily pick out the best land. And when settlers came west, land was viewed in a pragmatic Jeffersonian light. Aridity defines these western landscapes, and those who would last would be those who held claim to water. Early homesteaders occupied creek bottoms and river valleys first and did what came naturally. They stuck a plow in the ground and farmed. In deep alluvium, farming worked, as it did on vast plains well watered by perennial rivers and streams. But many who came later dug the plow into lands that should never have felt such rough surgery. An early leader in the cattle industry, R. S. Van Tassell, said at the turn of the century, "I won't live to see the day, but many of you will, when people will regret that they ever plowed up this buffalo grass sod." In 1934 another ranching industry icon, Dugald Whitaker, said to his fellow ranchers, "We have lived to see that day."

Seven decades later, we continue to see the effects of these conversions yet are unable to recognize the same progression in our own communities. Succession of a single ranch is driven by economic reality—by the fact that the note at the bank cares little for drought, disease, or decision. And like the newfound wealth in electronic marketplaces, *volume* is essential to the economic integrity of a ranch. A cowboy who can handle fifty cows can handle five hundred; the pay's the same. When volume is limited by access to forage—whether on federal land that is regulated or on private land priced out of reality—time is the only factor remaining. When cows grazing native plants are no longer a viable option, maximizing output per acre leads to farming. And when farming is rendered inefficient by loss of soil, or markets, or cost of inputs, houses replace cornstalks up and down alluvial valleys once known as riparian areas.

In the succession of ranching, lands once grazed were plowed in order to extract a greater return per acre. Native plants and animals were now found in secondary states of succession, often blasted by herbicides to keep them in check. Pheasants did really well. Bluebirds met unbridled hell. When the concept of higher returns per acre failed, it was the result of people in pastoral economies being reduced to poor farmers on poorer land. The farms grew smaller as pieces were sold off in reverse of their productive capacity for hobby farms and homesites. This process, too, is an intricate web of life and death, a response to economic and social pressures that has a massive effect on biological diversity and even ecological potential. At its earliest roots, the business of ranching was perhaps one of the simplest mimics of natural process in the history of human civilization.

None other than Aldo Leopold made it clear that mandating a land ethic would fail. His admonition that the prayers and resolutions of the public would do naught ended with a simple statement: "All the non-farming public can do is to provide information and build incentives on which farmers may act." This notion is particularly salient today. My friend Gregg Simonds calls it "rational behavior," the sane reaction of people to economic signals they receive. Right now the main economic signals ranchers receive relate to domestic animals and hay. Many if not most ranchers would be happy to raise wild sheep, bluebirds, mountain plovers or frogs, instead of cattle, but markets for wild creatures are almost solely consumptive, not at all unlike markets for Abbey's "stinking, bawling cows" or Muir's "hooved locusts." Markets for livestock are pretty simple. Two or three companies process all the calves raised throughout the country, and when they want to pay for cattle, the guy who raises calves and plovers gets more money. When they want to not pay, the guy on the land receives not.

Markets for wild things aren't a whole lot different. If the wild thing you feed and sustain grows horns, or swims and fights like heck on three-weight line, or flies straight enough to be blasted with scattered shot, you may become economically viable, sustainable, even visionary. But these markets exclude a portion of society from access to resources the public owns, and they offer little or nothing to species less desirable on the den wall. That may be just as well; women's hats and men's watch fobs contributed mightily to the extinction of the Carolina parakeet and ivory-billed woodpecker.

Economic signals for plant and wildlife conservation are perhaps just as logical and convoluted as cattle markets. In Texas, great big white-tailed deer are a cash crop, bigger than the beef market for some. Warblers and vireos, though far more important to the web of life in ranching landscapes, are viewed by some as a nuisance to development. White-tailed deer are under no pressure to survive and might in fact qualify as "pests" in a strict reading of the law. The standard line encourages ranchers to look for ways to capture the economic values of wildlife habitat, and these lines are becoming as flawed as a monopolistic cattle market. In the sagebrush behind my house, there are lots of potential dollars in elk and mule deer. But there is nothing in the marketplace that tells me to leave grass for grouse, brush for song sparrows, or willows for flycatchers.

Therein lies a tenuous ground between what is ethical and what is economical. Many have chosen to forgo the money and maintain the spirit of community, but this posture will not last in the face of economic pressure. The time has come to develop markets that reward stewardship, not in the traditional image of cost-share, subsidy, or bailout, but in a framework where raising vireos and warblers is honorable and necessary. The lands of the West are interconnected into a myriad of ecosystems. Loss of single pieces is an immense threat not only to species, but more importantly to *process* on a landscape scale. There will be people on the land. If these people are ranchers, they will likely be willing to forgo wealth. These are the stewards who offer opportunity at the species level, at the landscape and natural process scale, but only if we develop a marketplace that captures value in nature in the same manner ranchers sustain a business with cattle or sheep. It is not a question of which will win out. It is, instead, a matter of placing economics on a par with our intellectual and emotional value system. In a world of untold wealth in stocks, dotcoms, and other ventures, ranching remains a passion, a grossly illogical pursuit where millions' worth of capitalized value return mere pennies on the dollar. The work is hard, the line between sustainability and failure razor sharp.

There are still people willing to accept this responsibility, though they may be highly irrational. But so too are mice, and native fishes, and birds that sing sweetest when free to fly.

Chapter 13

Making a Living in the Age of Wal-Mart

Tom Field

There once was a meadow. The meadow and its occupants, the most noticeable of which were the herd bulls of a local ranch, marked the changing seasons for Gunnison. We drove past them on our way to a day of skiing in Crested Butte as they lay in the snow chewing their cuds, their gentle and rhythmic breathing releasing small clouds of vapor in the cold winter morning. As the snow gave way to the warmth of springtime, the bulls would begin their annual rite of jousting with each other like great horned warriors. They snorted, rubbed their heads against the ditch banks, and sparred in preparation for the breeding season. And all about them the meadow was transformed into an array of color, the greens of timothy and brome grass, the reds of clover, mixed with the violets and yellows of wildflowers. The bulls were moved to the high country for breeding season and the meadow blossomed and the grasses grew tall. The return of the bulls to the meadow and the ever so subtle browning of the landscape signaled that autumn would bring the seasons full circle.

Then one day the cattle were gone, the fences cut, and the earthmovers roared across the meadow until it was no more. In less time than a single season of the calendar, the hulking, gray, square trademark of a Wal-Mart emerged, its pavement and concrete incapable of marking the valley's seasons.

If it were only a single meadow giving way to "progress," perhaps there would be no reason for comment. For the western landscape, however, this is a recurring scene that ought to spark more than a passing comment from those who desire to make more than just a living but a life in the West. The conversion of meadow to mall is tragic both environmentally and culturally. The loss of open space, wildlife habitat, and agricultural land has become an American habit. Beyond the environmental consequences, these changes are damaging community dynamics and eroding the cultures that have valued land for both its aesthetic and its functional characteristics.

What forces lead us to choose superstores over meadows? Why do longtime ranchers call it quits? These are big questions for the West and its people. The American West and ranching have never been isolated from the forces of change or the agonizing choices required when decisions have to be made about what ought to be saved and what should be left behind. There is a story about a newly appointed officer in a British artillery unit during World War II that sheds light on the dilemma faced by those who care about the West and depend on its resources to make a living.

After the disaster at Dunkirk, which resulted in a high level of attrition in the officer ranks, relatively inexperienced soldiers filled leadership positions in the British army. One such young officer was placed in charge of an artillery unit. He observed the batteries during training and noticed that five soldiers manned each artillery piece. Two were responsible for loading, one for firing, and the other two simply snapped to attention prior to firing. When he questioned the training officer about the two men who only stood at attention and offered no other assistance to the unit, the noncommissioned officer replied that he had been trained to organize each battery in just this way. Not wanting to change tradition without due inquiry, the young officer passed his question up through the chain of command. At each juncture he was curtly informed that the procedure was the "Army Way" of operating. Several weeks later he encountered a veteran of the Boer War who had served in an artillery unit. He questioned the old man about the function of the two soldiers. "It should be obvious," said the old man. "They are there to hold the horses."

Such is the dilemma for ranching: which traditions to preserve and which to abandon? This is not a new question. Nor will its contemporary answer be sufficient in the future. Change has always been part of existence, and so it is west of the 100th meridian. Ranching is caught between the romantic notions of its past and the escalating demands of the consumer age. Many of us are fond of Thomas Jefferson's idealistic agrarian concept of a nation largely populated by farmers and local merchants. But as consumers we have not uniformly supported this agrarian ideal of localized food production. We cling to an idealistic image of the family ranch but shop at the superstores of Wal-Mart and the other multinational conglomerates that offer lower prices, more choices, and greater convenience.

MEANWHILE BACK AT THE RANCH

Traditional ranches have relied on cattle production to generate a living. Where climatic and geographic conditions allowed, hay production, small-grain farming, and timber sales supplemented the cash flow. And in communities with Scottish, Greek, Spanish, or Basque influence, sheep and wool production were incorporated into the enterprise mix. Regardless of the products, ranchers function under a commodity pricing structure not all that different from the one faced at the end of the trail drives in the late 1800s.

For the uninitiated, commodity selling is akin to playing in a poker game when the other players control the cards and make bets for you. In short, selling calves or yearlings under the conventional auction market system means a rancher is in the undesirable position of being a price-taker, not a price-setter. Prices for commodities, such as cattle and sheep, are typically cyclical in nature and the average rancher manages to break even over time. Cyclical markets yield high prices when demand is relatively high compared to low supplies. When prices are rising, ranchers respond by increasing production. Eventually the meat production overwhelms the level of demand and prices fall. As a result of falling prices, production falls and the cycle repeats itself. Under a commodity pricing system, profitability is variable: ranchers find profits attainable in periods of high prices and more difficult to capture when prices are low. Cyclical markets taken in combination with the effects of random weather conditions make it clear that ranching is a risky business at best.

Individual ranchers lack the power to affect prices in a commodity system, as any individual decision is absorbed by the decisions of the masses. Livestock producers, lacking control over prices, are thus left just a few options to attain profitability over the long term. The first option is to increase the *volume* of production through increased numbers of animals or increased productivity of each animal. The task of improving production received great attention in the sixty years following the Depression. Technological advances and improved efficiency have resulted in levels of individual animal productivity that when coupled with the impact of the North American Free Trade Agreement have allowed the U.S. beef industry to produce nearly 14 percent more beef in 1999 than in 1980—with nearly 5.5 million fewer cows in the national inventory.[1] Increasing the volume of production may yield favorable results in the short term, but it can turn out to be a bad decision in the long run. Two consequences stand out. First, increasing the quantity of production is rarely free from cost. Second, if increased production is a widely adopted strategy then price declines in a cyclic market may be more pronounced.

Lowering the *cost* of production is the second option. In a cyclical commodity market, the low-cost rancher has the advantage with the greatest number of opportunities to generate a profit while the high-cost rancher waits for cyclical peaks in price before profitability is attained. Lowering the cost of production is often the most attainable solution. But this strategy has limitations if the efforts to lower production costs result in production quantities that fall beneath profitable levels. And, just as in a game of limbo, production costs can only go so low.

NEVER ASK A COWBOY THE SIZE OF THE SPREAD

Despite Jefferson's vision, the economies of scale factor into the survival of ranches. The economic power associated with large enterprises was made most evident to me by a conversation with a manager of a large eastern seaboard farrow-to-finish hog enterprise. When I inquired about the effects of increased environmental regulations on his business, he said that increased regulation would deliver even more market share to the company because the costs associated with new regulation could be borne by the large organizations but not by the small to mid-sized farms that would be forced out of business. This is not an isolated example. Economies of scale are having a significant impact on the structure of agriculture and rural communities across the United States, and ranching is not immune.[2]

Many benefits arise from capturing economies of scale: opportunities to lower costs via the advantages of high-volume purchasing power (which lowers per unit costs of inputs), greater access to useful new technology, the ability to spread fixed costs over higher levels of production, and greater access to markets as a result of scale. In the beef industry, ranchers with herds larger than 500 head have about one-half of the production costs to produce a weaned calf compared to small herds with fewer than 50 head.[3]

Consolidation is occurring at every level of the industry—and the net effect is that the biggest players control more and more chips in the game. Most of the cow-calf enterprises in the United States are small (less than fifty head) but control only about one-third of the national inventory. Only 10 percent of cow-calf enterprises have more than a hundred cows, but these ranches account for about one-half of the total beef cows in the country. At the packer level, economies of scale have driven consolidation that has resulted in 80 percent of the market cattle from feedlots being harvested by the four largest companies. At the feedlot level, less than 15 percent of the feeding companies account for nearly 70 percent of all fed cattle marketed in the United States.[4] The mom-and-pop grocery store on the corner has given way to the supermarket. In fact, just five retail companies account for some 50 percent of all grocery store sales. At the ranch level, increased consolidation is driven by survival of the fittest. In this case the fittest are those ranches that can function as low-cost producers. Increased consolidation also results when ranchers choose to fold their cards and sell out rather than adapt to the new rules of the game.

Increased consolidation does have its positive effects: lower production costs at the ranch level, lower food prices for consumers, and a more competitive position for U.S. agriculture in the global market. But consolidation also forces changes that are undesirable: dramatic changes in the structure of rural communities may result when local businesses and services are unable to compete with the multinational conglomerates; ranchers find themselves increasingly disadvantaged in the marketplace; and mega-outfits may lack the cultural and historical connections required to sustain the integrity of rural life.

Structural changes in the food industry have come in response to consumer demand for inexpensive foods that are not only of high nutritional value but are also offered in abundance, in a variety of forms and brand names, with a high degree of convenience and packaging, and without the need for much time or effort in cooking. Furthermore, consumers want livestock products that are produced in a way that contributes to environmental health, food safety, and animal welfare. In the beef industry and ranching, consolidation has been driven by consumer expectations of cheap and plentiful food. Instead of paying 21 cents of each earned dollar for food, as was the case fifty years ago, American consumers now pay 11 cents.[5] The corporate superstores, Wal-Mart and all the others, are part of the economic landscape because they meet consumer demands.

THE COWBOY WAY AND THE NEW RULES

Ranchers have several alternatives in the age of Wal-Mart. These alternatives should not be uniformly applied in all cases nor are they mutually exclusive. Nonetheless, because the rules of the game have changed, ranchers, like the British artillery, must alter their way of doing business. Beyond attaining a position as a low- cost producer, the clearest options seem to be: (1) capture profits from participating in the process that adds value or creates brand name products; (2) diversify the economic activities of the ranch; (3) develop a source of off-ranch income; or (4) capture the remaining equity in the ranch by selling to the highest bidder, usually a developer. While all these alternatives are largely financial decisions, it is essential to recognize that factors other than money play an important role in the decision-making process for many ranchers. As well, there are cultural considerations that involve community and family commitments. Ranching has as much to do with how people live on the land as making a living from it. Lynn Sherrod, who ranches with her husband in the Elk River valley of Colorado, captures the essence of living on the land well: "There is something about getting your hands dirty with soil on your own land, gazing across hay meadows rippling in the breeze and seeing that same hay has been baled and is ready for winter, seeing a calf be born and struggle to its feet instinctively seeking its mother's milk, realizing and understanding that daily this rhythm and pattern of life is repeated, reinforced, and reaffirmed for the future."

Neither ranching nor society will be well served if we ignore traditional values. What we need is a delicate balance of the central mission of generating long-term profits via superior business skills with a passion for excellence and sustained cultural traditions. Without a sense of emotion the concepts of good stewardship and careful husbandry are not possible. Without an understanding of tradition we cannot sustain healthy communities. Without stewardship, husbandry, and community the business of ranching would be less worthy of our investment of time and resources.

Nevertheless, the message to ranchers is stark: "Get big, act big, or sell out." The development of partnerships is an effective way to gain the advantages associated with economies of scale and to participate in the financial rewards (and risks) that come from adding value to raw ingredients. These partnerships can take a variety of forms ranging from contractual agreements to loosely knit alliances. They can focus on both traditional products (livestock and hay) and nontraditional products (recreation, carbon sequestration, endangered species habitat, open space protection). There are distinct advantages to partnering: opportunities to capture economies of scale in both the purchase of inputs and access to markets; opportunies to secure higher prices by adding value to products; and establishment of customer loyalty via the delivery into the marketplace of brand-name products that consistently meet consumer expectations. But there are disadvantages as well: acceptance of more market risk; loss of independent decision making as a result of agreeing to predetermined production and marketing specifications; and the cost of gaining access to the infrastructure required to add value.

One of the biggest challenges for such alliances is acquiring the expertise needed to participate fully in the value-added supply chain. And there are infrastructure issues to be dealt with—acquisition of human resources, capital, and processing capacity, for example. Often ranchers seek opportunities to build or purchase processing plants. This approach has rarely worked. A better tactic has been to capture plant capacity via partnership or contractual agreements. Making the transition from supplying raw ingredients to delivering value-added products to consumers requires a different mindset and new skills.

Alliances have become a hallmark of the livestock industry in recent decades. Efforts have ranged from large-scale approaches such as U.S.

Premium Beef to local efforts such as Yampa Valley Beef. Some of these alliances between ranchers, feeders, packers, wholesalers, retailers, and food service will succeed. Others will fail. But their presence does give livestock producers a way to participate in the creation of branded products. In a diverse marketplace, demand niches create opportunities for a variety of approaches to capturing a share of the consumer's dollar. Creating brands that are attached to specific ranches (CO Bar Beef in Arizona; Ranchers Renaissance headquartered in Colorado), efforts to preserve open space and agricultural lands and livelihoods (Yampa Valley Beef in Colorado), or demand for organic products (3BR Beef in Texas or Coleman Beef in Colorado) have found at least moderate success.

The emergence of business agreements between elements of the beef industry—pacts that coordinate activities to ensure the consistent delivery of value-added products to consumers—should not be viewed as a passing fancy. Furthermore, the formation of alliances will extend beyond the mechanics of food production. Cooperative partnerships will tie other values to food products as well. Certification programs are likely to develop whereby ranchers with a strong record of environmental stewardship will have access to participation in a brand-name product supply chain that merchandises environmentally friendly products. These changes will require significant adaptation by livestock producers. Supply chain systems will have more stringent requirements with respect to product specifications and production standards. Therefore, managers will have to become more focused on information, risk strategies, and the business environment. Ranchers who wish to participate in branded product approaches will value flexibility, creativity, and relationships over business as usual.

Access to these alliances will not be limited to the largest producers. While the largest ranches are typically targeted in the early stages of alliance formation because of the volume they bring to the table, small and mid-sized enterprises can gain access by joining forces. Cooperative agreements between smaller producers allow them to gain access to market opportunities and take advantage of economies of scale by acting large through partnering.

For most ranches, cash flow tends to be seasonal in accordance with historical marketing strategies. Significant sales may only occur once or twice a year. Diversifying the ranch's economic activities is often an effective solution to the cash flow problem. The possibilities, however, depend on the ranch and its resources. The options available to a ranch depend on its geographic location, resource base, and facilities, as well as the manager's motivation to initiate new enterprises. Innovative enterprises may in fact offer opportunities that increase cash flow and promote the ranch's ability to use its resources fully. As ranchers evaluate opportunities, they will have to conduct an honest assessment of the financial ramifications, hidden costs, risks, and required skills. Moreover, ranchers must learn to recognize the full range of products and services that can be offered: guiding and outfitting, Christmas tree production, native plant nurseries, nontraditional animal enterprises such as bison or elk, wildlife viewing, and a host of activities for which the public may pay to experience ranch life. Understanding the consumer's perception regarding the value of a particular resource may point to unique opportunities. In short, it is important to look at ranch resources from a different perspective in the search for new enterprises.

Seeking off-ranch income is a common decision. USDA data give us some insight into the dependence of families on outside income. The reliance on income generated outside of farming is also related to scale. As the gross sales from an agricultural enterprise increase, the percentage of total income derived from off-farm sources declines. This effect is particularly significant once gross sales of $250,000 are exceeded.[6] Although the decision to have family members work outside the ranch yields income, it may also increase stress as people try to juggle responsibilities to family, ranch, and the off-ranch job.

Finally, ranchers can always capture the value of their resources by selling. In some cases, this may well be the best decision from a financial perspective. But from a long-term view, the continuing exodus of agricultural landowners sets off a chain reaction that is dramatically altering the West's landscape, community structure, and culture. When a ranching family leaves the land, more than the enterprise is lost. A lifetime of knowledge about the resource is severed—perhaps several lifetimes—and the intimate relationships with the land and its inhabitants are broken. Often they are supplanted by those who easily tire of the responsibility for stewardship of a working piece of land or have only a short-term profit motive with little interest in either the community or the landscape. The loss of ranches in the West is in many ways a financial problem. But failing to find a solution will create a crisis in terms of environmental and social issues. If we cannot find a way to make it profitable for people to stay on the land in a productive capacity that also protects the natural landscape, then we will continue to sacrifice meadows for superstores, malls, and condos. And the West will be a much poorer place for our failure.

Even when ranches are profitable, passing the legacy on to the next generation is problematic. In almost every case, the costs associated with estate taxes have stacked the deck against family ranchers wishing to pursue agriculture in the future. For the future of agriculture and the western landscape, the most significant policy measure would be estate law reform that reduces the burden of intergenerational transfer of agricultural lands.

Ranches provide more than food and fiber. They maintain open space, wildlife habitat, and a profound connection to the history and heritage of the West. Easements offer another tool to help protect ranchlands from development. Easements can take a variety of forms that designate the land's use for periods of time into the future. Through the sale or donation of easements, ranchers can help sustain rural communities while gaining estate tax advantages from designating lands as agricultural use and thus lowering the taxable value. Agricultural conservation easements aren't the silver bullet for everyone. But without innovations that protect working landscapes, Americans can look forward to a future of depending on foreign sources of food as they depend on fossil fuels today.

THE UPSHOT

So what are we to do? The answers do not come easily or uniformly. The solutions come one conversation, one partnership, and one step at a time. Recently a group of us sat on the back porch at Jay Fetcher's ranch near Clark, Colorado. Jay, his neighbor Lynn Sherrod, and C. J. Mucklow, the Routt County extension specialist, shared their vision for ranching and the community in which they live. They told how conservation easements were making a positive difference for ranchers on the western slope. They discussed the creation of a value-added wool program to boost income for sheep producers in the area. They spoke of how they had forged partnerships with active and retired business professionals in the community to launch a local branded product called Yampa Valley Beef. As we listened to the conviction and passion that drove their efforts, it became apparent that Thomas Jefferson's spirit of hope and self-reliance still lives.

Just like that young British officer, they had questioned their assumptions, taken off their blinders, and begun to search for better approaches to the dilemmas that confront them. We will never be able to catch ranching in a freeze frame and hold it changeless against the tides of economic, political, and social dynamics. Such a notion is unreal. Instead we will have to learn new skills and unlearn those old perspectives that hinder our ability to forge partnerships, build communities, and contribute to healthy and productive landscapes. Nothing good ever comes without the effort of motivated people, and creativity is the best salve to heal our wounds. The answers to good ranching west of the 100th meridian will not come from the agencies or experts. Nor will they come from blaming the forces of change. The answers will come from the creative energy of people empowered to act in their local communities. Only then can we assure that meadows, not an addiction to consumerism, define the seasons.

NOTES

1. U.S. Department of Agriculture, Economic Research Service. Productivity changes occurred due to the following factors: improved genetic selection, increased utilization of European breeds of cattle, better nutrition, increased importation of Canadian feeder calves, and increased utilization of technology and information systems.
2. M. Drabenstott, "Consolidation in U.S. Agriculture: The New Rural Landscape and Public Policy," *Economic Review* 1(1999): 63–71. Consolidation into the hands of larger firms is widespread. The largest four companies control 62, 76, 57, and 74 percent of the country's flour milling, soybean crushing, dry corn milling, and wet corn milling.
3. R. Lamb and M. Brasher, "From the Plains to the Plate: Can the Beef Industry Regain Market Share?" *Economic Review* 4 (1998): 49–66.
4. Cattle-Fax, *Cattle Industry Reference Guide*, Englewood, Colo., 1999.

5. A. Barkema and M. Drabenstott, "Consolidation and Change in Heartland Agriculture," in *Economic Forces Shaping the Rural Heartland* (Kansas City: Federal Reserve Bank of Kansas City, 1996).

6. U.S. Department of Agriculture, Economic Research Service, "Structural and Financial Characteristics of U.S. Farms," AIB-746, 1995, p. 51.

Chapter 14

Economic Survival of Western Ranching: Searching for Answers

Larry D. Butler

Today the optimism of passing a ranch from generation to generation is diminishing due to dimming optimism regarding the economic viability of ranching. When the ranch is in economic trouble, the ranch culture is in trouble also. When ranch economics are bad, the potential for harmful ecological effects on the landscape increases and the environment is in trouble.

Ranch culture, ranch economics, and ranch ecology may seem to be separate issues. They are not. These issues are interrelated and dealing with them requires a holistic approach. Here I present a few economic options, but each approach is linked to the culture of ranching and the ecology of the rangelands. Solutions that work will be solutions that complement all aspects of the ranching business and way of life. A workable economic solution must be a sound ecological solution and an acceptable cultural solution. Any solution that fails this test will be short-lived.

ECONOMICS AND THE ALLOCATION OF RESOURCES

Economics is the science that deals with the efficient allocation of scarce resources among competing uses. Economics is often called the science of choice because it offers methods to evaluate competing choices. Terms that generally come to mind are "net present value" or "internal rate of return on investment." These are the yardsticks by which investors measure an investment to determine if it meets their standards and is the best place to spend their money.

Financial resources are not the only resources that ranchers must allocate. Ranchers must make many decisions in their day-to-day, season-to-season, year-to-year, and generation-to-generation choices. The ranch's survival depends on how well these decisions are made with the information at hand. In addition to financial capital, other scarce resources such as grass, forage, and hay must be allocated. And then there is the matter of personal time and family time. These too are part of the fabric that make up ranching culture and their allocation is just as important as the allocation of financial capital. Thus all ranching decisions require the use of economic principles when determining the appropriate course of action. But the science of choice is not just about dollars and cents.

FEASIBILITY OF RANCHING

Is ranching economically feasible? Is it economically efficient? To answer these questions, we must define ranching. If ranching is raising livestock, then there are times when it is not feasible and, depending on the rancher's minimum acceptable rate of return, it may never be the economic choice for investment of funds. But ranching can be defined in a broader context. A ranch is a business enterprise that produces goods and services from the management of financial, biological, and physical inputs inherent to the ranch landscape. What do ranchers produce? What can ranchers produce? Are there viable markets for the products or services? What mix of products and services should be produced? All these questions must be answered, not only in economic terms, but also in ecological and cultural terms. Products and services must be profitable over the long term; they must be produced in a manner that is ecologically sustainable; they must be a compatible mix when utilizing common land, labor, capital, and time; and they must be acceptable to the culture of the rancher and the public.

WILL WESTERN RANCHING SURVIVE?

More and more people these days, both in and out of the industry, are asking, "Will ranching survive in the West?" Many describe the rancher's plight in economic terms; others speak of environmental issues. Some have pointed out that the ranching community must strive to see that all its members do a proper job of grazing management and must inform fellow citizens about the many values that properly managed rangelands and pastures can provide. All of us with an interest in these resources and the West, as well as a desire to sustain its culture and improve its economic status and environment, must do our part.

Three basic concerns must be addressed if ranching is to survive: economics, environment, and culture (which includes education). One concern does not necessarily take priority over the others; all three areas must be addressed, often simultaneously, as quickly as possible. If a ranching operation is not an economically independent unit, it needs supplemental income from other sources for it to survive. Each ranch should be operated in an environmentally sound manner. Ranch operators should help to educate the public about the benefits the public receives from the ranch's resources when the grazing lands are well managed. The most obvious values are food and fiber. Others include clean, abundant water, healthy fish and wildlife with a healthy habitat, clean air, open space, scenic landscapes, and recreational opportunities. In addition to informing the public, ranch operators should represent a positive model for other ranchers who may not be doing a satisfactory job in the economic and environmental areas.

ECONOMICS AND RANCHING CULTURE

What is "return on investment" to the ranching industry? Not only is it the interest earned on a dollar invested over time, but it also can be thought of as the "value added" to a dollar. Therefore, thinking of return on investment as value added puts economic principles in practice when the concept is applied to living on a ranch. There are many values added to the ranching family, its individual members, and the members of rural and urban communities over the years. This may sound like an aspect of ranching culture. Indeed it is.

The historical settlement of the American West conjures up images of cowboys, vast herds of cattle, and wealthy cattle barons. The economic and environmental conditions of the 1880s helped create this image. Yes, the cowboy and his image are still with us. And let's hope for the sake of American culture that they always will be. But the economic conditions and environmental concerns are different today. Today's western family ranch with a cow-calf operation typically needs more than 300 mother cows to be considered a viable economic unit. These family-sized ranching operations are struggling to stay in business amidst a complex and ever-growing world around them. Ever-increasing costs of operation—without increasing prices received for livestock products—have put many ranches in an economic bind.

The average western ranch operation has historically yielded about 2 percent annual return on investment. A typical 300-cow breeding herd ranch in the western United States has required at least a million-dollar investment and in many places much more. This investment consisted of land, grazing permits, buildings and improvements, machinery and equipment, and livestock. An average 2 percent annual return would be about $20,000. It would be much easier to place the million dollars in a simple interest-bearing account earning 5 to 10 percent and even more with diversified investments. Such an investment would earn an average return of $50,000 to $100,000 a year. Why, then, do ranch families continue to labor under this economic model? How can they continue to ranch? Many can't. In fact, many of today's ranching families are struggling to stay in business. Those who are making it have done so through several methods: refinancing their ranches; postponing the depreciation of capital investments; taking other jobs to support the ranch operation; using some of the benefits of ranch life to sustain themselves; or diversifying.

Today's rancher has to be a prudent businessperson to continue ranching and receive a positive return. Since one rancher has little effect on the prices received for livestock products, the ranchers must concentrate on reducing the cost of current operations or find a new mix of business enterprises to operate on the ranch. Laborsaving methods must be used whenever possible. These techniques may involve making the haying operation more efficient or totally changing the ranch's grazing strategy.

VALUE OF WESTERN RANCH CULTURE

Obviously no one would ranch for a return of 2 percent when a much greater income could be achieved through investment—unless that person was dedicated to the lifestyle and culture of ranching. For many families the overriding factor in the decision to ranch is love for the land and the ranching way of life. Closeness to the land, the link with their parents and grandparents, makes ranching a precious opportunity to give children a heritage filled with values that many families wish to duplicate. Lessons taught by drought, floods, wildfire, predators, depressed markets, and life and death are learned through ranching.

The enjoyment received when riding the range, whether on horseback, pickup truck, or four-wheeler, cannot be easily reckoned in economic terms. The greening of the land in spring, the sounds of newborn calves and their mothers, and the smell of rain in the air—these are experiences for which many would pay dearly. And many are indeed paying for these experiences as ranches throughout the West are diversifying their business with tourism.

SOLUTIONS THROUGH DIVERSIFICATION

Many ranchers are diversifying and beginning new enterprises to supplement their livestock operations. Diversification can come in many forms. The enterprises may produce goods, services, or experiences. The goods produced on a ranch are most often animal or plant products, but some ranchers are turning in new directions. Services can vary from contract farming to food and lodging; experiences may be entertainment and educational activities. Enterprises range from harvesting and selling grass seed to such nontraditional ventures as recreation and tourism. Guide services for hunting on public land and access fees for private hunts are among the most popular enterprises that ranchers are adding to their operations. Although many cowboys cringe at the thought of "dude wrangling," for some ranches it has become essential. The sights, sounds, smells, and feelings of nature that are so cherished by the cowboy are also marketable to the urban dweller. Sharing nature through these business enterprises can keep many ranches in business and many cowboys in the saddle.

Often the enterprises are based on livestock, wildlife, water, plants, geology, heritage, history, facilities, and other natural resources such as beauty. The real test for an enterprise is this: Does it return an acceptable profit without causing an equal or greater loss from another enterprise? All enterprises need to be evaluated for their effects, both positive and negative, on other enterprises and ranch goals. These various sources

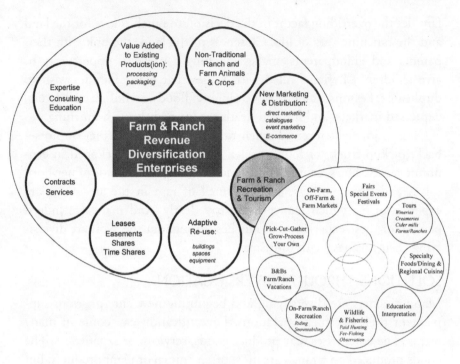

FIGURE 14.1. The major categories of ranch revenue diversification.
As the diagram indicates for Farm and Ranch Recreation & Tourism,
all categories can be further subdivided.

of revenue from products, services, and experiences can be classed follows (Figure 14.1):

• Value-added revenue from existing products—marketing and packaging the ranch's own brand of beef, for example, or finding a market for what was once considered a waste by-product such as wheat straw woven into decorative craft items.

• Nontraditional animals or crops—bison, longhorn cattle, llamas, or mushrooms, for example. The producer must take special care to conduct a long-term marketing and feasibility study when entering such markets.

• New marketing and distribution. Some ranchers are moving away from their traditional price-taker position at the local auction barn and are setting their own prices and marketing their products in nontraditional ways. Catalog sales and Internet marketing are two examples.

- Farm and ranch recreation and tourism—hunting, fishing, and camping for a fee, for example, as well as photography, special festivals, working ranch vacations, tours, and bed & breakfasts.

- Adaptive reuse of facilities, equipment, buildings, and resources. Many barns and bunkhouses are finding new uses as hunters' quarters, weekend retreats, and gift stores. Other ranch resources can be used at off-peak times in multiple enterprises. For some ranch owners, adding another ranch enterprise can justify itself by employing valuable ranch labor that might otherwise have to leave seasonally for employment elsewhere.

- Leases and easements. Some ranches are opting for permanent easements to reduce a tax burden. Others are leasing their ranch out for a weekend to wanna-be ranchers.

- Contract services. Ranchers can contract with others to raise beef or process ranch products.

- Consulting fees. Many nontraditional owners are entering the ranching business, and some of them need expert advice on animal husbandry and range management—areas where a traditional rancher might begin a consulting business.

CRITERIA FOR RANCHING SUCCESS

Whether a new business enterprise is based on a traditional product the rancher is planning to market in a new manner or is based on recreation and tourism, all successful diversification must meet a number of criteria:

- There must be a real market. The product or service cannot simply sound good or be something that has succeeded elsewhere. A market evaluation is needed.

- The rancher must have a market orientation. Ranchers must learn a new market just as they learned the livestock market.

- Products, services, or experiences must be accessible to the market. A market may indeed exist, but access to the ranch may be too difficult or too expensive.

- The market must perceive the value of the product or service to be great enough to cover the rancher's cost and provide an acceptable profit.

- Nontraditional alliances must be established. Not only may ranches have to form a cooperative, but partnerships with other community businesses such as motels, tourism businesses, and restaurants may be desirable.

- The philosophy of operation must focus on service and quality. Just as a rancher takes pride in providing an excellent livestock product to traditional buyers, the rancher must take the same appraoch to ensure quality in other products and services from new enterprises. Word of mouth among customers can result in success or failure.

- There must be a business approach, not a hobby approach, if long-term success is desired.

- Stewardship is essential. Taking care of the resources will provide for long-term success whether the ranch is in the cattle business or the tourism business. Cattle need clean water and healthy forage to produce high-quality offspring for the livestock enterprise. A tourism business needs clean water and healthy vegetation to enhance the landscape and attract customers for the recreational enterprise.

When these criteria are met, market development, relationship building, profits, and resource and ranch sustainability can be expected.

Can ranching survive in the West? The answer is yes. But for this to happen, four things must occur. First, ranchers need to implement ecologically sound resource management. Second, ranchers need to reduce their costs and receive a fair market price for their products and services. Third, ranchers need to diversify their operations in traditional and nontraditional ways that complement one another. And fourth, the public needs to be informed about the benefits it receives when rangelands are well managed with grazing animals. Change is inevitable. But changes on ranches can protect ranching's cultural values. When this is done through sustainable and economically successful ranching, society benefits too.

Chapter 15

Saving the Family Ranch: New Directions

BEN ALEXANDER AND LUTHER PROPST

Owners of ranchland are being forced to get in front of the tide of change and to plant their feet on new ground. For the first time, a range of landowner-driven solutions are providing us with hope to control our destiny and survive change.

—Ann Patton, Lone Mountain Ranch, San Rafael Valley, Arizona

Every four minutes an acre of agricultural land in Colorado is converted to development. Numbers like this reveal the impact of over 3 million Americans relocating from urban areas to the small towns and open spaces of the rural Rocky Mountain West in the past two decades. In the wake of this change, more and more ranchers are abandoning operations because of burdensome estate taxes, suburbanizing landscapes, attractive offers from developers, low commodity prices, and the increasingly high cost of buying out family members and partners. Throughout the West—from the arid grasslands of Arizona to the mountain meadows of Montana—working ranches are being converted into small tracts of recreational and residential homes, creating serious social, ecological, and economic problems.

What do we lose when a ranch landscape is carved up into 40-acre ranchettes? For the individual ranch family, it is often a personal tragedy as generations of family history are lost forever. For society in general, we lose the wide open spaces, the pure uncluttered sweep of nature that defines the American West. We also lose the viability of the agricultural economy that is the lifeblood of many rural communities and an essential element of the West's sense of place and neighborliness.

Piecemeal subdivision of ranch landscapes also threatens the viability of dynamic ecosystems. The heart of most ranches is precisely the land that's most sought after for development: their flat, open meadows and scenic riparian areas. With subdivisions quickly replacing large, intact ranch lands, the most productive wildlife habitat in the West is fragmented, and natural forces that shape the landscape—fire, flood, herbivory—are suppressed. Most important, the relationship between people and land is altered. On subdivided land, people no longer enter into an active, living relationship with the natural processes of the land. They are no longer stewards of the land but rather its temporary tenants.

The ranchers who will survive in today's West are the ones Wallace Stegner called "stickers." They are the ones who are open to working with their neighbors and adapting to the changing economics and land-use patterns that are shaping the West. Seizing new opportunities is at the heart of their approach. As prominent stewards of the West, tomorrow's ranchers must be ready to use all the private-land tools at their disposal: easements, estate planning, limited development, voluntary zoning districts, collaborative planning, and business diversification.

Today ranchers are discovering that they don't have to compromise their property rights, financial status, health of the land, or quality of life to stay in business. This has become a reality because the list of options for marketing all the values ranchers produce on their land is becoming longer, more flexible, and more diverse. Most encouraging of all is the fact that some of the same people who once were fighting to remove ranchers from the land are now working to broaden these options. This emerging consensus recognizes that preserving working ranches in the West depends on securing long-term land tenure based on viable economics and cooperation.

This essay explores a variety of voluntary approaches that ranchers are using to preserve their land and meet their personal, financial, and ownership goals. These options do more than prevent the fragmentation of agricultural lands. They give hope to a growing number of ranchers who are finding ways to combine financial resilience with ecosystem health. As the West becomes more urban, agricultural landowners are taking ranching in new directions.

CONSERVATION TOOLS FOR WORKING LANDSCAPES

With generations of work invested in land, the primary concern of many agricultural producers is to keep the ranch in the family. This strong connection to the land is often marked by a commitment to maintain working ranches along with the rural lifestyle and natural values it supports. But too often ranching families are forced to sell their land just to pay estate taxes to multiple heirs. Appropriate combinations of estate planning tools—such as a unified credit trust, minority shareholder discounting, life insurance trusts, family limited partnerships, and creative charitable gifting arrangements—present a variety of options to keep a ranch intact and in the family.

Conservation Easements

One of the strongest measures to prevent a forced sale and ensure that land is permanently protected as a working agricultural landscape is a conservation easement. Concerned about the rapid pace of change, a growing number of ranchers in the West have responded by voluntarily placing agricultural conservation easements on their ranches.

A conservation easement is a voluntary contract that permanently limits the type and intensity of future land use while allowing landowners to retain ownership and control of their property. To understand how conservation easements work, it is necessary to understand the nature of property. Real estate consists of a bundle of property rights: the right to farm or ranch, to subdivide the land, to construct buildings, to restrict access, to harvest timber, to sell the water, or to mine. In many instances these rights can be separated from the bundle and transferred to another party. Mineral and water rights, for example, are commonly bought and sold separately from surface rights.

Conservation easements involve the donation or purchase of a property's development rights. In general, conservation easements limit the amount and location of future structures and define the permissible land uses. Easements used to preserve farming or ranching operations are generally referred to as agricultural conservation easements and allow agricultural activities to continue. They do not grant public access unless the landowner specifically wishes to permit it. With a conservation easement, the landowner can reserve the right to carry out specified activities, such as limited development and commercial use of part or all of the land (guest ranching, logging), so long as these activities do not unduly affect the land's conservation value. Like all property instruments, conservation easements are recorded with the county clerk or recorder so that future owners and lenders will know about restrictions when they obtain title reports. The land remains on the tax rolls in private ownership.

Donating an Easement

Most landowners who place conservation easements on their land donate them outright to a land trust or public agency and continue to live on the property. In addition to safeguarding the property in perpetuity, landowners who donate easements may gain substantial savings in estate and income taxes. The donation or bargain sale of a conservation easement is a tax-deductible gift provided that the easement is donated in perpetuity to a qualified nonprofit organization or public agency for conservation purposes. If an easement meets IRS criteria—by providing open space, agricultural lands, and wildlife habitat—the landowner qualifies for a charitable deduction.

Surging real estate values and the resulting estate taxes have made it difficult for many landowners to pass property from one generation to the next. Federal estate taxes can be as high as 55 percent of a property's value. Many ranching and agricultural families have experienced estate taxes so high that they are forced to sell all or part of their property just to pay the taxes. Conservation easements reduce property values, however, thereby lowering estate taxes. Even if a landowner does not want to restrict a property during his or her lifetime, the owner can still specify by will that a conservation easement be made to a qualifying organization upon the owner's death.

To qualify for a federal income tax deduction, easement donations of more than $5,000 must be verified by a qualified appraisal. The value of the easement is based on the difference between the property's fair market value before and after the easement is established. If an easement reduces a property's fair market value from $500,000 to $200,000, for example, the charitable gift would be valued at $300,000. The federal tax deduction is 30 percent of the adjusted gross income, and any unused amount can be deducted over the next five years. Landowners typically receive deduction values associated with the grant of a conservation easement between 20 and 50 percent of a property's fair market value. This deduction variation is a function of specific provisions in the easement (the number of homesites reserved for example) and the difference between a parcel's agricultural value and its value for development or speculation.

Conservation easements can either be sold or donated to a qualified conservation organization (typically a private land trust) or public agency who serves as easement holder or grantee. These organizations assume the responsibilities spelled out in the easement, which include annual monitoring and, if necessary, enforcement. Over the past ten years, the number of land trusts in the Rocky Mountain West has more than doubled, reflecting a growing concern to save the region's open spaces and ranching heritage. Working together with landowners, land trusts across the country have thus far protected nearly 6.5 million acres of land—an area larger than the states of Connecticut and Rhode Island combined.

In 1981, for example, the Grimes-Kleckner family, fourth-generation ranchers in southwestern Colorado, faced a bleak yet all-too-common predicament: How could they pay the monumental estate taxes on their 480-acre ranch and pass it on to the next generation? As the surviving owner of the ranch, Mary Grimes worried what would happen to her land. With the growing demand for second homes in the scenic San Juans surrounding Pagosa Springs, the ranch seemed slated for eventual development. Intent on keeping the land in the family, however, her daughter-in-law, Virginia Kleckner, explored strategies to minimize the looming estate tax burden. Just as she was about to give up, she learned about the estate tax benefits associated with donating a conservation easement. The Trust for Public Land helped the Grimes-Kleckner family and other Pagosa Springs ranchers set up a local land trust—Upper San Juan Land Protection, Inc. (later renamed the Southwest Land Alliance)—which accepted Mary Grimes' easement donation of 480 acres.

Deemed a valuable part of the agricultural and natural resource system of the Piedra River watershed, the San Juan National Forest, and the

Upper San Juan basin, Mary Grimes' ranch qualified as a tax-deductible donation under the IRS code. The provisions of the easement allowed for continued ranching and agricultural uses, hunting and recreational activities, as well as the construction of two single-family residences for her extended family. The easement prohibited public access, subdivision development, or commercial logging. Most important, this arrangement allowed Mary Grimes' son, Carl Kleckner, and his wife, Virginia, to inherit the family ranch and keep it. Almost two decades later, Virginia is the remaining survivor on the ranch. Although she isn't sure which son will continue to ranch, she has the comfort of knowing that her land will not be subdivided.

Selling an Easement

For a growing number of farmers and ranchers who are unable to take advantage of the income tax benefits associated with a donated easement, selling an easement is an attractive option. As an alternative to protecting land through fee-simple acquisition, the federal government and an increasing number of state and local governments are now purchasing easements from ranchers and farmers to protect core agricultural areas and critical open lands. This approach appeals to many ranchers because it generates immediate income that can be used to retire debt, cash out siblings or heirs, or expand an operation. As with donated easements, land remains in private ownership and agricultural and conservation values are safeguarded in perpetuity.

Purchased easement programs differ in the lands they aim to protect. Some focus on big-game habitat and wildlife migration corridors. Others emphasize historic rural landscapes and agricultural production. These programs have been particularly successful in regions and states experiencing rapid growth and conversion of rural land to urban or suburban uses. In the West, purchased easement programs are frequently administered by the U.S. Fish and Wildlife Service, the Forest Service, and the Bureau of Land Management, in addition to local and national land trusts. Some western states are running their own programs. In Montana, for example, the legislature recently created the Montana Agricultural Heritage Program, a purchased-easement program specifically authorized to protect critical farm and ranch land in the state.

Counties in the West are initiating purchased-easement programs as well. Concerned about the rapid conversion of agricultural lands in the Yampa River Valley in Routt County, Colorado, a coalition of ranchers, conservationists, and business leaders spearheaded a county initiative to create a purchased-easement program. In 1996, local residents passed this measure with a one-mill (0.001) property tax increase for a ten-year period. This funding supplements a $3.2 million grant from Great Outdoors Colorado (funded by state lottery funds) and a $250,000 start-up fund from the city of Steamboat Springs and Routt County. In the spring of 2000, the county purchased its first conservation easements on the Stanko and Robinson ranches, protecting them from development and allowing these longtime ranching families to continue to raise cattle and protect open space.

Conservation Buyers

Conservation buyers are affluent people who value—and try to protect through their purchases—the open spaces, ranching traditions, and healthy, natural ecosystems of the West. Unlike land developers and speculators, conservation buyers are often allies of ranchers. Many conservation buyers seek scenic, wildlife-rich properties for riding, hiking, hunting, fishing, and other recreational activities. They generally purchase large tracts of desirable land which they then protect with conservation easements. Conservation buyers compete with developers for the right to own such property. When conservation buyers outbid developers, the land often remains in agricultural production and is leased by neighboring ranchers. There are several sources for finding conservation buyers: a local land trust, agricultural trade magazines, and a growing number of real estate brokers who specialize in conservation deals.

Take, for example, the Sun Ranch in Madison Valley, Montana. With the advent of ranching in southwestern Montana in the late nineteenth century to supply nearby miners with beef, the Sun Ranch became one of the region's signature livestock operations. Originally created through the aggregation of smaller homesteads, in more recent times portions of the ranch have been sold off by an interim owner who was a real estate speculator. In a county with more than 3 percent annual growth and no land-use planning, there were concerns that more of the ranch might be subdivided to meet the demand for recreational homes. In 1998, Roger and Cynthia Lang bought the Sun Ranch with the intent of keeping the land in one piece.

Upon buying the ranch, Roger hired a sophisticated ranch manager, Rich Hewitt, and together they set about inventorying current land conditions with an eye toward restoring land health and running an efficient cattle operation. The Sun Ranch's land stewardship plan establishes the following mission: "The Sun Ranch seeks to enable its 25,000-acre natural resource base to function as an intact, healthy ecosystem. Each resource present will be treated with care and respect for its integral role. Ecological principles will guide the operation of the livestock enterprise, which is to fit within the greater framework of environmentally sound land management."

With this clear mandate, Roger, Cynthia, and Rich hope to turn the Sun Ranch into a model of ranch management and land stewardship for others—newcomers and old-timers alike—to emulate. In the short span of two years they have achieved an impressive list of accomplishments. They are resting overgrazed pastures. They have developed stock wells to keep cattle out of riparian areas. They are in the process of installing wildlife-friendly fencing that will allow for implementation of an intensive, rotational grazing system. They are restoring native fisheries and have constructed a pond to rear endangered Western Slope cutthroat trout. They are aggressively treating weeds, including knapweed and hound's tongue, with a combination of herbicides and intensive goat grazing. They are working with federal and state agencies, as well as private entities, to ensure the health of 3,000 elk and a number of predators, including wolves and grizzly bears, that live on the ranch seasonally. And, finally, they are participating in The Nature Conservancy's conservation beef program to support environmentally sound grazing standards and value-added beef production.

The Langs are a model for other conservation buyers who come to the West and want to become more than absentee property owners. Even though they only live on the Sun Ranch part-time, they have gone out of their way to get to know and cooperate with neighbors and have become advocates for farming and ranching in the region. Roger sits on the board of the Madison Valley Ranchlands Group, a local rancher-led organization striving to find ways to accommodate ranching and new development, and offers pasture on his ranch as a grassbank to local ranchers in need of additional forage. With Rich's help, he is working to turn the Sun Ranch into an education resource for sound livestock/wildlife/human interactions.

Limited Development

The concept of limited development is not new. For years ranchers have been selling off a few homesites to meet their cash needs. What is new is the concept of protecting the rest of the ranch from future development—thereby allowing a rancher to make more by selling a few carefully selected lots than by selling off 40's. Today's limited development plans include restrictions on the location and total number of homesites enforced by conservation easements or less secure instruments such as mutual covenants. Under this arrangement, ranchers can generate more income with fewer homesites because the value of each site increases substantially when the land around it is protected forever. Moreover, a growing body of evidence demonstrates that conservation-minded development has higher appreciation rates, faster rates of sale, and lower infrastructure costs than conventionally designed subdivisions. Often a portion of the tax liability from the sale of a protected homesite can be offset by using a conservation easement as the device for restricting development.

By selling a homesite with limited recreation access to the rest of the property, ranching families are generating revenue to pay off debts while retaining their agricultural rights. A pioneering example of this approach is two fourth-generation ranchers, Zach and Patty Wirth of Wolf Creek, Montana. With the help of American Conservation Real Estate and the Montana Land Reliance, the Wirths granted a conservation easement on their ranch that restricted new development to a couple of cabins in the headquarters area plus a single homesite at the other end of the ranch. The Wirths sold this 21-acre homesite along with a deeded parcel of land and limited recreation access to the rest of their 1,000 acres. Except for a 3-acre building envelope around the new homesite, the Wirths retained exclusive agricultural rights to the buyers' homesite parcel.

The buyers got what they wanted—the privacy and amenities of ranch ownership—and the Wirths got the cash needed to capitalize their operation, making it possible for them to continue ranching. Lane Coulston of American Conservation Real Estate remarks: "By placing a conservation easement on their land, the Wirth family is making a personal statement about their commitment to the future of ranching. This family along with many others is helping to create a climate where other ranchers are more likely to grant conservation easements, thereby ensuring the long-term land tenure needed to appropriately manage an agricultural operation." The key to this transaction was the conservation easement. It assured the buyers that the recreational, open space, and wildlife amenities of their investment would remain forever unimpaired by further development. It also gave the Wirths a substantial premium on the sale price.

WORKING TOGETHER TO STAY IN BUSINESS

Settlers who came west in the days of the frontier soon discovered that its image as a land of fiercely independent loners was more myth than reality. Though some who made a go of it in the West were able to do so because of their ability to take care of themselves, survival in such a rugged land required cooperation. The need to work together was so great in the early West that smoldering enmities and even all-out hostilities were routinely shelved when it came time to brand the calves, build corrals, or put up hay.

The West today is no different. Though its disputes are still sensationalized, shoot-outs have been replaced with lawsuits. Behind the scenes and out of the headlines, however, people are sitting down face to face to find realistic solutions that capitalize on cooperation and hard work. This section features a number of these collaborative efforts that offer a glimpse of how they came to be and what they have been able to achieve.

Diversifying Among Neighbors: Hatfield's High Desert Ranch, Oregon

When it comes to creating innovations that have taken ranching into the twenty-first century, the achievements of Doc and Connie Hatfield, who own and operate their High Desert Ranch in southeastern Oregon, stand at the top in a number of categories—above all, conflict resolution. The Hatfields helped put together the Trout Creek Mountain Working Group, one of the first and most successful efforts at bringing ranchers, environmentalists, and agencies together as problem solvers rather than warring factions. Through the efforts of this group a dispute over an endangered fish—the Lahontan cutthroat trout—was transformed from a sure bet for a costly court battle into an opportunity to form an ongoing working group that continues to pull polarized interests together in southeastern Oregon and northwestern Nevada.

But the Hatfields know it takes more than resolving environmental conflicts to keep ranching afloat. There's the matter of economic sustainability as well. In this too they took the cooperative high road. Sustainability has long been a concern of the Hatfields. It was the reason, in 1974, why they left their Montana farm that was using too much fossil fuel, fertilizer, and labor to move to the high desert of eastern Oregon. Doc and Connie describe the sagebrush, bunchgrass, and juniper-covered hills that made up their new ranch as a dream come true. As soon as they got there they began applying their creativity to make sure their dream was sustainable.

Their first move was to start breeding "fault-free" cattle. To the Hatfields this meant cattle that could perform well on what the ranch provided naturally. In plain terms it meant thrifty cattle that calved without help, that were good mothers, and that could live on rangeland forage with a minimum of supplemental winter feed and still rank high in market value. The Hatfields have achieved that goal sufficiently well that their strain of a Tarentaise base crossed with Red Angus and Hereford blood is in high demand as breeding stock.

The next lesson was clear: Raising cattle efficiently, effectively, and appropriately on the land doesn't guarantee economic sustainability. In 1986 the cattle business was threatened by low prices and nationwide campaigns trumpeting the hazards of eating red meat. Instead of "stonewallin' it," the Hatfields saw this as an opportunity in disguise. Their response to the low prices and political assaults on their product was to join with thirteen other ranchers to form Oregon Country Beef—a marketing cooperative offering beef certified to be free of growth hormones and antibiotic food supplements. This solution got Oregon Natural Beef into health food stores in the Pacific Northwest and northern California and into the markets of Japan. And it created yet another opportunity in disguise.

Just when everything was finally going smoothly, the Hatfields received a call from the owner of one of their health food outlets saying there were people in his store dressed up in cow suits claiming that he was selling a cruel and environmentally destructive product. The Hatfields' response was typical of their open and honest way of handling problems: They asked the store owner to invite the demonstrators out to the ranch. "One of them actually came," Connie says. This encounter and others like it have led to the latest innovation to come from Doc and Connie and their collaborative community. To affirm their commitment to ranching practices that improve the environment rather than exploit it, the members of Oregon Country Beef (now also known as Country Natural Beef) have developed a set of principles. And they invite anyone to come out and see if they're living up to them.

As word of the Hatfields' success has spread, more and more ranchers across the West are pioneering creative solutions: conflict resolution through community-building initiatives, cattle management that achieves ecological as well as economic goals, and niche marketing of beef that is certified as a natural food. As a result, Doc and Connie are in big demand as speakers wherever ranchers are looking to turn problems into opportunities and confrontation into cooperation.

Preventing an Avalanche of Development: Upper Elk River Valley, Colorado

Sometimes even the best of ideas can come back to bite you. When John Fetcher started a ski resort in Steamboat Springs, Colorado, he said he did it to save his cattle ranch, which was "going down the drain financially." At the time Fetcher had no idea he might be creating an even greater threat to his way of life by building a resort. But that is just what happened. Upper Elk Valley turned into one of the fastest-growing recreation communities in Colorado. Recently John Fetcher and his family and their neighbors have found themselves looking for ways to keep the valley's meadows and foothills from being inundated with an avalanche of recreation homes attracted by the mushrooming resort.

First Fetcher and his neighbors got together for a goal-setting session. What they agreed on was a common vision that surprised no one:

They wanted the Upper Elk River Valley to remain a landscape of working ranches. To achieve this goal, Fetcher and his neighbors brainstormed a strategy of "protective development" and elicited help from Marty Zeller, a landscape architect from Denver. Working with the American Farmland Trust, Zeller helped the Fetchers and some of their neighbors set aside a limited number of building sites on their ranches in areas where they would have little or no impact on ranching operations and would not detract from the landscape's scenic or natural values. Then the ranchers donated conservation easements on the undeveloped remainder of their land to the American Farmland Trust.

By designing the homesites so they are secluded and scenic enough to demand top dollar, the easements have enabled participating ranchers to create a maximum amount of value while opening a minimum amount of land to development. The Upper Elk Valley Compact, as this plan has come to be called, even includes provisions for affordable employee housing so that rural community members aren't entirely displaced by wealthy urbanites.

Conservation easements have also contributed in what may be an even more important way to the ranchers' ability to maintain the security and sustainability of their property. The easements have reduced the taxable value of participating ranches sufficiently that when it comes time to pass these ranches on to the next generation, as another Colorado rancher, T. Wright Dickinson, puts it, the families won't "have to buy them back from the government first."

Community-Created Zoning Districts: Jefferson County, Montana

For many rural people, zoning is a dirty word—an intrusion of urban regulation into country lifestyles. In a growing number of rural areas, however, ranchers are discovering that zoning can be a useful tool to maintain the rural character of their community.

Western Montana's Jefferson County, just outside of Bozeman, is an area of rolling wheat fields and pasture with big sky vistas rimmed by surrounding mountains. Until recently it was also, as are so many areas like it, a county with no development controls. Attracted by the scenery as well as the cheap land and lack of development regulations, a couple of speculators bought isolated land sections within the county in 1992 and split them into 20-acre lots with no amenities: no water, no utilities, no access, not even surveyed boundaries. Then the speculators began an aggressive national marketing campaign and the lots began to sell. Neighbors did not find out what happened until buyers started showing up and looking for their land. That was enough for some county residents to see the writing on the wall. They had only to look to Bozeman, a few miles to the east, to see the logical outgrowth of what had begun to happen in this community. Around Bozeman, subdivisions are rapidly gobbling up the valleys and foothills that were once the home of family farms and ranches.

Convinced that quick action was needed, the board of county commissioners and a handful of local residents hired Bozeman consultant Keith Swenson to help them develop a comprehensive county plan. But some Jefferson County residents like Terry Murphy, a wheat farmer and former Montana legislator, didn't want an agency dictating what could or could not be done with their land. Swenson advised them to make use of Montana's 1953 Special Zoning Act—which empowers local residents to form their own zoning district if 60 percent of the landowners in the proposed district petition for it. The group then took the necessary steps to set up their own special zoning district to protect the rural nature of their homelands. The most effective way to do so, they decided, was to designate a minimum lot size of 640 acres—one full section. Smaller lots already in existence were exempted. Because the participants cherish their private property rights, they included a provision that only willing landowners would be subject to the zoning district. At the time of its formation, 84,000 acres were included in the special district. Now it is up to those who formed the district to inform their neighbors of its value and persuade them to join. Those who participated in the process are pleased that the solution was put together by community members rather than imposed by a government body. "The secret for farmers and ranchers is to get ahead of the game," says Jack Dawson. "I'm the third generation on this ranch, and maybe my kids will be the fourth."

CONCLUSION

The rapid change in the West today brings both challenges and opportunities for livestock producers looking to stay in business and leave an enduring conservation legacy. The tremendous pressure to develop scenic ranchlands, tight profit margins, and complex family and estate situations make it difficult to maintain the large, unfragmented landscapes needed to stay in operation and provide healthy wildlife habitat. At the same time, innovative pioneers are finding solutions to the challenges of our day. In cooperation with partners in land conservation, landowners are successfully experimenting with strategies that range from conservation easements to land-use planning and limited development, business diversification to new land-management techniques. The common thread that links the success stories in this chapter is a commitment to integrate inherited wisdom with new ideas. The most exciting trend is a balance between land protection strategies, a newly strengthened land ethic, and low-cost operations that are constantly on the lookout for new market opportunities. These mutually reinforcing approaches offer hope that we can sustain a vital tradition—productivity and land health.

Chapter 16

Cloudy Sky over the Range: Whose Home and Why It Matters

W. WILLIAM WEEKS

First an admission. Early in the process of making this book, one of our goals was to assemble an objective body of thought on the culture, ecology, and economics of ranching. I liked that goal. Pleased to be asked to contribute, I accepted the invitation. When it came time to deliver my essay, however, I realized that I am not objective.

I am biased. And the source of my bias is my commitment to conservation and my particular interest in the conservation of biological diversity. But I do believe I can be objective about the question of what ranching means to conservation. Indeed, my job and my interest in the conservation of biodiversity demand that of me.

RANCHING AND BIODIVERSITY

For readers who spend more of their time thinking about a few species and subspecies of the genus *Bos* than they do the global extinction crisis, I offer the following quick tutorial on biodiversity. Many biologists now conceive of biodiversity in terms of four or five levels of organization: from genes (the variation within species upon which evolution is built) to species (the most frequently cited standard of biodiversity) and natural communities (associations of species) and ecological systems (interacting combinations of natural communities) to landscapes. It's fair shorthand to say that if you want to achieve durable conservation at any of these levels of organization, you have to pursue it at the level *above* your target. But if you are committed to conservation, you can't afford to fail at any of these levels of biological organization. Conservation of biological diversity is a public good—not only because there is strong evidence that the public cares but also because it is difficult to reduce biodiversity to a private good that can be owned, bought, or sold.

The Nature Conservancy's mission is the conservation of biodiversity. I got interested in ranching because I kept running into ranchers as The Nature Conservancy pursued its mission in the West. At this point I want to add one more caveat with regard to my frame of reference. Unlike many contributors to this volume, I'm not an expert on ranching. Although I have used part of my time for a few years thinking about ranching and conservation, there is very little on the subject about which I am certain. And almost no point I will make here couldn't be improved by someone who knows more but doesn't happen to work for The Nature Conservancy.

Some years ago I concluded that those of us who are interested in the natural world would have to work with ranchers if we wanted to conserve biodiversity in the West. Today I am convinced that many ranchers serve a public purpose and provide a public economic benefit that is coincident to their basic work. This benefit is the management of land in a manner that helps to ensure the conservation of the West's biodiversity. With access to good science and good advice, many ranchers would do even better at serving this public purpose. I am not starry-eyed about ranching, and some of what I say here may not sit well with ranchers. But I suppose I am even less in step with the vocal current of environmental opinion today.

Maybe I have only gotten to know the best of ranchers. But a lot of the ranching folks I have met project a love of the land that makes them more like Nature Conservancy people than much of the rest of this country. The ranchers I know have a feeling for the land that is grounded in a deep and authentic knowledge of particular places. These ranchers are not attached to a mere image or a carefully edited series of images. Theirs is a real feeling for a real place: the real thing. I respect that. And I think it is a sound foundation for a durable commitment to conservation—maybe the only ground upon which a truly durable commitment to conservation of a lot of land can exist.

And to conserve biodiversity in the West, we have to conserve a lot of land. Since this is not a scientific paper, I will not worry too much about documenting my assertion that real conservation in the West means conservation of big landscapes. The aridity, the size of the unbroken pieces, the characteristic wildlife—all point to a scale of biodiversity that is bigger than the well-watered and naturally dissected East. As Arizona State University Professor Michael Rosenzweig and others have pointed out, over the long term the percentage of species we conserve will be approximately equal to the percentage of natural habitat available to them. In the United States, 60 percent of our land is no longer characterized by its native vegetation. If we push, we may be able to sustain, as a society, a lasting commitment to maintain as much as 15 percent of our country in parks and preserves. The rest of the land required to conserve our natural heritage must contribute what it can to conservation while it also fulfills other needs. Ranch land managed with environmental consciousness is better suited to this purpose than any other western land use we can foresee.

RANCH LAND'S VALUE AS OPEN SPACE

Ranching's potential gift to biological diversity conservation is not its only contribution to the public good. Ranching is a land use that occupies western ecosystems with a low-intensity economic activity that preserves an open feel, significant wildlife habitat, and scenic vistas. Society values these things. Certainly there are limits to our willingness to act on this value. On the one hand, The Nature Conservancy's million members and the increasing thousands of private land trusts are evidence of society's concern. Further evidence: The public will generally vote for bond issues to finance acquisition of parks and open space. And when asked, our diverse publics consistently equate quality of life with open space, healthy landscapes, and a vibrant natural heritage.

On the other hand, our reaction to abridging property rights with zoning is less positive. Moreover, we have been willing, as a society, to tolerate extensive conversion of ranches to subdivisions. (Indeed many of us buy homes in such subdivisions.) There have been efforts to resolve the implicit tension between our love of open space and our commitment to liberty of property. But our experience with proposals for publicly financed programs to purchase development rights is too recent to say whether most people will support that mechanism to preserve open space.

Some economists have tried to quantify, as a policy tool, the extent to which people value scenic open space. First economists ask them how much they would pay to go to a certain scenic place; then they repeat the question while altering aspects of the description or picture. The methodology strikes me as being about as exact as most polls—not very. Although the results clearly suggest that society places economic value on the kind of open space that ranching currently preserves in the West, they have not been useful in translating this value into a foundation for effective action to conserve open space. Routt County, Colorado commissioned a poll several years ago that endorsed ranches as a positive element in a visitor's experience in a western place. I suspect the basic result is generalizable: If you ask people whether they would like ranching to continue as a principal land use in much of the West—and do not suggest they will have to do something to make it happen—they will say yes, please, and thank you.

There are, of course, more conventional ways to measure the economic contributions of ranching in the West. The beef industry tells us that 20 percent of the nation's livestock grazes on public lands, most of which is west of the 100th meridian. I could not quite match that figure with the 2.3 million cattle said to be raised in thirteen western states—which would be just short of 7 percent of the 36 million cattle processed nationwide in 1995. In any case, business activity associated with cattle production, both nationally and across the West, is significant economically.

ECONOMIC CHANGE ON THE RANGE

On the whole, I don't think the demographic patterns and land-use trends we see in the West today threaten its economic activity. Where ranches are replaced by subdivisions, the beef economy will be replaced and even outperformed by a different one. The land and the quality of life will suffer, but not "the economy." Where subdivision is a less immediate threat, the beef economy will prevail but continue to change. As the Department of Agriculture has said: "As in all of agriculture, competitive pressure to reduce unit costs has brought a trend to fewer and larger cattle businesses." But there is a countervailing current: Apparently a lot of the beef processed in this country—one rancher told me half—comes from herds of twenty head or fewer and cattle operations that cannot represent anything more than incidental income to their owners. There is no particular reason to think that hobby ranchers will go out of business very soon. It is the family ranch of western tradition and public imagination that is vulnerable to the "competitive pressure" cited by the Department of Agriculture. Before exploring the nature of this pressure, I want to develop the theme about why we should care. Why should we care wheter ranching continues to contribute to a conservation whole and, specifically, whether family ranches remain a vital part of the ranching mix?

The twenty-head folks are not holding down landscape of the scale we need in the West. The big corporate ranches that are coming probably will. But the owners of these ranches will be motivated largely by raw economics. They are going to want to earn—their shareholders will usually demand that they earn—the highest short-term profit possible. Many of their decisions will be driven by the imperatives of the next quarter's earning report. When development makes more sense than raising cattle, the corporate ranch will sell for development.

This, incidentally, brings to mind yet another element of the economics of ranching. With regard to public services, ranches and farms almost always cost units of local government less to service than the ranchettes or subdivisions that are fast replacing them. This savings is often recognized by one of the few expressions of public favor for the industry: special status with respect to local property taxes. Because public acceptance of agricultural district taxing is not based solely on the service cost differential, but also on a desire to maintain agricultural land use and lifestyles, this is an area of public incentives for ranching that ought to be considered for enhancement.

Another often cited public economic benefit of ranching is its contribution to the control of exotic and invasive species. Invasives surely pose a serious threat to biodiversity. In fact, The Nature Conservancy considers them a major threat second only, perhaps, to residential development. There is no particular reason to prefer family ranches to corporate ownership on this ground: All ranches are potentially allies in the campaign to control invasive species as well as the reintroduction of fire to a landscape that thrived on occasional fire and is now generally deprived of it. Ranchers have not always been great stewards. Nor are all ranchers great stewards now. Indeed some ranchers, sometimes acting on recommendations from state and federal advisers, are still introducing exotic species into the West—often on the theory that doing so will speed recovery of the land from some past abuse. There is no quick cure for abused land. There is only a slow cure. As one rancher told me, you do not buy a perfect ranch, you build one—and it takes about forty years. And this, by the way, is also, in my estimation, the number of years it will take to secure a conservation future for any landscape we care about.

Much of the western range, it can be granted, is not as healthy or resilient as it would have been without poor ranching practices. But ranchers have always fought invasive species. And some ranchers conduct (and more can be persuaded to allow) prescribed burns. Without people to conduct this kind of active management, much of our western range will follow a course of plant succession that cannot be called natural and is, from a biodiversity perspective, less desirable than the likely future of that range under enlightened management by ranchers. It's hard to imagine maintaining and restoring working ecosystems in the West—a task of enormous magnitude—without a partnership with skilled people inclined to work hard outdoors.

Big corporate ranches and medium-size family-owned ranches alike provide suitable habitat for animals many people care about: elk, deer, pronghorn, game birds. I have to note here, however, that society also likes (at a distance) birds of prey, wolves, bears, big cats, and prairie dogs. Most ranchers are not great protectors of any of these latter elements of our western natural heritage. But good science, good communication, and economic incentives can change ranchers' minds on this subject, too.

Either corporate ranchers or family ranchers might respond in the short term to a well-made case for preserving the West's biodiversity. But I like our long-term chances better with family ranchers. The economic motivation to which families respond includes more subtleties than does the corporation designed to be responsive to absentee holders of the business's capital. Family ranchers have always taken, as part of the return they seek, the opportunity to offer their children and grandchildren the ranching life they so value. And many ranchers have always taken part of their return in the opportunity to live the ranch life themselves. They value the independence, the outdoor work, the open spaces, the scenery, the seasons, the wild and domesticated animals, and the ranching community. They do not have to prepare a quarterly report for shareholders; they can forgo the maximum return today for that better ranch a few years, maybe even forty years, from now. At best they need only answer to themselves and their sense of family commitment to a place when it comes to doing the right thing for the land.

For these reasons, at least, it is a matter of significant concern that the prospects for family ranching appear to be poor. Agriculture in general has been under economic pressure for the last twenty years. I compared the USDA's net farm and ranch income statistics for the years 1993 through 1996 to the USDA's figures on the value of farmland and buildings for the same years. The average return, 5.7 percent, overstates the return on equity because certain elements of capital costs, such as farm and ranch equipment, are not included. The *real* return on equity that agricultural businesses could offer was, on average, somewhere between one-fourth and one-third of the return generally required to attract capital to a business. Conversations with agricultural lenders, real estate people, and ranchers lead me to believe that returns on ranch equity in recent years have been, at best, a couple of percentage points below that overall agriculture figure. Surely most ivory tower economists would expect western ranching to have disappeared already.

There is more. There is an unmistakable trend toward globalized markets for products and commodities. If you are a rancher, you may think of global markets as a positive thing. And to date, they do seem to have been positive: The United States, with 10 percent of the planet's cattle, exports enough beef to supply 25 percent of the world market. But as we open our markets to beef raised elsewhere, there will be producers from other countries who can supply beef of acceptable quality for a lower price than western ranchers. And the "competitive pressure" will grow a little more intense.

KEEPING RANCHERS ON THE LAND

A year or so ago, I was listening to a business school professor discuss the Internet's impact on markets. By way of explaining that it would eventually eliminate less efficient producers, he claimed it would do the same thing to marginal producers that the railroads had done to family agriculture a hundred years ago. The implication was clear: Family agriculture was a barely remembered feature of times past.

Well, family ranches have not, in fact, quite disappeared. And despite what some ranchers say, we have at least a little time. (As a rancher once told me: "Ranchers love to complain about how bad things are. Some people even believe them.") But there isn't anything imaginary about the general trends I have cited. So what is to be done? If we, as a society, want to secure the public benefits that western family ranches offer, it seems to me we have some bargains to strike. I realize that by saying so, I've parted company with half the ranchers who read this—and half the environmentalists.

The ranchers I have lost are saying that I have just finished making the outlines of a case for the good things they do and the problems they have doing them. To them it seems clear that society ought just to do the right thing and compensate them for providing these benefits (or at least stop making it harder for them to provide them). They aren't excited about the insulting, wasteful, and often ill-fitting constraints of "deals with the public." And the environmentalists are saying that nobody should have to give anything to ranchers for conducting their business in a way that accords minimal respect to the land and its native inhabitants.

To the offended ranchers I say: The public cares about western ranching. But not that much. It won't pay very much just to keep family ranching alive. It might, however, pay to guarantee that ranching continues to provide direct and indirect support for a functioning western landscape that the public cares very much about indeed.

To the environmentalists I say: We need the part of the landscape now held down by ranches as part of our conservation portfolio in the West—and we have no assurance that we can continue to count on it. If we can strike a bargain that makes a compatible kind of ranching better able to withstand the increasing competitive pressures of development, we will get, and keep, more of that kind of ranching. The alternative—for the next generation anyway—is not a pristine landscape. It is a landscape characterized mostly by three land uses that are far less promising for conservation than compatible ranching: corporate ranching oriented toward short-term profit and long-term speculation on eventual sale for development; degraded range overrun by exotic invasive species and woody replacements for native grasslands; or sprawl and ranchette development. I like the idea of making some deals better.

I cannot say with confidence how well any of the arrangements I'm going to outline would work. On balance though, I have decided to go ahead and present them in the hope that doing so will serve the causes we care about because someone will take the rough sketch presented here and make a better one. The first three bargains are public. And they are deals that will probably not be made by ranchers or conservationists working alone, but might be made if we work together.

I have already mentioned one possible bargain that could be struck with ranchers at the local level: Keep your land in agricultural use, and we'll grant you a concessionary property tax rate. The terms of this well-established bargain could be refined and improved. We ought to examine the qualifying definitions of agriculture with large-landscape conservation in mind. There ought to be recapture provisions that require payment of at least five years of back taxes at the development rate if there is development. And perhaps the taxing authority ought to guarantee a low and stable rate for a long term upon the recording of a permanent commitment against subdivision. Low property taxes will not resolve the issues facing family ranching. But they will send the right signal, and one that is economically meaningful on the margin.

A second tax incentive, potentially more powerful, would have to be forged at the federal level. Ranchers frequently cite estate tax bills as the blow that forces subdivision. Sometimes selling ranch land is the only way to raise the cash needed to pay big tax bills on land that isn't generating a competitive return on the equity and will be taxed in an intergenerational transfer. Farmers and ranchers could get relief under provisions of a tax code amended to permit the transfer of agricultural land at agricultural value—if it is maintained in that use for ten years following its transfer. But the upper limit on the land value that can be sheltered under these provisions is significantly short of the value of many ranches of the size that ranchers and conservationists would like to see kept intact. Perhaps we ought to consider exempting from estate taxes any land committed permanently to agriculture or conservation use. Some people who might support this idea are disinterested because they expect Congress to repeal estate taxation altogether. And it may, after a struggle. But this lesser reform might be adopted more quickly. And how much land could we save if we could market this incentive for conservation and agriculture right now? How many costs of inappropriate development could we avoid?

I will do no more than mention a third option. Recently I heard Senator Tom Harkin propose that the nation replace farm price supports and agricultural bailouts with a dependable system of stewardship payments. Though prospects for this idea are dim in the short term, the proposal is worthy of serious conversation. Coming up with a half-decent set of stewardship standards that would qualify farmers and ranchers for the payments would be a messy process that would have to be pursued in a decentralized fashion. But I think it could be done. Ranchers haven't traditionally received federal support comparable to that available to farmers. But the impact on the natural world of paying ranchers for land stewardship west of the 100th meridian would be at least as great as that which could be achieved by paying the nation's crop farmers. For public-land ranchers, these payments might not even require appropriation. Instead they might come as part of a package of requirements associated with lowering or eliminating grazing fees. Those who can hardly imagine a new public policy that might prolong grazing on public land need to take a big leap of imagination. Imagine how the public lands might look if we gave a competitive advantage to the ranchers who accommodated the full spectrum of values we hope to get from these lands. There are arid lands on which, it must be admitted, any commercially remunerative grazing substantially compromises biodiversity conservation. Prolonging that grazing is a compromise worth considering, though, given the substance and effect of increasing sprawl and commercial development throughout the West.

My confidence in public processes and institutions is no more robust than that of most Americans these days. So to those who insist that federal bargains are bound to generate disappointment and disillusionment in the end, I would defer—but only after trying them. For this reason and others, The Nature Conservancy and some collaborators, principally a Montana nonprofit called Artemis/Common Ground, have been developing a three-way bargain involving ranchers, conservation organizations, and conservation-conscious consumers. Some years ago we polled a statistically acceptable group of people across the country to ask whether they would be interested in buying high-quality beef that was raised to conserve western landscapes and the family ranching tradition. To the astonishment of food marketing professionals, most people we surveyed said yes—and most said they would pay a premium for beef that met our product description.

Our advisers told us that people buy food to eat, not to save the world. And they weren't all wrong. The survey made it clear that people weren't interested in a new source of mediocre beef at a premium price even if conservation came attached to it. Indeed, they ranked the elements of our product description in this order: delicious beef, conserve western landscapes, family ranching tradition. Twice as many people cited delicious beef as most important than those who cited landscapes, and landscapes drew three times more support than family ranching. But the consumers seemed to see a relationship between all three elements. They believed they might well get better beef if it was raised to satisfy the other two elements of the description. And they surely thought someone might be able to supply better beef than the beef they were currently buying.

Armed with these expressions of market interest, we started working with ranchers in the Madison and the Big Hole valleys in Montana, the Yampa Valley of Colorado, and the Malpai Borderlands region in the Southwest to try to define "Conservation Beef." We conceived of it as a product that could support a consistently profitable price to ranchers, allowing them to legitimately plan on being able to sustain lives and families on their land. And if The Nature Conservancy were willing to design and monitor the conservation elements of the product, consumers would be assured of the legitimacy of the conservation claim and could find a way to express their interest in all the public benefits of ranching. As the program took shape, it incorporated a group of stewardship commitments that focused on land, water, vegetation, soil, and wildlife. And it required that participating ranchers agree to significant disincentives against subdivision. Along the way, the folks in the Yampa Valley blazed their own path, setting different standards with many of the same overall objectives, and have had a promising start marketing Yampa Valley Beef in Steamboat Springs.

We tested our own product and marketing in the fall of 1999 with a limited program of seasonal sales to upscale restaurants and a 140,000-

piece direct mail retail program. We sold—at prices that could sustain the business—all of the marketable steaks from the ninety or so animals we bought for the test, and we sold about as much ground beef, at premium prices, as steak. People liked the product so much that a remarkable 30 percent of our buyers specifically told us so by returning a customer survey we mailed out a few months later. And in response to a neutrally phrased question about the product's purpose, our customers wrote essays. They got the idea. They care how food is produced and they liked the terms of the bargain we were testing.

We have a lot of work to do—and a lot of burger to sell at a premium price—before we can say we have a real business and a fair bargain to offer family ranchers. But the test showed enough promise that we're going to continue the project.

A FAIR BARGAIN

At this time, we don't have a fair bargain to offer ranchers. No one can say whether the market we have targeted will be developed fully or will last. Yet we are insisting, as we think we must, on a robust conservation package that includes significant disincentives against subdivision—disincentives that aren't linked to the life of the Conservation Beef business.

A tough-minded analyst might point out that we'll simply sign up ranchers who are already committed—those who just need an excuse to commit the land they love to the uses they really want to save it for. Several ranchers considering the program have pointed out that even if we are successful, the higher cattle prices we offer won't service the development value of the ranch in exchange for the commitments we require against development.

To the argument that subdivision restrictions eliminate a big part of the only serious item of value that many ranchers have to pass on to their children, I have two responses. First, ranchers can exclude some parcels for limited development that interferes as little as possible with agricultural and ecological function. Second, many of us would just as soon the kids not go out and buy the Mercedes with some developer's dollars when we're gone. Because we know that the land that's a part of us (and vice versa) will still be there and ought to survive us.

You can see that it isn't an easy bargain to strike. A rancher has to care enough about the land and the future of the West to decide to make subdivision hard or impossible, knowing there are risks we can't be certain about. You'd only do it if you thought that keeping the land open and a little wild was likely to be as right or more right in the future as it is now.

This brings us to the interwoven subthemes of this book. We're compelled to talk about return on investment, the development value of ranches, and economics in general. The content of the book reflects our experience as well as the power of our habits. Culture, ecology, and economy really are related. Economic analysis is useful in helping us understand our society and predict its direction. But we should not leave this topic without asking whether that's really the way we want to look at the problem.

My sixteen-year-old son, having read during the past eight months all of the Kurt Vonnegut there is to read, suspects there is no purpose to life. Although I am inclined to differ with him, I'm less certain than past generations that our purpose includes inexorable progress toward some better destination. But at least he's considering the question. One thing I do know is that the purpose of life cannot be to make the most money possible. Maybe the purpose is as simple as for us to live well in the place where we live. What purpose makes better sense?

Living well doesn't mean cultivating the tastes of an epicure. It means living in the best possible harmony with the physical and biological environment—our human community, the associations of plants and animals that surround us, and the geological setting for all of that. By this standard, public and private bargains in support of the best kind of ranching look like a pretty good idea. Because ranching the way some family ranchers are doing it is not an anachronism. It's a different answer to the questions the rest of us face all the time. And we ought to be paying attention.

Part Five

EPILOGUE

Going to Buy Heifers
The Death of Jesse Parker

DRUMMOND HADLEY

We turn onto a dirt road
Calves scamper away toward the West
Tail hairs flying shimmering in the sunlight
I'll bet those little farts'll weigh 500 pounds
In the fall if it rains Bill Bryan says
It's been 40 years since I been down this road
Paloma my girl friend lived right through that gap
We turn on the road to Terlingua
We stop to look toward some brindled brahma cross cows
Come in out of the desert country to Terlingua Creek
To shade up under the cottonwoods at noontime
Here by this willow spring Bill Bryan says
I'll bet my grandaddy watered his horse a few times
He's buried in that country toward the southeast
Near Boquillas by the Big Bend
His grave is by the side of the new paved road
Jesse Parker was his name
He was cutting whyula on a ridge top
When his horse came home in June
That was the first they knew something was wrong
It's quite a ways from here to Boquillas
Hot as it gets in June
By the time the horse showed up
His body sure must have been a mess
Blue Bonnet blooming beside the road
Yellow poppies just barely swaying
A butterfly crossing in the morning sunlight
Nobody knows what happened

Chapter 17

Why This Book Matters

ED MARSTON

This is a loving book, but not a sentimental book. Like ranching, this book is tough love. The first thing we do is declare ourselves for ranching. Then we invite all those we think can help ranching and disinvite all those who we think could hurt ranching. We respect the sincerity of those who wish to see pristine western lands and the sincerity of those who wish to see pristine private property. But we who wish to see ranching and landscapes and communities thrive know that for the moment our search for direction will go forward better without them.

And, by the way, they are not the only ones who are treated toughly. Several essayists tell ranchers that the strongest currents of the modern world—the Wal-Mart culture; an economic system that prizes cheap food; the rancher's hunger for personal wide open spaces—are flowing against them and their industry. The essayists also say that, to survive, ranchers must continue to live a marginal economic existence while changing many of their most cherished beliefs and ways of doing business. To take one example, they must cease thinking of themselves as primarily producers of red meat and start thinking of themselves as providers of an array of goods and services that urban society wants—biodiversity, healthy watersheds, and open space, for instance.

More painfully, ranchers must learn to go back and forth between their rural world and the urban world in order to sell themselves, their livestock, and their social values to our society at large. They can no longer live solely in remote, rural spaces, congratulating themselves on their quality of life and lack of responsibility for what goes on in the congested urban world. The price of maintaining ranches and a rural life will be a growing interaction with urban people and urban ways.

And these prescriptions come from the self-described "friends" of ranching. Having friends like us may be enough to send most ranchers in search of a real estate developer (who several writers here assure us are prowling the West with big bucks to pay for pretty, subdividable ranch land).

In fairness to the book, and in the hope of stopping the rancher/reader before he or she sells out, the writers are even tougher on nonranchers. The most consistent pounding is delivered to the consumerist culture—a culture from which family ranchers are largely excluded by their low cash incomes. Tom Field, for example, asks: What kind of society would prefer a Wal-Mart to a meadow? And if the example of Wal-Mart lets you—the reader—off the hook, then substitute a Subaru showroom or factory, or the many coffeehouses in the West, or the offices of your favorite nonprofit organization, or the local REI store.

And a few chapters are very tough on the environmental movement's tendency to see cows as the source of all evil. It starts with Paul Starrs in Chapter 1 writing of the extremes of the wilderness movement: "Even more insidious today is the percolation of that benevolent pro-wilderness, antihuman sensibility steeped into those of us who grew up in the 1970s, started college in the 1980s, and graduated to become observers and students of the public domain in the 1990s. We watched, agape and eventually aghast, as the sides spread wide apart, ever intransigent, often absurd in their militancy (or militant in their absurdity?)."

If this makes the book sound as if it's against ranching and against ranching's opponents, then I've misled you. These writers are not taking the easy way out. They are not painting with broad brushstrokes. They are looking at the devil—at the details. Each chapter searches for the strengths in ranching and points out its weaknesses. And the essayists are honest about their relationship to ranching. Bill Weeks of The Nature Conservancy makes it clear that he can take or leave cows. But Weeks and The Nature Conservancy are committed to protecting large stretches of land in the most natural state possible. And that leads him to line up with those who wish to reform and preserve ranching. Herds of livestock and western grasslands, in the hands of skilled and committed and knowledgeable ranchers, are one of the best ways Weeks and his organization know to protect and restore land.

This book won't be a best-seller. Best-sellers are full of dramatic questions followed immediately, breathlessly, by dramatic answers. This book asks excellent questions, but there are no sweeping answers announced with a drum roll. The questions it asks, often implicitly, include the following: Are there people who believe that the environmental movement can gain long-term political control of the West's federal and private rangelands? And if so, would a centralized federal bureaucracy then be able to restore the land by imposing its ideas on the land and the associated communities? The people who are attracted to this book will admit that long-term control of federal lands lies beyond the ability of a national environmental movement. Environmentalism, the movement, has done a wonderful job of making Americans conscious of the 29 percent of the nation that is federally owned. But elections still swing on the economy and on racial policies and on "choice" or "abortion," as you choose. Federal lands will always be a tail wagged by national politics so long as control of these lands is centralized in Washington, D.C. Public land policies make abrupt tacks left and right each time someone new moves into the White House or appoints a new chief of staff or secretary of interior.

Should we therefore put our faith in privatizing the federal lands? It might work—anything might work—but it's not going to happen. Thanks to the environmental movement, the American people have become incredibly attached to the public lands. Moreover, the law of the land—the 1976 Federal Lands Policy Management Act—dictates that the U.S. government will retain the federal lands. Privatization, either politically or legally, is no longer a possibility.

These twin realities—the inability of centralized control to plot a long-term path to a sustainable future and the impossibility of privatizing federal lands—force us to seek a mix of public and private, local and national, communitarian and legalistic. In other words, we are all in Bill Weeks' place: We can't have exactly what we want; but the platter of options before us should satisfy most appetites and meet most needs.

The options are laid out here: conservation easements, economic diversification, conservation biology, and the integration of ranching—as food producer and protector of biological systems and open lands—into society at large. But the book also points the way in a human sense. Because these chapters, like ranching itself, are about community. A diverse group—academics, ranchers, environmentalists, economic developers—has come together here to grapple with a problem that society must solve if it is to become the kind of society they wish to live in.

To pursue this goal, to join this community, they make sacrifices. The academics remain authoritative but work hard to speak plainly to a mixed audience. The environmentalists declare themselves clearly in favor of a working landscape and in favor of people, ranchers, they often fight. The economists apply themselves to an economy most of their colleagues wouldn't deign to bother with, so low is its economic "output" in terms of dollars. But the ranchers take the biggest and hardest step of all: proud, self-reliant, inward people going before a bunch of outsiders and declaring themselves in need of help.

It will be hard for some to see community in a collection of essays. But those who attended the May 2000 meeting at Colorado State University in Fort Collins, where these and other essays were first presented, will understand. When rancher and nonrancher gatherings first began a decade ago, they were always self-conscious and self-congratulatory: "Isn't it amazing we were actually here without shouting at each other?" Two exotic species looked at each other across lunch and conference tables.

But at CSU those days were long past. Of course we'd come together to solve this problem; we understood that when we signed on. Of course we knew we needed researchers and poets and ranchers and environmentalists. We are all part of the problem; we have to be part of the solution.

And of course we knew we weren't going to come out of a three-day meeting with a single solution. We are grown-ups in a grown-up community, even if it's a new community. And although we prize the concept, we weren't going to waste time talking about consensus and collaboration because that's what we do as naturally as we used to fight.

The value of this book lies in the tools and perspectives it offers. It stands as a marker in a long road toward a healthy, beautiful, biologically diverse western range peopled by healthy, beautiful human communities. To paraphrase Wallace Stegner's wonderful line, we are taking a few steps on the road to a society that may, someday, match its scenery.

| Contributors

Ben Alexander is director of the Working Landscapes Program at the Sonoran Institute. He manages an integrated program of research, outreach, and place-based work designed to maintain and improve the health of agricultural landscapes in the West. Alexander works out of the institute's Northwest Office in Bozeman, Montana. He holds a B.A. in history from Tufts University and an M.A. in American studies from Yale.

Mark Brunson is a professor in the College of Natural Resources at Utah State University, where he specializes in the human dimensions of natural resource management. His research and writing have focused on the relationships between people's knowledge of nature, their attitudes toward natural resources and their management, and their behaviors in natural and political settings. A former environmental journalist, he once lived on a small hay-and-livestock farm in Montana.

Bob Budd is director of stewardship for The Nature Conservancy in Wyoming and manages the 35,000-acre Red Canyon Ranch near Lander. Before attaining that position in 1993, he spent fifteen years with the Wyoming Stock Growers Association and Wyoming Beef Council, ten as executive director. Budd has been recognized for his work in rangeland management and ecology in the western United States and has received stewardship awards from the U.S. Forest Service, Bureau of Land Management, Wyoming Riparian Association, and ReNew

America. He is currently president-elect of the Society for Range Management. He has written four business histories and two popular books of western humor: *Send Fresh Horses* (1987) and *A Wide Spot in the Road* (1990). He and his wife Lynn have three children, Joe, Jake, and Maggie.

Leah M. Burgess is presently a program assistant for the American Farmland Trust. She has worked for public land management agencies in the West and as a protected-area manager in the Philippines. Her degree is from Colorado State University.

Larry D. Butler is currently director of the Grazing Lands Technology Institute of the Natural Resources Conservation Service in Fort Worth, Texas. He provides national leadership to the NRCS in the development and transfer of technology pertinent to rangeland and pastureland with personal expertise in enterprise diversification, range economics, wildlife and recreation enterprises, and nontraditional uses of all types of grazing lands. Previously he served as a range conservationist for the NRCS across much of the West. He has a Ph.D. in range science from Utah State University.

Wayne Elmore is currently team leader for the Interagency National Riparian Service Team charged with implementing an approach to cooperative riparian restoration and management. Formerly he served as field manager for the National Riparian Program at the Bureau of Land Management. Elmore has a broad background in forestry, fisheries, wildlife, and range management. He has given over 500 presentations on riparian function, potential, and management. He has been recognized with numerous achievement awards including the Chevron National Conservation Award and the National Fish and Wildlife Foundation Chuck Yeager Award.

Tom Field is an associate professor in the Department of Animal Sciences at Colorado State University. He serves as the director of the Beef Industry Leadership Master's Program. A native of Gunnison, Colorado, he grew up on a high country ranch. His research efforts are focused on beef cattle management systems designed to generate sustainable profits.

Wendell C. Gilgert is a wildlife biologist with the Wildlife Habitat Management Institute of the Natural Resources Conservation Service in the Department of Fishery and Wildlife Biology at Colorado State University. He received his undergraduate and graduate degrees in biology and plant and soil science at California State University–Chico. Since going to work with the NRCS he has served as a soil conservationist and district conservationist in northern California. Gilgert is a past president of the Watershed Management Council and is certified as a wetland scientist. A native of California, he was reared on a fourth-generation family farm in the northern San Joaquin Valley where farming that promotes wildlife is a family tradition.

Drummond Hadley is a rancher and poet. After graduating from the University of Arizona with a master's degree in English, he worked on ranches in New Mexico, Arizona, Wyoming, and Old Mexico. In 1972 he and his family bought the Guadalupe Canyon Ranch in southeastern Arizona. He has published three books of poetry—*The Webbing* (Don Allen's Four Seasons), *Strands of Rawhide* (Goliard Press), and *The Spirit by the Deep Well Tank* (Goliard Press)—and is working on a book of narrative poems based on the voices of the people of the borderlands. He recently created the Animas Foundation to purchase the 500-square-mile Gray Ranch, a working wilderness in the borderland country of southwestern New Mexico. He is a founding member of the Malpai Borderlands Group.

Linda M. Hasselstrom earned her living by working on the family cattle ranch in South Dakota and from freelance writing and conducting workshops in writing and publishing. She holds an M.A. in American literature from the University of Missouri. Her nonfiction titles include *Windbreak, Going Over East,* and *Land Circle.* Her most recent works include the coedited *Woven on the Wind: Women Write About Friendship in the Sagebrush West* and two collections of poems, *Dakota Bones* and *Bittercreek Junction.* Since 1992 she has spent winters in Cheyenne, Wyoming, writing from a changed perspective, but her writing still centers on the ranch she now owns.

Lynn Huntsinger is an associate professor in the Department of Environmental Science, Policy, and Management at the University of California–Berkeley. Over the last fifteen years she has examined the transformation of ranching in California as urbanization advances across the state's millions of acres of private rangeland. She has surveyed and interviewed ranchers in California, Nevada, Utah, and southern Oregon, asking them why they ranch and how they cope with the new neighbors, new problems, and new opportunities presented by the values, lifestyles, and goals of California's growing population.

Jeff R. Jones is the Rocky Mountain field director for the American Farmland Trust. In this position he provides research and technical assistance and carries out land demonstration projects for the Rocky Mountain region. His work experience includes working as a stewardship forester for the Colorado State Forest Service as well as research and conservation planning in Sri Lanka under the Fulbright Junior Scholar program. Jeff Jones has a J.D. from the University of Denver College of Law and an M.S. in natural resource planning from Colorado State University.

Richard L. Knight is a professor of wildlife conservation at Colorado State University. His research interests deal with the ecological effects of the conversion of a West best defined as a workscape to the New West, perhaps best termed a playscape. He sits on the board of governors for the Society for Conservation Biology, the Natural Resources Law Center, the Colorado Wildlife Federation, the Colorado Cattleman's Agricultural Land Trust, and the Science Advisory Board of the Malpai Borderlands Group. He has coedited *A New Century for Natural Resources Management*; *Wildlife and Outdoor Recreation*; *The Essential Aldo Leopold*; *Stewardship Across Boundaries*; and *Forest Fragmentation in the Southern Rocky Mountains*. He was recently named an Aldo Leopold Leadership Fellow (Ecological Society of America) for his work in communicating scientific information to a diverse audience. With his wife Heather he practices community-based conservation with their neighbors in Livermore Valley, Colorado.

Page Lambert, still in love with her native Colorado, has lived for the last fifteen years with her husband (a fifth-generation rancher) and their two teenagers on a small ranch in the Black Hills of Wyoming. Author of the Rocky Mountain nonfiction bestseller *In Search of Kinship*, as well as *Shifting Stars*, a novel of the West, Lambert has presented more than a hundred workshops and readings throughout the West and Canada. She was one of fifteen women writers selected from around the nation to contribute to *Writing Down the River: Into the Heart of Grand Canyon* and has contributed to numerous anthologies: *Leaning into the Wind: Women Write from the Heart of the West; Woven on the Wind: Women Write About Friendship in the Sagebrush West; The Stories That Shape Us: Contemporary Women Write About the West; Tumblewords: Writers Reading the West;* and the upcoming anthology *Deep West: A Wyoming Literary Guide*. She is currently at work on three books: *In Search of Story: Exploring the Writing Landscape; Lifeblood: Rivers of Living Water;* and *Confluence*, a contemporary novel set in Denver.

Steve Leonard is the range ecological and grazing systems specialist on the Interagency National Riparian Service Team. Previously a range specialist for the BLM in Reno, Nevada, he has worked on the Range Health Indicator Project, served as rangeland coleader for the Interior Columbia Basin Science Assessment, and provided inventory and monitoring advice as a National Range Program field representative. With ten years on the National Soil-Range Inventory Team (BLM/NRCS), Leonard's experience extends throughout the West. He has been a state range conservationist in Utah and a range and natural resource specialist in Colorado and New Mexico. Prior to that he managed a cattle operation in North Park, Colorado.

Ed Marston has been the publisher of *High Country News* since 1983. *HCN* is a regional biweekly newspaper covering public land and natural resource issues in the western United States for 22,000 subscribers. Marston, a New Yorker by birth, received his B.S. from City College of New York and his Ph.D. in experimental physics from the State University of New York at Stony Brook in 1968. He and his wife, Betsy, have lived in Paonia, Colorado, a coal-mining and fruit-growing town, since 1974. He has written or edited four books. His "Colorado Memoir" appeared in *Colorado 1870–2000* by W. H. Jackson and John Fielder. Marston is on the Advisory Council of the Rocky Mountain Office of Environmental Defense and is serving his fifth term as an elected board member of the Delta-Montrose Electric Association, a rural electric co-op serving 25,000 families and businesses in Delta and Montrose counties.

Luther Propst is executive director of the Sonoran Institute, a nonprofit organization based in Tucson, Arizona. He has coauthored two books: *Balancing Nature and Commerce in Gateway Communities* and *Preserving Working Ranches in the West*.

Allan Savory, founding director of the Allan Savory Center for Holistic Management, was born in southern Africa where he pursued an early career as a research biologist and game ranger in the British Colonial Service of what was then Northern Rhodesia (today Zambia), and later as a farmer and game rancher in Southern Rhodesia (today Zimbabwe). He served as a member of parliament in the latter days of Zimbabwe's civil war and was leader of the opposition to the ruling party headed by Ian Smith. Exiled in 1979 as a result of his opposition, he emigrated to the United States where he co-founded the Center for Holistic Management with his wife, Jody Butterfield. Their most recent book, *Holistic Management: A New Framework for Decision-Making*, was published in 1999.

Paul F. Starrs is a writer and geographer who teaches at the University of Nevada, in Reno. An alumnus of Deep Springs College and the University of California–Berkeley, his knowledge of ranching has been learned first hand. His special interests are people, natural resources, and the landscapes and communities they generate. Author of *Let the Cowboy Ride: Cattle Ranching in the American West*, Starrs has also written some eighty articles, essays, and reviews. He lives in California and Nevada with his two daughters and his wife, Lynn Huntsinger.

Martha J. Sullins is a research associate with the American Farmland Trust. She has a master's degree from Michigan State University in agricultural economics.

David T. Theobald received his Ph.D. in geography from the University of Colorado. Presently he has a Smith Fellowship from The Nature Conservancy. He is coeditor of *Atlas of the New West: Portrait of a Changing Region.*

George Wallace is an associate professor in the College of Natural Resources at Colorado State University. His teaching, research, and outreach efforts focus on land-use planning, park and protected area management, and land stewardship. He works both nationally and internationally on a variety of research, training, and technical assistance projects through CSU's Center for Protected Area Management and Training. He is a member of the IUCN's World Commission on Protected Areas. A third-generation Coloradan, Wallace is a planning commissioner and co-chairs the Agricultural Advisory Board in Larimer County. With his wife, Nancy, he owns and operates a farm north of Fort Collins, Colorado.

W. William Weeks practiced law with an emphasis on securities and antitrust litigation in Indianapolis between 1979 and 1982. In 1982 he joined The Nature Conservancy as director of its Indiana program and in 1988 was named The Nature Conservancy's chief operating officer and assumed management responsibility for some 2,000 employees involved in science and conservation programs in the United States, Latin America, and the Pacific. Between 1990 and 1994, he led The Nature Conservancy's movement toward adopting an ecosystem approach to conservation. Since 1995 he has directed the Center for Compatible Economic Development as a focal point for these efforts in The Nature Conservancy. He was appointed executive vice-president in 1998. His book on ecosystem conservation and compatible economic development, *Beyond the Ark*, was published by Island Press in 1996.

| Index

Abbey, Edward, 180
adaptive management, 38, 201
advocacy groups: animal rights, 82, 214;
    grazing and environment cooperatives,
    153–54; grazing associations, 125;
    litigation by, 152; on stream recovery
    with grazing, 151. *See also*
    environmental conservationists; ranchers
aged ranchers, 43. *See also* estate planning;
    estate taxes
agricultural district tax plans, 223, 227
agricultural trade magazines, conservation
    buyer contacts through, 209
agriculture, California's growth in, 79
alliances: economies of scale and, 189–90;
    nontraditional, 202. *See* collaborative
    planning; cooperative organizations;
    partnerships
American Conservation Real Estate, 211
American Farm Bureau Federation, farming
    perception poll by, 93–94
American Farmland Trust, 30, 215
Americans, Brenan on rootless nature of,
    13–14
animal impact, as rangeland management
    tool, 161, 167
animal–plant interactions, grazing and,
    119–20
animal rights, 82, 214
Artemis/Common Ground, 228–29
art on rock, ancient, 114–15

bald eagles, 62, 73
bankers, 40–41
Bar 99 Ranch, Fish Lake Valley, Nev., 6
Baum, L. Frank, 50
Bear Creek, Oregon, restoration of, 147–48
biodiversity: chaos, confusion and, 117–18;

in Europe vs. U.S., 15–16; grazing and,
    86; healthy rangelands and, 155–56;
    land use and, 14; ranching and, 219–21
bioregional ethic, Powell on, 12
birds, human-adapted vs. generalist species
    of, 132–34
birthing: cattle, 64–65, 66; sheep, 65–66
bison: landscape shaping and, 116, 117. *See
    also* buffalo commons
boomers (baby), rangeland development
    and, 132
brand name products, 188, 190, 192–93,
    200
Brenan, Gerald, 13
British army artillery, staffing for, 184–85,
    193
brittle environments: fires in, 162;
    nonbrittle environments vs., 157–59
Brown, Jim, 130–31
buffalo commons, 131–32. *See also* bison
Bureau of American Ethnography, 12
Bureau of Land Management: Bear Creek
    restoration by, 147–48; California
    rangeland management by, 78; easement
    programs of, 208; employees on Oregon
    rangeland, 83–84; Grand
    Staircase–Escalante Monument survey
    by, 96; grazing management mandate
    vs. practice by, 151; land management
    by, 26; ranchers' role in, 9
business diversification, 190–91, 199–201,
    202, 204, 237; protective development
    and, 215. *See also* income diversification

California Cattleman's Association, 86
California ranches, 77–90; changing
    economy and, 77; diversity in species,
    77–78; industry of, 78–80; land-use

251

Gilgert, Wendell, 134
goats, 86, 210
"Going to Buy Heifers: The Death of Jesse
  Parker" (Hadley), 233
Goodnight, Charlie, 38
government regulations: partnerships with
  ranchers and, 101–2; ranchers on,
  81–82. *See also* federal government;
  local governments; state governments;
  entries under U.S.
grain production, Midwest, 79
Grand Staircase–Escalante Monument, 96
grass-banking, 118–19
grasses in brittle environments, herbivores
  and, 158–59
grasshoppers, landscape shaping and,
  116–17
grassroots empowerment, 167–68
Gray Davis Preserve, Calif., 82
grazing: analysis of ecological effects of,
  127–28; animal–plant interactions and,
  119–20; benefits to plants of, 129–31;
  brittle environments and, 158–59;
  definition of, 115; ecological effects
  debate over, 123–24; landscape shaping
  and, 116–17; as rangeland management
  tool, 161, 167; short-duration, 163–64;
  social factors against, 150–52; stream
  recovery and, 146–50; weed control
  and, 210. *See also* grazing on public
  lands; livestock industry; overgrazing;
  rest from grazing
grazing associations, entrenched attitudes
  of, 125
grazing on public lands, 3, 94–97;
  availability of, 26; decisions about, 60;
  disputes over, 82; as environmental evil,
  91–92; expectations of wilderness
  visitors and, 100–101; fire management
  and, 85–86; rangeland decline and, 27;
  restrictions from, 9–10
Great Outdoors Colorado, 209
Grimes, Mary, 207–8
grocery stores, consolidation of, 187

Harkin, Tom, 228
Hasselstrom, Charley, 55
Hasselstrom, John, 47–51
Hatfield, Doc and Connie, 212–14
herbivores: brittle environments and,
  158–59; evolution of, 156–57. *See also*
  cows/cattle; goats; sheep

Hewitt, Rich, 210
High Desert Ranch, Ore., 212–14
Hispanic ranchers, 9
hobby ranches, 80, 103, 150–51, 202, 223.
  See also ranchettes; subdivisions
Hobson, Rich, 38–39
holistic goals, 165–66; decision-making to
  meet, 166–67, 169–70; grassroots
  empowerment to enable, 167–68
horse(s): Lambert family, 61, 62–63, 65,
  68, 70; Mongolian, 72
humanity: as large-animal hunters, 157;
  reshaping natural world, 16. *See also*
  public

Iliff, John, 38
income diversification, 86. *See also*
  economic diversification
In Search of Kinship (Lambert), 59
insects, nonbrittle environments and, 158
interagency Proper Functioning
  Assessment, 153
intermediate disturbance hypothesis, 15
Internal Revenue Service, 206. *See also* taxes
Internet marketing/sales, 200, 225–26
invasive species control, ranches and,
  223–24
Ishmael (Quinn), 178

Jackson, Wes, 121
Jefferson, Thomas, 11, 93, 178, 185
Jefferson County, Mont., 215–16
Johnson, Al, 125

Kleckner, Carl, 208
Kleckner, Virginia, 207–8
knowledge vs. landscape economy, 14
Krutch, Joseph Wood, 51

Lambert, Mark, 59–60; calving and, 65;
  Christmas tree and, 74; U.S. Forest
  Service and, 60–61
Lambert, Matt, 60; animals birthing and,
  66; howling at coyotes, 65; orphan steer
  of, 69; Romie and, 75
Lambert, Sarah, 60, 62; animals birthing
  and, 66; Christmas tree and, 74;
  Mongolians and, 72; Romie and, 75;
  tending animals, 65
land: biodiversity conservation and, 217;
  economical uses of, 28–29; future
  strategies for, 30–31; intimacy with,

Whitaker, Dugald, 179
wilderness areas. *See* public lands
wildlife: adequacy and vigor of, 42;
economics of, 180–81; fires and, 69–70;
herds of, 156–57; landscape shaping
and, 114, 116; preservation, ranches
and, 224; slash piles and, 74; in spring
and summer, 67–68; in winter, 61–62.
See also specific animals
wildlife biologists, 10–11
Wilkinson, Charles, 137
Williamson Act, 81, 85, 87
Wirth, Zach and Patty, 211–12

women ranchers, 56–57
Wonderful Wizard of Oz, The (Baum), 50
wood, for fires, 71
"Work, The" (Hadley), 109

Yampa River Valley, Colo., 209
Yampa Valley Beef, 190, 193, 229
Yucca Mountain, Nev., nuclear waste
under, 10

Zeller, Marty, 215
zoning districts, voluntary, 204, 215–16,
221